# THE FANTASY
# FAMILY

# THE FANTASY OF FAMILY

Nineteenth-Century Children's Literature and the Myth of the Domestic Ideal

ELIZABETH THIEL

Routledge
Taylor & Francis Group

NEW YORK AND LONDON

First published 2008
by Routledge
711 Third Avenue, New York, NY 10017

Simultaneously published in the UK
by Routledge
2 Park Square, Milton Park, Abingdon, Oxon OX14 4RN

*Routledge is an imprint of the Taylor & Francis Group, an informa business*

First issued in paperback 2011

Typeset in Minion
by Keystroke, 28 High Street, Tettenhall, Wolverhampton

*Library of Congress Cataloging in Publication Data*
    Thiel, Elizabeth.
    The fantasy of family: nineteenth-century children's literature and the
    myth of the domestic ideal / Elizabeth Thiel.
        p. cm. — (Children's literature and culture; 51)
    Includes bibliographical references and index.
        1. Family in literature. 2. Children's stories, English—History and
    criticism. 3. English fiction—19th century—History and criticism.
    4. Home in literature. 5. Domestic relations in literature. 6. Social problems
    in literature. 7. Values in literature. 8. Idealism in literature. 9. Literature
    and society—Great Britain—History—19th century. I. Title.

    PR878.C513T55 2007
    820.9′355—dc22                                          2007019503


ISBN 10: 0–415–98035–6 (hbk)
ISBN 10: 0–415–89937–0 (pbk)
ISBN 10: 0–203–93551–9 (ebk)

ISBN 13: 978–0–415–98035–7 (hbk)
ISBN 13: 978–0–415–89937–6 (pbk)
ISBN 13: 978–0–203–93551–4 (ebk)

In Memory of Olivia Hutton (1915–2007)

# Contents

# Series Editor's Foreword

Dedicated to furthering original research in children's literature and culture, the Children's Literature and Culture series includes monographs on individual authors and illustrators, historical examinations of different periods, literary analyses of genres, and comparative studies on literature and mass media. The series is international in scope and is intended to encourage innovative research in children's literature with a focus on interdisciplinary methodology.

Children's literature and culture are understood in the broadest sense of the term *children* to encompass the period of childhood up through adolescence. Owing to the fact that the notion of childhood has changed so much since the origination of children's literature, this Routledge series is particularly concerned with transformations in children's culture and how they have affected the representation and socialization of children. While the emphasis of the series is on children's literature, all types of studies that deal with children's radio, film, television, and art are included in an endeavor to grasp the aesthetics and values of children's culture. Not only have there been momentous changes in children's culture in the last fifty years, but there have been radical shifts in the scholarship that deals with these changes. In this regard, the goal of the Children's Literature and Culture series is to enhance research in this field and, at the same time, point to new directions that bring together the best scholarly work through the world.

Jack Zipes

# Acknowledgments

I am indebted to Roehampton University for the funding that enabled much of this research and to Jenny Hartley and Lisa Sainsbury for their invaluable assistance throughout the project. I would also like to thank Kim Reynolds and Gillian Lathey for their enthusiasm and help, Geoff Thiel, Laura Atkins, Mary Sebag-Montefiore, Noga Applebaum and Michele Gill for their encouragement, and the many other individuals who have generously shared their knowledge and expertise. I am grateful too to the relatives of nineteenth-century author 'Brenda' who provided memories and memorabilia and so facilitated the earlier research that ultimately led to this book. Numerous libraries and organizations have proved immensely helpful and I owe particular thanks to The British Library, Senate House Library, The Shaftesbury Society and Roehampton University library. Finally, thank you to Jack Zipes and the staff at Routledge New York for their support.

# Introduction

"By a process of selective amnesia the past becomes a historical equivalent of the dream of primal bliss." (Samuel 18)

As social theorist and historian Robin Gilmour suggests, we remain late Victorians: "[w]e are still the spiritual great-grandchildren of that century and look back to our Victorian ancestors with conflicting feelings of envy, resentment, reproach and nostalgia" (1993: 1).[1] The greatest of these, it would seem, is nostalgia. At Christmas-time our yearning for the past finds form in greetings cards emblazoned with Victorian family fireside scenes or sleigh rides, while countless town centers herald the festive season with Victorian shopping evenings and costumed carollers. Moreover, our desire to incorporate elements of what we perceive as our Victorian past is not merely a seasonal phenomenon. Our nineteenth-century homes, stripped back to basics, proudly display their original features, while our television screens consistently play host to celebrations of the Victorian period, ranging from the feats of nineteenth-century engineers to the lives and works of the era's literati. James Walvin's 1987 comment that "[t]he tourist industry's emphasis on certain aspects of British history has led to claims that the nation might soon need a curator rather than a prime minister" (p. 163) remains entirely relevant, and although we may be aware that child labor and immense poverty existed within the Victorian world, our nostalgia is essentially of a rose-coloured hue—sanitized, packaged and marketed to accommodate twenty-first century sensibilities.

However, as late Victorians we have also implicitly inherited and internalized various and diverse ideologies spawned during the nineteenth century. Today's middle class remains, in many ways, the direct descendant of the Victorian bourgeoisie, and political discourse, specifically among more right-wing politicians, has utilized this inheritance, often to great effect. The notion of "Victorian values," championed vociferously by Margaret Thatcher in the approach to the 1983 Parliamentary elections, has skulked on the periphery of British middle-class consciousness ever since, reappearing spasmodically to remind the country of the endangered, or indeed vanished, mores that were once the backbone of

1

Britannia's being. Raphael Samuel, writing of Margaret Thatcher and Victorian values in 1990, asserted that Victorian Britain "[had been] constituted as a kind of reverse image of the present . . . a testimony to the decline in manners and morals, a mirror to our failings, a measure of absence" and that, by metaphorical extension, "Victorian values" had passed from "the real past of recorded history to timeless 'tradition'" (1992: 18). It has continued to be so. More than a decade later, our passion for all things "traditionally" Victorian and our nostalgia for a golden age of national pride celebrated by united, supportive families remains potent, but it serves primarily to engender a sense of loss.

The image of the "traditional," but "lost," family has been a particularly powerful force within a contemporary Britain that perceives itself as beset by societal ills. Diana Gittins, in her seminal study *The Family in Question: Changing Households and Familiar Ideologies* (1985), proposed that the gap between reality and ideology had contributed to the contemporary sense of crisis in the family; in *A World of their Own Making: Myth, Ritual and the Quest for Family Values* (1996), John Gillis explains that when we subscribe to the idea of the family in terms of tradition, "[we project] a static image of family onto a particular past time and place [and] we immediately begin to describe change in terms of 'decline' or 'loss'" (p. 4). Media coverage of family issues continues to exacerbate concerns that contemporary British family life is failing. In September 2004, for example, the *Daily Mail*, a newspaper that has been described as writing in one of two styles—either sycophantic praise of middle-class lifestyles or moral outrage at the ever-increasing wickedness of the modern world (www. Britishnewspapers.co.uk)—was swift to comment on an Institute of Psychiatry report that showed a decline in the mental health of British adolescents. According to social affairs correspondent Steve Doughty, "the British experience ha[d] closely followed the demise of the traditional family" (p. 10), while columnist Melanie Phillips compared the single-parent family with those who are "intact" (p. 12). The "traditional," "intact" family was clearly the desirable norm.

It is this assumption of normality that underlies contemporary perceptions of the "traditional" family, yet this supposed normality is entirely counterfeit because it is flawed at root. While "[i]n many ways the modern understanding of the family was a creation of the nineteenth century" (Davidoff et al. 1999: 101), the Victorians too were seeking a perfect paradigm which, in time, evolved into the myth of the domestic ideal and was ultimately transmitted to future generations. The inclusive, supportive family[2] had been in existence for centuries, but it was the Victorians who sought to elevate its status to that of an icon and, in so doing, to create a sense of permanence and stability in a country beset by social anxieties. As Leonore Davidoff and Catherine Hall state in *Family Fortunes: Men and Women of the English Middle Classes 1780–1850* (1987), the early nineteenth century in England was "a time of heightened fear about both social and economic chaos" and, partly as a reaction, the middle strata became fascinated with "carving up their world into discrete categories and classes"

(p. xiii). In the wake of revolution overseas and in the midst of industrialization and modernization at home, it was scarcely surprising that the Victorians were preoccupied with order and classification, and their conceptualization of the family as the lynchpin of society from which all else emanated was a palliative; it promised the recreation of a mythical age in which all was secure. As Gillis suggests:

> Feeling themselves ravaged by time . . . [the Victorians] imagined earlier families to have been large and cohesive, inclusive of kin as well as multiple generations, rooted in place and tradition and more deeply religious than themselves. From those sturdy foundations all else descended or more accurately degenerated, because for the Victorians, as for us, the past offered the authentic original of family life, so perfect that they could do no better than build on it. (1996: 6)

## The Divine Home

According to Victorian ideology, the idyllic home was eminently achievable for all and the family within its hallowed walls could, and should, be suitably perfect. John Angell James' *A Help to Domestic Happiness* (1828), a series of overtly prescriptive sermons that addressed the duties of various household members from husbands and wives to children, foreshadowed the numerous writings of the Victorians in its celebration of the family and home. James' emphasis is on piety and duty to God, and he asserts throughout that by adherence to the guidelines of what he terms "The Family Constitution," supreme happiness is freely available:

> A family! How delightful the associations we form with such a word! How pleasing the images with which it crowds the mind, and how tender the emotions which it awakens in the heart! Who can wonder that domestic happiness should be a theme dear to poetry, and that it should have called forth some of the sweetest strains of fancy and of feeling? . . . The domestic constitution is a divine institute. God formed it himself . . . Domestic happiness, in many respects, resembles the manna which was granted to the Israelites in the wilderness; like that precious food, it is the gift of God which cometh down from heaven . . . dispensed alike to the rich and to the poor. (pp. 1–3, 10)[3]

One of James' favourite authors, Sarah Stickney Ellis, probably "the best-known idealogue of domesticity" (Davidoff and Hall 1987: 182), continued the theme with her influential publications *The Women of England and Their Social Duties and Domestic Habits* (1839), *Family Secrets, or Hints to Those Who would make Home Happy* (1841), *The Wives of England, their Relative Duties, Domestic Influence and Social Obligations* (1843) and *The Daughters of England, and their*

*Position in Society, Character and Responsibilities* (1845). Later, and most famously, John Ruskin's "Of Queen's Gardens" (1865) definitively extolled the virtues and attainability of home as "the place of Peace; the shelter, not only from all injury, but from all terror, doubt and division" (p. 59).

Yet this ideology was fundamentally problematic. If "home" was indeed a divine phenomenon, "a sacred place, a vestal temple, a temple of the hearth watched over by Household Gods" (Ruskin 1865: 59), or the creation of God, as James avowed, it was a phenomenon that demanded maintenance through constant vigilance: "The Victorians had taken on the cultural project of creating and sustaining their own symbolic universe" (Gillis 1996: 71) and, by necessity, it needed to remain steadfast and strong. Consequently, the political and philosophical voices that extolled home and family were forceful and persuasive and allowed no deviation from the ideological stance. Speaking in 1872 on "Conservative Principles," Disraeli asserted:

> England is a domestic country. Here the home is revered and the hearth is sacred. The nation is represented by a family—the Royal Family; and if that family is educated with a sense of responsibility and a sentiment of public duty, it is difficult to exaggerate the salutary influence they may exercise over a nation. It is not merely an influence upon manners; it is not merely that they are a model for refinement and good taste—they affect the heart as well as the intelligence of the people. (Behlmer 1998: 22)

The family was already ideologically representative of the Divine Family, with father the God-given head and mother the angelic administrator, a notion that was established prior to the Victorian crisis of faith, but that became ever more potent as fundamental religious beliefs were challenged. Now it was also perceived as influential in the formation of strong nations, albeit that conceptualization of Victoria as mother of Empire required some moderation of the truth:

> What few Victorians could have known was that the Queen herself, paragon of domesticity, compared a woman giving birth to a cow or a dog; loathed the "terrible frog-like activity" of newborns; despised "baby worship"; and deemed the subject of breast-feeding "horribly disgusting." (Behlmer 1998: 22)

However, other unpalatable truths that challenged the idyllic images of home and family so fondly portrayed by those in power *did* come to the public's attention. The various social studies of London's poor—Henry Mayhew's *London Labour and the London Poor* (1861) and John Hollingshead's *Ragged London in 1861* (1861) for example—as well as the multitude of social and highly popular commentaries by authors such as Dickens, were incontrovertible evidence of another world in which home was sometimes the site of violence, suffering or despair:

Within a few doors of [an illegal sporting theatre] is a family who were found ... without food, without fire or any other necessary, in a room nearly bare, their furniture having been seized for rent. There were a father, mother and several children standing shivering within the bare walls, the children having nothing on them but sacks tied round their bare waists ... In Old Nichols Street, a turning in this district leading off from Shoreditch, we have a specimen of an east-end thieves' street ... its houses are black and repulsive. (Hollingshead 1861: 41, 42)

These too were images of family and home, but images that entirely subverted the "domestic constitution" ostensibly formed by God and embraced by the middle classes. Furthermore, even *within* the supposed safety and sanctity of middle-class domesticity, there were anomalies that threatened the myth of familial bliss. The campaign against The Contagious Diseases Act of the 1860s, led by Josephine Butler who "refused to countenance [the notion] that working-class women were created to minister to the sexual needs of gentlemen" (Jordan 2001: 2) and, later, the exposure of young girls sold into prostitution, often to satisfy "gentlemen," shook the very foundations of Victorian family ideology. But although fiction, non-fiction and newspapers alike sometimes suggested, although implicitly, that the myth of the domestic ideal was fragile, the continuing vision of an idealogically perfect Monarch and her family and the wealth of popular journalism that celebrated domesticity and that flourished during the mid 1800s, from Dickens' *Household Words* to *The Home Companion* and *The Englishwoman's Domestic Magazine*, served as an effective counteraction to unease and reaffirmed the centrality of home and family.

## Acculturating the Child

This constant reaffirmation of domestic values was of vital importance in maintaining the ideological status quo for Victorian adults, but if it was to endure, it was essential that subsequent generations subscribed to a similar doctrine. The myth of home and family that resonated throughout the early part of the century had simultaneously been replicated through popular children's literature to create a template for a world in which father and mother, devoted to the moral and/or spiritual well-being of their offspring, were ever-present and ever-mindful of their duties. The family-centered, moralistic tales of Maria Edgeworth (1767–1849) and Mary Martha Sherwood (1775–1851), for example, popularized in the early years of the nineteenth century, continued to be widely read throughout the latter part of the Victorian period. Edgeworth's tales, founded on the principles of Locke and Rousseau, were located in a middle-class world and encouraged children to learn through choice and experience. Careful parenting was implicit to Edgeworth's scheme, although her message was subtly relayed; Rosamond, the child protagonist of several of Edgeworth's stories is encouraged to be cautious, but is ultimately allowed to make her own mistakes. In "The Purple Jar" (1796), she is torn between a new pair of badly needed shoes and a purple jar that she spies in a chemist's shop. Her mother forbears to influence her choice, remaining coolly objective, but nevertheless attempting to guide her daughter towards a wise decision:

> "Oh!" said Rosamond, looking round [the shoe shop], "there is a pair of little shoes; they'll just fit me, I'm sure."
>
> "Perhaps they might," [said her mother] "but you cannot be sure till you have tried them on, any more than you can be quite sure that you should like the purple vase exceedingly, till you have examined it more attentively." (pp. 4–5)

Rosamond finally chooses to buy the purple jar and is mortified to discover that it is plain glass filled with colored liquid. Moreover, the results of her folly continue to unfold; without soles to her shoes, she cannot go for walks with her mother and her father refuses to take Rosamond on an outing with her brother because she is "slip-shod" (p. 8). Together, and separately, both husband and wife guide their daughter toward a future of wiser decisions.

In contrast, Mrs Sherwood subscribed to a Calvinistic doctrine and emphasized that parental guidance was crucial to the child's moral and spiritual well-being. *The History of the Fairchild Family* (1818), her most successful and popular series of stories, is characterized by didacticism and religiosity; for the Fairchild parents and their three offspring, Hell is an ever-present threat, sinners can only be saved by knowing and loving God and Jesus, and it is the duty of the Fairchild parents to ensure that their children achieve salvation. If the family was indeed a divine phenomenon, parents clearly had an obligation to preserve and nurture God's creation and to join together to raise their children in an appropriately devout manner.

In "Story on the Sixth Commandment," Mr Fairchild attempts to impress the dangers of arguing on his children by taking them to view a gibbet and the grisly remains of a man who killed his brother. His wife condones his actions:

> After dinner, Mr Fairchild said to his wife:
>
> "I will take the children this evening to Blackwood, and show them something there, which, I think, they will remember as long as they live: and I hope they will take warning from it, and pray more earnestly for new hearts, that they may love each other with perfect and heavenly love."
>
> "If you are going to Blackwood," said Mrs Fairchild, "I cannot go with you, my dear, though I approve of your taking the children." (p. 35)

Mrs Fairchild would appear to comprehend the implications of a visit to Blackwood, but cannot, or does not wish to accompany the group, and entirely defers to her husband's decision. As patriarch, he clearly holds the dominant position within the family; although his wife approves of his actions, her acquiescence is unnecessary because Mr Fairchild has already determined that he "will" take the children to Blackwood. Nevertheless, the unity of the Fairchild parents establishes them as exemplary and responsible carers of their children—characteristics that are implied, although less overtly displayed, in Edgeworth's tale. Edgeworth and Sherwood may propose different methods of parenting, but both portray the world of the middle-class child as a secure place of order in which routines and patterns of behaviour are clearly delineated, where Mother is a mainstay, always loving and attentive, and Father presides over all, offering guidance and discipline in equal measure.

This notion of the family as a secure, organized and patriarchal unit in which roles were clearly apportioned was further perpetuated in non-fiction for children, as exemplified by Agnes Giberne's *Sun, Moon, and Stars: A Book for Beginners* (1879).[4] Giberne (1845–1939) was a prolific author for children and wrote more than a hundred books, many of them evangelical tales for the Religious Tract Society, but she was also interested in the natural sciences, describing herself in the 1881 British Census as "Author Fiction Science,"[5] and wrote a number of texts about the natural world. *Sun, Moon, and Stars* is primarily an informative scientific work "for 'beginners' of all kinds, whether children, working-men or even grown people of the educated classes" (preface n.p.), yet it also explicitly colludes with the doctrines of Victorian family ideology.

Part 1 of Giberne's book is devoted to depicting the solar system as a family, with the earth being "one of the little sisters." The "head" of the family is the sun, referred to throughout as "he," and he is instrumental in uniting the family: "a certain close family tie; or, more correctly . . . the powerful influence of the head of the family" binds the system together (p. 23). The planets of the solar system are "the leading members" of the family, the moon characterized as a particular friend and attendant who "has proved herself constant and faithful in her attachment" (p. 56), while comets are visitors, shooting stars and meteorites are little servants, and neighbors are other systems and seasonal constellations. Giberne, as the author of a text for beginners, may have devised a useful metaphor for her readers, but her recourse to such a model simultaneously validates the family as a concept that extends beyond earthly boundaries.

Like John Angell James in *A Help to Domestic Happiness*, Giberne proposes a link between the "traditional" family and divine creation, and emphasizes this relationship throughout by introducing each chapter with a suitable biblical quotation. The fact that *Sun, Moon and Stars* is a non-fiction text further endorses its sentiments; as a "serious" study authenticated by a learned Oxford professor, it is seemingly eminently reliable. However, Giberne's text, for all its ideological emphases, ultimately portrays the universe as a non-traditional family group. There is no mother figure present in Giberne's depiction of the earth and its "relatives," although this is never mentioned in the text; the sun, as father, is apparently a single parent. While the impression initially gauged from Giberne's book is one of familial "normality," there is clearly a tension within her work that implicitly challenges the construct of the domestic ideal.

It was a construct that had been granted official government status; the Census of 1871 declared: "The natural family is founded by marriage and consists, in its complete state, of husband, wife and children" (Behlmer 1998: 26). But by idealizing the "natural" family that existed in a "complete state," the Census statement also acknowledged the existence of incomplete units, the transnormative family groups, that comprised at least a part of the Victorian social world.

## The Transnormative Family

The term "transnormative family" is original to this work and identifies those family units headed by single parents, step-parents, aunts, uncles, grandparents, siblings or the state that exists in opposition to the "natural" and "complete" family of husband, wife and children. These are not merely extended family units. They may incorporate kin, but the transnormative family is identified primarily by the temporary or permanent absence of a natural parent or parents, often by the presence of a surrogate mother or father, who may or may not be related to the child, and, frequently, by the relocation of the child to an environment outside the "natural" family home.

Although "transnormative"[6] is an expression sometimes employed to denote that which is forbidden, particularly with reference to sexuality, it assumes an altogether different emphasis when coupled with "family." As a compound, "transnormative family" characterizes a familial unit that is outside of the established order, and so simultaneously situates such "incomplete" families within the broader frame of Victorian ideology. They are, by implication, "beyond the norm." Moreover, and perhaps most significantly, there is a suggestion of deviance in "transnormative" that is less explicit in the more usual and pedestrian epithets of "alternative" or "fractured" and that consequently renders "transnormative" an entirely appropriate nomenclature within this study. The nineteenth-century transnormative family was deviant in that it challenged the verisimilitude of the domestic ideal by depicting paradigms of family that existed beyond the desirable norm.

There is little published data specifically on transnormative groupings in Victorian Britain, but Michael Anderson's definitive 1988 work on household structure, "Households, families and individuals: some preliminary results from the national sample from the 1851 census of Great Britain," gives a clear indication of the many varieties of household that existed in the mid-century. For Anderson, private households were "the most important locale" in which society chose to place those who were unable to provide for themselves—widows, orphans, single parents and other groups—and his findings, using a one-fiftieth cluster sample of the Census figures, demonstrate that it was only *just* the majority of mid-Victorian households that consisted entirely of conjugal family members. In homes populated by non-conjugal kin, the greatest group of relatives was grandchildren and, overall, there were numerous children living apart from their parents. As Anderson explains: "Many were clearly orphans (or children who had lost one parent and whose surviving parent had remarried) and the numbers were thus a consequence of the high Victorian rates of mortality" (p. 426).

Research such as Anderson's is invaluable in conceptualizing the variety of family groups in mid-century Britain, but the actualities of transnormative clusters are more elusive. While, as Anderson states, "nieces and nephews and grandchildren seem to have been an especially significant element in the household structure of Victorian Britain"(p. 437), there is scant information on the causes of such arrangements, nor definitive evidence as to the frequency of such family types. Prior to the 1926 Adoption Act, informal fostering or adoption was largely outside the aegis of the record books but children were nonetheless rehomed, and for various reasons—the death or absence of a parent or parents, or perhaps because lonely relatives needed a young person about the house for company or as an heir. Many of the texts discussed in this book deal with such scenarios; in the course of my research I discovered numerous stories, many by once-popular authors, that were written between 1850 and the turn of the century and that center on transnormative family groups. The sheer volume of such books, and the fact that they were often penned by acclaimed children's writers, such as Hesba Stretton (1832–1911), "Brenda," otherwise Georgina Castle Smith (1845–1935) and Mary Louisa Molesworth (1839–1921), suggests that transnormative families were well within the experience of the mid-Victorian child, either personally or through acquaintances. Moreover, with the exception of the orphans of street-arab tales, children in the midst of grief or those confronted with a new mother following the demise of their own mamas, the central characters of these essentially middle-class novels rarely complain about their situation and the narrators of the tales are similarly unperturbed; the child is frequently presented as living with grandmother or aunt with scarcely a mention of his or her natural parents.

This apparent complacency, when coupled with the Victorian predilection for the domestic ideal, is puzzling. Furthermore, the relative dearth of mid-Victorian children's fiction that focuses on what has been perceived as the ideal family of mother, father and siblings, is equally perplexing. Although the mid-to-late-Victorian child was seemingly surrounded by an ideology that privileged the concept of the idyllic family group, the fiction that was available to her often presented an entirely different scenario. The transnormative family, essentially the antithesis of the idealised "natural" paradigm, was frequently depicted as commonplace and unremarkable. However, and significantly, representations of transnormative units often aped more ideologically conformist representations of the family.

Many Victorian children's novels that focus on transnormative families are characterized by what appears to be an ideological subterfuge in which alternative family groups are portrayed as akin to the "natural," idealized family model. There is a sense of collaboration with prescribed family ideology as authors attempt to impose an idyllic façade onto tales of transnormative families, but the result of this merger is often less than convincing. Despite their supposedly "happy endings," such texts are characterized by what seems to be an implicit "conflict between rhetoric and thought" (Cuddon 1982: 55), and these *aporia* suggest that while authors strove to achieve a semblance of ideological conformity, the less palatable realities of orphanhood, stepfamilies and foster homes, situations that prevailed throughout all social classes, created a tension between reality[7] and ideology that could not ultimately be disguised. In essence, the transnormative family could rarely, if ever, replicate the domestic ideal, despite the enthusiastic assurances of children's authors.

The responsibility for creating this semblance of domestic harmony within what was clearly an often less than harmonious situation, lay primarily with women writers who, by 1850, were becoming a notable force in the children's publishing world. These writers are infrequently acknowledged beyond the field of children's literature, but they and their books were often powerful agents of social legislation and reform. Stretton campaigned for the impoverished children of the streets, while Brenda's work apparently inspired the social reformer Lord Shaftesbury, who was one of the founders of the Ragged Schools Union (Thiel 2002: 17). Furthermore, while such texts may sometimes superficially suggest adherence to Victorian ideological dogma, they are often subtly subversive, although it is generally impossible to gauge whether this is a conscious or subconscious authorial stance. Nonetheless, it is a trait that exists throughout the literature for children written by women that is explored within this book, regardless of the author's status. My research covers a broad range of texts by renowned authors, from Charlotte Yonge (1823–1901) to Stretton and Molesworth, and also examines the work of largely forgotten writers such as Brenda and Harriet Childe-Pemberton (1852–unknown), whose texts are given particular emphasis. Such scope not only offers the opportunity for recovering overlooked authors, but simultaneously exposes the complexities that different writers faced as they attempted to comply with mainstream ideological tenets, while addressing the realities of transnormative family life.

### An Enduring Legacy

The Victorians' apparently steadfast adherence to prescribed ideology, despite the realities of bereavement, orphanhood and fostering, is paradoxical, yet its effects have endured. The family ideology nurtured in the nineteenth century permeates British culture today, despite political and social emphases on the "normality" of transnormative family groups; the construct that was perpetuated one hundred and fifty years ago is, in many ways, as potent now as it was then. In examining the evidence from the past and thereby achieving a greater understanding of a bygone era, we, as late Victorians, can implicitly illuminate the prejudices and preoccupations of our own century. Moreover, while the literature of the Victorians is a fundamental resource for researching the period, it is crucial to access the whole spectrum of popular literature, of which children's literature is a significant part, in order to achieve a comprehensive understanding of the past. Nineteenth-century children's literature both reflected and engendered the culture of the time, and offers unparalleled insights into Victorian life and ideology, although it has often been overlooked by scholars working on the recovery of the nineteenth century. However, ideological positions are frequently overt in writing for children, as John Stephens points out in *Language and Ideology in Children's Fiction* (1992), because it is essential that the beliefs of a culture are internalized swiftly and thoroughly by its offspring if that culture is to flourish (p. 3). Thus, in children's literature, the anomalies inherent to propaganda, for that is essentially what these ideological texts must be, can often be more easily identified.

In investigating the fantasy of family through examination and discussion of children's literature, speculations and suppositions are inevitable, and questions of subjectivity must invariably arise. In *Knowing the Past: Victorian Literature and Culture* (2001), Suzy Anger comments that "epistomological scepticism [dominates theoretical debate] . . . and the conception of truth that allows for the possibility of objective knowledge has come to be regarded as naïve and suspect" (p. 1). However, while recognizing the impossibility of engaging with and examining texts from a Victorian perspective, I believe that valuable information can be gleaned by a twenty-first-century reader. Like Anger, I also subscribe to Carlyle's notion that by striving "to penetrate a little . . . into a somewhat remote century . . . and [looking] face to face on it" it is possible to "perhaps illustrate our own poor century thereby" (p. 2). The discrepancy between ideology and reality, evident in Victorian children's literature on the transnormative family, is mirrored by the gap between our own contemporary desire for the ideal and the reality of a society partly comprised of transnormative family groups that are still perceived as "different." Frederic Jameson asserts that "a crisis in historicity" has reduced the collective human record to empty images of nostalgia (McPheron 1999: 4), but while this critique offers an explanation of the postmodern condition and our desire for an idealistic past, it clearly fails to adequately address the similarities that exist between Victorian and contemporary idealism.

## Scholarship and the Family

In many ways my theoretical perspective is founded on new historicism, particularly the models propounded by Michel Foucault and Mitzi Myers, as succinctly explored by Tony Watkins in "Space, history and culture: The setting of children's literature" (1999: 54, 55). Foucault's emphasis on the re-situation of literary texts alongside non-literary discourses and representations as a means of exploring contemporary social issues is highly pertinent to my study, while

Myers' assertions, with their focus on children's literature as a force for the legitimization or subversion of dominant ideologies, have proved especially useful. Traditional family theory has, perhaps, been less valuable; although it offers a foundation for comprehending family structures, there is little published work on transnormative families, particularly those represented in nineteenth-century children's literature by female authors. My research addresses this imbalance by fusing new historicism with elements of family theory and gender studies to offer a socio-historic and literary perspective in which nineteenth-century British female writers for children predominate. Indeed, I have based my work entirely on female authors; I believe that it is from once-popular but frequently overlooked texts that new insights can arise. While canonical male writers such as Carroll, Kingsley and MacDonald are often prioritized in research into Victorian texts for children, culture is shaped in eclectic ways and the examination of works by both acknowledged *and* effectively forgotten female writers can provide original and valuable evidence for current and future scholars.

There is, and has been for some time, substantial and sustained scholarly focus on the recovery of the Victorian past, particularly through exploration of the literature of the period, but, to date, there has been only limited use of children's texts. Nevertheless, a number of recent studies have provided insights into the Victorian family from a variety of theoretical and critical perspectives and have, by default, established the parameters for my own research. There have been numerous socio-historical approaches to the family since the 1970s, an era that might be perceived as the heyday of family sociology, ranging from Lawrence Stone's *The Family, Sex and Marriage in England, 1500–1800* (1977), to Mary Abbott's thought-provoking and accessible *Family Ties: English Families 1540–1920* (1993), yet none has focused to any discernible degree on the trans-normative family, nor has there been any published work on transnormative family groups in children's literature. This conspicuous absence identifies the transnormative family as a new subject area for research, but one that clearly engages with and adds a further dimension to the socio-historic material already available, much of which has provided a foundation for my study. Previous scholarship on nineteenth-century family ideology, marriage, childbirth and pauperism has implicitly identified those areas that are fundamental to an exploration of transnormative family groups and this book is consequently both a response to and an extension of earlier work.

Michael Anderson's *Approaches to the History of the Western Family, 1500–1914* (1980) has long provided a starting point for socio-historic research and is dealt with in some detail in Chapter One because it usefully documents the primary theoretical perspectives that have often informed studies of the family. However, since the publication of Anderson's text, other theoretical permutations have developed, most notably in 1987 with Leonore Davidoff and Catherine Hall's *Family Fortunes: Men and Women of the English Middle Class 1780–1850* (1987). Davidoff and Hall's text remains pertinent to any study of the family for its sheer breadth of scholarship and stimulating commentary on class, gender differences and the economics of the family sphere. Devised in the wake of feminism, it acknowledges the centrality of women within the middle-class family, but, perhaps equally importantly, foregrounds the family as an eternal variable. For Davidoff and Hall, there is no absolute "family" as such, but rather a shifting organism that might comprise both immediate and distant kin and therefore implicitly blurs the boundaries between the concepts of "household" and "family," terms that often informed earlier demographic studies. It was, perhaps, Davidoff and Hall's emphasis on the flexibility of the family group, and Davidoff et al.'s subsequent work, *The Family Story: Blood, Contract and Intimacy, 1830–1960* (1999), a collaborative publication that explored specific relationships within the domestic space, that encouraged further research on the family which resulted in academic interest in the public and private spheres of the Victorian familial group.

The duality of the Victorian family, as both a romanticized ideal and a publicly scrutinized entity, provides fertile ground for scholarship, and the contrast between Victorian ideology and the realities of nineteenth-century life remains intrinsic to my own research. Karen Chase and Michael Levenson's *The Spectacle of Intimacy: A Public Life for the Victorian Family* (2000) reveals how the family became the subject of the public gaze and the way in which private pleasures were subsequently exposed. The covert power of the British female novelist and her influence on the emergence of the middle classes informs Nancy Armstrong's *Desire and Domestic Fiction: A Political History of the Novel* (1987), while the impact of public discourse on what were seemingly private matters forms the basis of Mary Poovey's *Uneven Developments* (1989). George K. Behlmer's *Friends of the Family: The English Home and Its Guardians, 1850–1949* (1998) takes the discussion beyond the feminist emphases of Armstrong and Poovey to more broadly explore the public and private worlds of the Victorians through examination of the "ideal home," focusing not only on the self-regulating practices of family members, but also on the interventionist policies of government to show the interrelatedness of social dictate and the myth of the family ideal. Behlmer ventures into the realm of what he terms "artificial families," but his interest is largely in the pauper, poor laws and charitable organizations, although he provides extensive details on those topics and substantiates his facts with individual case studies. Overall, his book argues convincingly that the family has never truly been free of state interference and that the notion of the domestic idyll has been and continues to be a potent and forceful political tool, despite the fact that "the rhetoric of family values transcends party affiliation" (p. 322). It is those same "family values" with their intangible nature and questionable heredity that permeate my work and although I agree with Behlmer's assertion that "an explanatory black hole" from which no real enlightenment can escape exists "at the centre of our fantasies about a family golden age" (p. 322), I would also suggest that knowledge of the past provides at least some guidance for the future. John R. Gillis in *A World of*

*Their Own Making: Myth, Ritual and the Quest for Family Values* (1996) comments that recognition of the family ideal as a myth, and understanding of "our own engagement with myth and ritual," can only be achieved by comprehending the ways in which earlier generations engaged with theirs (p. 19), a perspective that would seem to be imperative, if we are ever to truly accept the diversity of contemporary family units without an accompanying sense of loss.

However, in order to understand the Victorian family and its ideologies, it is important to comprehend the complexities of such a group, and the different individuals that inhabited the nineteenth-century domestic space have also become a popular subject for scholarly scrutiny over the past fifteen years. Recent studies, both socio-historical and literary, have focused on particular aspects of the family, from its fathers and sons to its unmarried aunts, and have consequently yielded additional insights into the ideologies and realities of family life. In *A Man's Place: Masculinity and the Middle-Class Home in Victorian England* (1999), John Tosh, who has long been at the forefront of nineteenth-century masculine studies, proposes that the home life of the Victorian male was essentially a product of his gender and Tosh's most recent work on nineteenth-century male lives, *Manliness and Masculinities in Nineteenth-Century Britain* (2004), exposes the insecurities and frailties of the Victorian man through incisive examination of various perspectives, ranging from etiquette to Empire. Tosh's awareness of the complexities of the Victorian male, as both a product of and a response to his social and ideological environment, foreshadows my study of the bachelor uncle, an individual whom Tosh has not explored to date, but who embodies the contradictions inherent to the Victorian masculine ideal. Part man, part child, he exists in a limbo. He may be forceful and parental with his charges, but he also remains an immature playmate and is ever denied "manly" fulfillment by dint of his single status; he might be comparable with the feminized angelic boys discussed by Claudia Nelson in *Boys Will be Girls: The Feminine Ethic and British Children's Fiction, 1857–1917* (1991). He is, however, generally more kindly perceived than his female counterpart. In *Independent Women: Work and Community for Single Women 1850–1920* (1988), Martha Vicinus asserts that the single woman was frequently a powerful individual, largely in control of her own destiny, but it is also evident that the middle-class spinster who was dependent on the beneficence of family members was something of a social problem. Pat Jalland's and John Hooper's *Women from Birth to Death: The Female Life Cycle in Britain 1830–1914* (1986) brings together primary source material on women and women's health and exposes nineteenth-century pity and prejudices toward those who failed in their maternal, "natural" duties—an attitude that is embodied in W.R. Greg's 1862 indictment of the unmarried state (cited in Vicinus 1988),[8] and that is mirrored in a number of the children's texts discussed in the following pages. Moreover, the spinster was not merely to be pitied; as editor Laura Doan discusses in the introduction to *Old Maids to Radical Spinsters: Unmarried Women in the Twentieth-Century Novel* (1991), the single woman was also viewed as potentially dangerous, a suggestion that is sometimes echoed in Victorian children's literature.

It is the dangers to society, those elements of the population who fail to conform to nineteenth-century ideology and so challenge its most basic precepts, that often provide a veritable treasure trove for researchers of nineteenth-century society. The Citizenship Past Consortium's website, *Hidden Lives Revealed* (www.hiddenlives.org.uk), is a vast collection of archive material on poor and disadvantaged children who were cared for by The Waifs and Strays Society and covers the period from 1881 to 1918. Although names are withheld, the site's volume of information and photographs include the details of real children's lives and their sometimes appalling histories. Jane Jordan's biographical work *Josephine Butler* (2001), a study of both a courageous campaigner and the prostitution trade, and Jeannie Duckworth's *Fagin's Children: Criminal Children in Victorian England* (2002) offer compelling glimpses beyond their primary subjects into the juvenile underworld of nineteenth-century Britain, and provide a contemporary, and largely less political perspective, on Mayhew's and Hollingshead's Victorian commentaries. My eventually fruitful search for original material on "the problem of the poor" revealed not only the plight of the destitute, but the extent to which the middle classes feared the impoverished masses, particularly their children.

It is likely that scholars will continue to unearth new information; Victorian London and nineteenth-century texts for children that focus on destitute children are always fascinating subjects for students, perhaps because they contrast so vividly with contemporary Western life and/or because they supplement the Dickensian images with which we are so familiar, and so validate our preconceptions of the Victorian underclass. Nancy Cutt's *Ministering Angels: A Study of Nineteenth-Century Evangelical Writing for Children* (1979) and Jacqueline Bratton's *The Impact of Victorian Children's Fiction* (1981) demonstrate a comprehensive understanding of street-arab tales and those authors who most famously composed them, but neither Cutt nor Bratton thoroughly explore the alternative and subversive messages at play in these frequently sentimental and didactic texts. If the poor were a problem, they needed to be eradicated, either through socialization into middle-class sensibilities or through emigration, as Philip Bean and Joy Melville suggest in *Lost Children of the Empire: The Untold Story of Britain's Child Migrants* (1989), and the ideologies that informed many street-arab stories effectively validated such actions.

Laura Peters' *Orphan Texts: Victorian Orphans, Culture and Empire* (2000) investigates the poor from an altogether different perspective, yet one that is clearly allied to my research. Peters does not address children's literature per se, drawing largely on canonical texts and those from popular culture, but her work, which persuasively utilizes the Freudian notion of the *unheimlich*, effectively relates the figure of the orphan to the Victorian desire for a reaffirmation of family identity. Peters' methodology, which fuses socio-historic material with canonical and popular literature of the period, illustrates an increasingly popular tendency in critical analysis and informs my own study, while echoing that of several other relatively recent works: Shirley Foster and Judy Simons' *What Katy Read: Feminist Re-readings of "Classic" Stories for Girls* (1995), an exploration of the often subversive ideologies implicit to English and American juvenile texts; Anna Davin's *Growing Up Poor: Home, School and Street in London 1870–1914* (1996), which focuses on children's books and social history to chart the intricacies of urban life; Catherine Waters' *Dickens and the Politics of Family* (1997), an examination of the ideology of family through Dickens' work; and Carolyn Dever's *Death and the Mother from Dickens to Freud: Victorian Fiction and the Anxiety of Origins* (1998), an analysis of works by authors including Eliot, Collins and Darwin. My own research employs a similar methodology.

Dever's exploration of the dead mother in adult Victorian fiction is a seminal text, for its interpretation of the iconic maternal figure and its psychoanalytic analyses usefully extend and complement the more factual emphases of Pat Jalland's *Death in the Victorian Family* (1996), as well as echoing, in part, the Jungian theories of Jacqueline Schectman in *The Stepmother in Fairy Tales: Bereavement and the Feminine Shadow* (1993). Both psychoanalytic interpretations are inherently allied to Bruno Bettelheim's *The Uses of Enchantment: The Meaning and Importance of Fairy Tales* (1976) which, although primarily concerned with fairy tale, offers paradigms of motherhood that are satisfyingly applicable to maternal figures, whatever their provenance. Although little of my research draws on psychoanalytic theory, it is a particularly viable and rewarding approach when discussing maternal death and the Victorian preoccupation with the mother. However, as I suggested earlier in this chapter, no single theoretical stance dominates my work. While I have found children's literature theorists helpful—particularly Barbara Wall's excellent analysis of narrative techniques in nineteenth-century literature in *The Narrator's Voice: The Dilemma of Children's Fiction* (1991) and John Stephens' exploration of more contemporary children's books in *Language and Ideology in Children's Fiction* (1992)—the breadth of my material has often demanded an amalgam of theoretical approaches, from feminism to Marxism, which has allowed me to fully explore my subject without the confines of too rigid a framework.

## Concept and Content

The underlying concept for this book developed from my earlier work on Brenda (Thiel 2002), whose influential street-arab tale, *Froggy's Little Brother* (1875), appears spasmodically on university reading lists. Little was known about the author[9] although, as my research revealed, she had been a popular children's writer and had published a total of twenty-three books. As I investigated her life and works and examined Victorian publishers' lists, I realized that she was only one among many productive women writers for children who had effectively been silenced by dint of their omission from literary directories and, consequently, were in danger of being forgotten. Furthermore, it became apparent that our impressions of Victorian life and culture had been gleaned primarily from the works of a selected, approved elite and that we had accepted these offerings as truly representative of the time. Instead of seeking access to the whole spectrum of popular literature and striving to expand our knowledge of the Victorians, we had been satisfied with preconceptions and with the preferences of a canonical and ideological regime.

It was ultimately through exploration of domestic narratives by other female children's authors, both those who had been acknowledged and others who had virtually been forgotten, that the tension between the myth of the domestic ideal and the realities of transnormative families began to emerge. It has since become evident that the nineteenth-century family was as varied a unit as the family of today.

My work seeks to realign our perceptions of the past and, by implication, our understanding of the present, by interrogating the myth of the Victorian family through exploration of Victorian children's literature of the mid-to-late nineteenth century. It redefines received notions of Victorian life by recovering and analyzing representations of the transnormative family as portrayed in literature for children written by women, and explicitly challenges our pre-conceptions of the nineteenth-century. In doing so, it demonstrates that Victorian children's literature provides valuable insights into nineteenth-century ideologies and that these overlooked resources and concepts for historical, social and literary research enable a greater comprehension both of the Victorians and, by inference, of contemporary society.

Chapter One is primarily a review and reappraisal of existing sociological methodologies and contemporary literary discourses relating to the Victorian family, including those on maternal loss and parentless children. Pertinent methodologies are discussed and evaluated, including those identified by Michael Anderson in *Approaches to the History of the Western Family 1500–1980* (1980), and there is critical analysis of recent literary discourses on the family. While these publications offer valuable concepts through which to examine the Victorian family and offer some insight into the historical story, it is evident that information on the transnormative family is conspicuously absent, although these groups were relatively commonplace in nineteenth-century Britain. There is little quantitative data on the transnormative family, as the second section of the chapter explains, and so its focus is initially on existing qualitative evidence of alternative nineteenth-century family groups. Part Two is divided into sections on children of the Empire, parental death, widows and widowers, and children alone, and the emphasis of each section is largely socio-historic, although a number of children's texts, including titles by Frances Hodgson Burnett (1849–1924), Ismay Thorn, the pseudonym of Edith Caroline Pollock (1853–1919), and Harriet Childe-Pemberton, as well as excerpts from *The Girl's Own Paper* (1880–1941), are introduced to demonstrate how the transnormative family, and its problems, were represented in both fiction and non-fiction. For the majority of children depicted in this chapter, "home" bears little resemblance to the domestic ideal of loving parents and offspring, but for many middle-class children there was at least the refuge of a transnormative family that equated, in part, with more traditional images.

The focus of Chapter Two is on Victorian texts for children that feature those popularly termed "street arabs" and explores how authors attempted to underwrite middle-class ideology within tales of the destitute underclass. Original sources have been incorporated to illustrate both the extent and the nature of the street-arab problem as perceived by mid-to-late Victorian commentators, and the nineteenth-century methods employed to resolve the destinies of the thousands of largely homeless children. As well as implicitly questioning the philanthropic enterprise that sought to relocate the children of the streets, this chapter reveals the overt classism that depicted the poor as incapable of rearing children. Analyses of texts by Florence Montgomery (*Wild Mike and His Victim*: 1875), Stretton (*Jessica's First Prayer, Jessica's Mother*: both 1867 and *Lost Gip*: 1873) and Brenda (*Nothing to Nobody*: 1873 and *Froggy's Little Brother*: 1875) illustrate the different ways in which nineteenth-century children's writers approached what was clearly an issue for Victorian society and offered resolutions that generally urged the "rescue" of street-arab children from their inadequate homes and surroundings. It is a stance that clearly exposes the shifting, class-related value of the transnormative family. For the middle-class child, the transnormative family is usually portrayed as "second best" to the "natural" familial unit. For the destitute child, a transnormative family, infused with middle-class mores, is invariably depicted as superior to the child's "natural" family.

The figure of the stepmother is examined in Chapter Three, which discusses the impossibility of re-establishing the family ideal in the wake of maternal death and in the shadow of the perfection of the dead mother. Using original commentaries on stepmothering by Yonge and Mrs J. Bakewell, contributor to and editor of *The British Mother's Magazine*, later *The British Mothers' Journal and Domestic Magazine* (1845–unknown), the chapter also focuses on the relationship between the nineteenth-century stepmother and her wicked, mythical, fairy-tale counterpart to argue that children's texts ultimately serve to reaffirm the existence of a close association. The stepmother in her various guises is traced through detailed analyses of four children's texts, Yonge's *The Young Step-mother* (1861), Caroline Birley's *We Are Seven* (1880), Lucy Lane Clifford's "The New Mother" (1882) and Childe-Pemberton's *Birdie: A Tale of Child Life* (1888). While several of these authors attempt to conclude their texts with an image of family unity, each serves, albeit in different ways, to confirm that the nineteenth-century stepmother can never replicate the sainted persona of her predecessor, although she may, in some cases, achieve a semblance of the domestic ideal through manipulation.

Aunts and uncles as foster parents provide the basis for Chapter Four, which examines the spinster aunt and bachelor uncle as carers and reveals the gender bias that invariably privileges the male figure and condemns the unmarried aunt. While unmarried aunts are shown to have little or no skill in establishing a domestic idyll, are frequently insensitive to children and may be depicted as potentially harmful, the relationship between a child and her uncle, whether he is a bachelor or husband, is likely to represent an exemplary familial bond. Chapter Four is largely text-based, although there is extensive discussion of the spinster aunt as depicted in nineteenth-century non-fiction (with emphasis on Anne Penny's *The Afternoon of Unmarried Life*: 1858) and of the bachelor uncle, with reference to contemporary masculine studies. The chapter concludes that while authors largely ignore the problems inherent to transnormative families, including the absence or death of parents, they frequently offer a model of domestic contentment that is achieved, to differing degrees, through the benevolent single uncle. However, the uncle is often depicted as little more than a child and so is implicitly poorly equipped to assume the role of surrogate parent. Among the texts discussed are Catherine Sinclair's *Holiday House: A Book for the Young* (1839), Yonge's *Countess Kate* (1862), Brenda's *Lotty's Visit to Grandmama: A Story for the Little Ones* (1877) and *Little Cousins or Georgie's Visit to Lotty* (1880), Molesworth's *Rosy* (1882) and Childe-Pemberton's "All My Doing: or Red Riding Hood Over Again" (1882).

The emphasis throughout this book is on female authors, and Chapter Five centers on women as writers of children's literature. As nineteenth-century authors of domestic narratives, their focus was primarily the family and family life, and their foundation the familial ideal. Their perceptions were often based on first-hand experiences; as middle-class women, they were necessarily part of the world in which they lived and their preoccupations and anxieties were undoubtedly reflected in their writing. Furthermore, their role as author was inextricably fused with their gender identity. Their profession was not merely that of writer, but that of a writer who was a female and who "naturally" possessed the womanly characteristics demanded of her sex—a caring nature, transferable motherly tendencies and skills, and an ability to resolve crises. The role of the female author was in many ways maternal and the female author of domestic fiction was essentially a surrogate mother with responsibilities for both educating and edifying future generations. This chapter revisits four texts, Molesworth's *Rosy*, Brenda's *Froggy's Little Brother*, Yonge's *Countess Kate* and Clifford's "The New Mother," to examine the way in which the narrative voice assumes the role of parent, aunt, friend, or potential foe, and the extent to which this voice perpetuates or subverts the nineteenth-century domestic ideal.

Although biographical information on many of the featured authors, including the "forgotten" female writers of children's literature, has been incorporated throughout where appropriate, there are further biographical details in the Appendix, although some individuals have proved more elusive than others. It is information that serves to further illuminate the identities of these writers and, more importantly, counteracts the Victorian proclivity for idealized womanhood that has largely been responsible for conceptualizing such individuals as little more than ciphers. Ismay Thorn, for example, wrote numerous books for children, but was also the daughter of a Lord Chief Baron, was one of twenty-three offspring and was undoubtedly well-versed in the difficulties inherent to family life; Lucy Lane Clifford, referred to by Henry James as "Aunt Lucy" (Schlueter and Schuleter 1998: 108), apparently passed her childhood in the care of her grandmother and so patently understood the notion of the trans-normative family, which undoubtedly impacted on her writing for children. To expose these authors and their books to the critical gaze is to begin to acknowledge the existence of a substantial body of work that has yet to be fully investigated but that offers often explicit and unparalleled insights into the past and its ideologies. As late Victorians it is essential that we comprehend the roots of our preoccupation with the ideal family if we are ever to move forward and normalize transnormative groupings.

# Chapter One
## Redefining the Past

PART ONE: THEORY AND THE FAMILY

> We must continue . . . to question the dominance which the nuclear family retains over our imagination and our ideas about family life . . . Such a questioning will pull in from the margins of history the very different patterns of family life, practices and relationships which have existed in the past but which have been silenced or overshadowed. (Davidoff et al. 1999: 269)

Reviewing three new books on family history for *The Journal of British Studies* in 2002, Ellen Ross suggested that "the subdiscipline of family history [was] going through a mid-life crisis; indeed [that it might] actually be ready for retirement" (p. 537).[1] Her suggestion was based on the notion that the concept of the family had "been challenged so successfully and from so many angles, that its ontological status [was very shaky]" and that for those concerned with "unquantifiable changes in the emotions, divisions of labour, power relations, or sexual experiences in domestic and nondomestic settings, it [was] disorienting to be working with what seem[ed] to be, at least in the theoretical sense, a vanished entity" (p. 537). However, Ross was not deriding the notion of yet *more* research into the family, but rather highlighting the fact that, as a concept, the family was no longer useful; she suggested that it should be replaced for scholars by "such areas as intimacy, sexuality, fathers, mothers, regulatory policies and the like" (p. 544).

To propose further detailed quantitative research on the development of the family as a concept would indeed appear to be somewhat superfluous—there are numerous texts that have more than adequately done so. Furthermore, approaches to the study of the family have evolved; as Ross also states, the last few years have witnessed a blending of quantitative and qualitative material that incorporates both demographic and socio-historic evidence (p. 537), and it is within this sphere that academic research into the family is currently located. Writers such as George Behlmer (1998), Leonore Davidoff (1987 and 1999) and John Tosh (1999 and 2004), are evidence of a contemporary approach to the history of family life that focuses on the myriad diversities and intricacies of the nineteenth-century family and frequently does so with reference to both quantitative and qualitative sources. Whether the central focus of such texts is gender-related, as with Davidoff and Tosh, or, as in Behlmer's case, concerned with issues of social control and regulation, research into the family has clearly broadened, although it often acknowledges, to varying degrees, the earlier work of important social theorists such as Michael Anderson.

## Sociological Methodologies

In *Approaches to the History of the Western Family, 1500–1914* (1980), Anderson points out that "before the mid-1950s, family history as we know it today was almost non-existent. Most work was limited to single families or small elite groups or was based mainly on impressionistic literary sources" (p. 17). Anderson identifies four methods for studying the family; the psychohistorical, the demographic, the sentimental, and the household economics approach. His classification remains useful for understanding sociological methodology, although Anderson virtually dismisses psychohistory, which seeks to understand historical events by providing a detailed psychological analysis of characters in literary works of the period (Reber 1985: 591): "the literary sources which formed the basis of most earlier attempts at family history are largely rejected on the grounds that their evidence is difficult to interpret reliably, often contradictory and above all is uncertain in its relevance outside a small elite" (Anderson 1980: 17). However and more recently, various critics investigating the past through analysis of the literature of the period, have assimilated the theories of new historicism to establish a revised methodology that often juxtaposes the social discourses of the nineteenth century and its literature, and so attempts to illuminate the parallels and tensions between ideology, representation, and practice. My own research utilizes a similar historical approach, while drawing on earlier theories, but also includes demographic information where appropriate.

The demographic approach, as identified by Anderson, seeks out and analyzes historical data, and has continued to build on the techniques of demographers working in France in the 1950s where parish registers of baptisms, burials, and marriages were located and families linked together. Spearheaded in the UK by Peter Laslett, Roger Schofield and Tony Wrigley, demographic techniques have proved to be of significant value to studies of social change, providing analyzes of major events within a particular area, from birth and marriage to death. Although by its very nature the demographic approach is specific and can consequently be problematic when trying to gauge social structures on a broader scale, demographic investigations have often exposed the inaccuracies of earlier assumptions about the family. For example, and as Gittins states, work undertaken by Peter Laslett, Philip J. Greven and John Demos during the 1970s demonstrated that prior to industrialization most people lived in relatively small households that corresponded to what we might today term the nuclear family, while Anderson's work on mid-Victorian Preston, *Family Structure in Nineteenth-Century Lancashire* (1971), illustrated how kin helped one another, co-residing for periods of time (Gittins 1985: 6).

Researchers employing the sentimental approach "reject the argument that crucial changes in the Western family over the past 500 years can be deduced from a limited range of demographic sources," according to Anderson. Instead, he says, they subscribe to the notion that a proper understanding of family history is concerned with the family "as an idea" (Ariès cited in Anderson 1980: 39). Literature in this area is dominated by four general surveys that have long been considered seminal texts: Phillipe Ariès' *Centuries of Childhood* (1973), Edward Shorter's *The Making of the Modern Family* (1975), Lawrence Stone's *Family, Sex and Marriage in England 1500–1800* (1977) and Jean-Louis Flandrin's *Families in Former Times* (1979). As Anderson explains: "the major authors in this group describe a gradual movement away from [the] relatively emotionless, open, undifferentiated and patriarchal family" (1980: 44). For Stone, the crucial change is one towards affective individualism which emphasizes feelings, emotions, and individual happiness while stressing the importance of the individual's relationship with others; for Shorter and Flandrin, sentiment and consideration become increasingly important; while for Ariès, the physical and emotional well-being of the child is a central concern.

Finally, Anderson identifies what he terms the household economics approach, inspired by theories drawn from social science "about the patterning of social relationships and of change in relationships" with particular emphasis on economic or other exchanges (1980: 65). Abbott asserts that household economics appears to be Anderson's own preference (Abbott 1993: 8); certainly his work on family structure in nineteenth-century Preston, with its contrast between rural and urban dwellers and his broad analysis of the 1851 census within the context of what he describes as "the long-term development of British patterns of domestic residence" (Anderson 1972: 436), offer insights into family groupings but also focus on labor supply and domestic production.

Anderson's work has long been of immense value in comprehending at least some of the patterning of nineteenth-century households, and has informed numerous other studies of the family, primarily because it uses evidence gathered during the Victorian period itself and, in this way, provides a substantial foundation for new insights into the notion of family. But because Anderson's agenda is largely restricted to recorded facts, his work is limited, taking little account of the qualitative material that features so prominently in contemporary research and that invariably contributes further insights into nineteenth-century life. In order to achieve a breadth of understanding about the Victorian period, I believe that it is essential to draw on a wide variety of available resources, and so I have chosen to focus on both quantitative data, such as Anderson's, and qualitative source material throughout my study.

## Literary Discourses

Notable among recent qualitative approaches is Catherine Waters' *Dickens and the Politics of Family* (1997), an exploration of the author and of his "fictional interest in fractured families" (p. 16). As Waters explains, her methodology "owes much to recent work within Victorian studies which has adopted a post-structuralist orientation to history and focused upon the power of representation to materialise ways of being—to produce subjectivity" (p. 25). My own methodology echoes that of Waters and her contemporaries, although Waters specifically examines the ideology of family life, "as distinct from families themselves" (p. 12). While much of my emphasis is also on family ideology, "real" individuals, as well as fictional creations, feature where appropriate in my research, primarily because the realities of nineteenth-century life can often provide a bridge between ideology and literary representation, and thus offer further insights.

Waters' work is a valuable source of information in exploring the tensions between ideology and fictional images of the family. Acknowledging the difficulties that exist in defining the family, Waters traces the emergence of nineteenth-century ideology, but also emphasizes that the concept of the family in the Victorian period was one characterized by fluidity. Despite the fact that:

> the family was taken to be the basic "social unit" in the . . . [1851 Census Report] . . . actual living arrangements varied widely, and the difficulty of accommodating these within the definitions proposed by the Register-General's office points to a revealing gap between ideology and social practice. [There was confusion among enumerators] . . . who were required by the Register-General's definitions to count those boarding in another man's house as part of his family, but to count lodgers as single families.[2] As a result of the confusion, in the Act for taking the census of 1851 a distinction was drawn between "occupiers" and "families", thus narrowing the definition of the latter to match more accurately the reported "type of family": namely, "the community in a house, consisting of the husband, wife, children and servants; but the most common of all particular cases is that of a husband, wife and children." (pp. 13–14)

Moreover, she points out that "the nineteenth-century specialisation of the term 'family' to describe the small kin-group occupying a single house, identified as the 'type' in the 1851 Census Report, is evidence of the hegemonic[3] definition of the family established by the middle classes" (p. 14), and adds: "What is important to note for the purposes of examining familial ideology in the nineteenth century . . . is the function of a normative conception of the middle-class family and home in shaping the expectations of the census takers" (p. 15).

This "normalizing" of the concept of family, essentially a middle-class creation, is a crucial element in Dickens' work, states Waters. Although Dickens was celebrated in his own time for a concept of the family that was "the ideal of domesticity"—for example, the description of the Cratchits' Christmas dinner—his fiction, Waters asserts, often "delineates families made memorable by their grotesque failure to exemplify the domestic ideal" (p. 27). It is, she says, an ideal that is implied almost everywhere as a standard against which the fictional families are gauged and herein "lies the explanation for the paradox involved in the apparent disjunction between Dickens' reputation as the celebrant of domestic bliss and his fictional interest in fractured families" (p. 27):

> What condemns Mrs Joe in *Great Expectations*, for instance, is her failure to embody the maternal ideal that goes with the worship of the hearth ... What makes David Copperfield's eventual choice of Agnes as his proper partner in marriage function as a sign of his maturation and moral development is the ideal of domesticity that underwrites this choice. (p. 27)

Waters' text provides clear indication of what she terms "the normalising function of middle-class ideology in Dickens' fiction" and she concludes that his novels trace a shift in notions of the family toward "a new ideal of domesticity assumed to be the natural form of the family" (p. 27). What is true for Dickens' work—and Waters' evaluation is both a valuable and an insightful addition to research on the family—would also seem to be true for the children's literature of the period. The ideal family, as espoused by middle-class ideology, is implicitly a normalizing device in a number of Victorian children's novels discussed here, but there is, overall, no evidence of a general acceptance of a new familial paradigm in such texts. The ostensible "success" of the transnormative family in children's tales is often accompanied, even in the final stages of closure, by an overarching suggestion of compromise, as in Charlotte Yonge's *The Young Step-mother* (1861) and Caroline Birley's *We Are Seven* (1880), both of which are discussed fully in Chapter Three. Dickens may well propose "a new ideal of domesticity," as Waters suggests and perhaps he is at least partially successful in doing so. Children's texts, however, would appear to be less convincing in their attempts to validate the transnormative family as a new and desirable domestic model, consistently underwriting the desirability of the traditionally idyllic family group, even, and perhaps particularly, in the wake of parental death.

## Maternal Loss

Carolyn Dever's 1998 publication, *Death and the Mother from Dickens to Freud: Victorian Fiction and the Anxiety of Origins*, situates parental death, specifically the dead mother, at the center of Victorian fiction and argues that this loss, as a narrative technique, is fundamental to numerous novels. Like Waters, Dever focuses her research on nineteenth-century ideology and fiction of the period, drawing on Freudian psychology to explore the loss of the mother and examining the way in which authors utilized such absence for both plot and characterization. According to Dever:

> The ideal mother is the ghost that haunts the Victorian novel. Para-doxically, the world of Victorian fiction, so preoccupied with women's power in the context of the domestic sphere, only rarely embodies that power in the figure of the mother. Instead, Victorian novels almost invariably feature protagonists whose mothers are dead or lost, swept away by menacing and often mysterious outside forces. The maternal ideal in fiction thus takes its shape and its power in the context of almost complete maternal absence, and I would argue, through the necessary vehicle of such a void. (p. xi)

For Dever, such maternal loss enables nineteenth-century writers to "consider complex questions of female subjectivity and sexuality" (p. 2). Furthermore, she asserts, "Victorian dead-mother plots facilitate a number of cultural pro-cesses, functioning most prominently, perhaps, as a means of addressing the question of origins in terms at once physical and psychological" (p. 6–7), all of which is a laudable argument when applied to adult texts of the period. There are clearly similarities between the mother figures that appear in nineteenth-century adult and children's fiction in terms of their iconic status, and Dever's theoretical approach is an often valuable resource in examining familial rela-tionships and the persistent presence of the dead mother in both adult and children's texts. However, although Dever's insistence that a void is necessary for the creation of the maternal ideal is largely validated by nineteenth-century children's fiction as well as adult texts, her assertion that it is also vital to the plot and the development of the central protagonist, is a less convincing claim when applied to Victorian children's literature.

There are numerous maternal deaths in the children's tales of the period, yet these deaths seldom enable the degree of character development that Dever perceives within adult fiction; the stories for children are primarily domestic tales engaging with potentially credible events. The death of the mother may precipitate the arrival of a stepmother and the protagonists' resistance to the intruder—and thus inform the narrative—but such tales tend to focus on learning to accept change and the child's realization that the maternal ideal can be found amongst the living. Furthermore, in children's literature, the dead mother figure sometimes serves as a manipulative device to persuade a child character toward a particular course of action or style of behavior. For example, in Harriet Childe-Pemberton's *Birdie: A Tale of Child Life* (1888), Birdie's step-mother, Lady Victoria, achieves victory over her wayward charge by suggesting that Birdie's dead mother would be sad in Heaven if her children "were not trying to be happy and good" (p. 188).[4] Would-be academic Ethel in Charlotte M. Yonge's *The Daisy Chain: Or Aspirations: A Family Chronicle* (1856) is subjected to a similarly persuasive argument and relinquishes her desire for a classical education when her sister Margaret reminds Ethel of what their mother would have wished:

> Would you give up being a useful, steady daughter and sister at home? The sort of woman that dear mamma wished to make you, and a comfort to papa . . . I don't think dear mamma would have liked Greek and Cocksmoor to swallow up all the little common lady-like things. (p. 84)

In both texts the absent mother is a powerful tool, but one that is wielded by others to validate their own point of view, or, as in *The Daisy Chain*, to consolidate that of the male members of the family. As Shirley Foster and Judy Simons suggest in *What Katy Read: Feminist Re-readings of "Classic" Stories for Girls* (1995), the "alternative model of girlhood" that the "submissive and self-negating" Margaret proposes has already been mooted by Ethel's father and is subsequently echoed by her brother Norman (p. 73). But it is Margaret's deployment of the dead mother that is most effective in prompting Ethel to examine her role and, finally, to concede to gender expectations. It is significant that neither Birdie nor Ethel argues against the supposed desires of a deceased icon; the mere mention of what "mother" would have wished is sufficient to quieten any suggestion of rebellion. However, the dead mothers of *Birdie: A Tale of Child Life* and *The Daisy Chain* have at least some relevance to their children's daily lives, albeit vicariously, as others interpret their wishes. In contrast, in Florence Montgomery's *Misunderstood* (1869), Humphrey's dead mama is little more than an angelic cipher who awaits her offspring at the portals of heaven:

> Everything seemed to be turning and whirling; and, as if to save himself, he opens his eyes. On what a sight did they fall! There, close before him, bathed in light, and a glory round her brow, stands the figure of his mother, looking down upon him with a smile. And with a glad smile of welcome, he stretched out his arms, and cried, "Has God sent you to fetch me at last, mother? Oh, mother, I'll come! I'll come!" (p. 320)

Rather than creating an enabling void, and sentimentality aside, the dead mother plot in children's literature appears to provide practical guidance for those left behind; whether that guidance be for the motherless child or for the stepmother faced with the task of forming relationships with her new family. As Dever points out, "the fictional investment in maternal morbidity" is largely a narrative device accommodating agendas "ranging from the misogynist to the proto-feminist" (1998: 17), and while these specific agendas are rarely overtly evident in children's fiction, the dead mother would certainly seem to provide the means whereby the child can be cajoled into conforming to ideological expectations. Whatever the didactic implications of such children's texts, maternal death, or indeed the demise of both parents, would seem to have been entirely acceptable to nineteenth-century children's writers. Dever claims that "the death rate of mothers in the Victorian novel is elevated far beyond the mortality rates among the same population of living women during this period" and asserts that it was far more dangerous to "give birth in a fictional world than any region, under any conditions, within any social class in Britain" (p. 11), but there is clear indication that the death of a parent, whether mother or father, was very much a reality for numbers of Victorian children, as is discussed in the second part of this chapter. For example, in *The Cambridge Social History of Britain 1750–1950*, Michael Anderson estimates that about 19 per cent of marriages in the 1850s would have been shattered by death within ten years, with the rate decreasing to 13 per cent by 1880 (cited in Jalland 1996: 230).

## Parentless Children

Laura Peters, like Waters, also focuses on nineteenth-century family ideology in *Orphan Texts: Victorian Orphans, Culture and Empire* (2000), but does so while exploring the figure of the parentless child.[5] Allied to contemporary methodology that seeks to examine the paradoxical nature of nineteenth-century social discourse and literary representation, and, in some ways, an extension of Waters' research on Dickens, Peters' text offers a fresh perspective on the orphan, asserting that the prevalence of the orphan figure in Victorian culture "can be explained by the central role which the family played at that time" (p. 1). She explains:

> Although one would expect that orphans needed a family, in short, the reality was that the family needed orphans. The family and all it came to represent—legitimacy, race and national belonging—was in crisis; it was at best an unsustainable ideal. In order to reaffirm itself the family needed a scapegoat. It found one in the orphan figure. (p. 1)

Through exploration of primarily mainstream literature of the period, including works by Dickens, Eliot and Charlotte and Emily Brontë, as well as lesser-known texts, Peters' analysis of the orphan figure highlights the fragility of the nineteenth-century domestic idyll and posits the orphan not as a being outside "the narrative of domesticity" (p. 22), but as both a product and essential component of the family. Drawing on the theories of Freud and Derrida, she identifies the orphan as *unheimlich* and *pharmakon*; and in both instances, as she points out, opposites are opposed. Thus, as she says, the *pharmakon* "both contains the threatening difference and is the process by which this difference is expelled" (p. 22) and the family, as locus, contains its opposite in the figure of the orphan.[6] Moreover, she explains:

> The notion of the orphan as *unheimlich* and by that nature repressed (either discursively or through criminalisation or emigration) indicates that the orphan as a figure continues to provoke in the larger family—society—fear, anxiety, guilt and inadequacy by its presence . . . The secret hidden nature of orphanhood manifests itself not only in foreignness but also often intertwines with illegitimacy. (23)

For Peters, as with Waters, there is a tension between middle-class ideology and the writing so frequently espoused by middle-class authors that focuses on "failed families, unorthodox families and domestic violence" (p. 5) and Peters proposes that this is a melancholic maneuver; "the keeping alive of an ideal through desiring it in the midst of loss" (p. 5). Although Peters' focus is adult literature, her comment and the suggestion that "a melancholic manoeuvre" exists within Victorian narratives about the family is equally appropriate to a discussion of children's texts; portraits of transnormative groups frequently expose that which has been lost, whether overtly or implicitly. Furthermore, Peters' conceptualization of the orphan as *unheimlich* offers, in part, a rationale for the Victorians' desire to keep such creatures at a distance by expelling them or assimilating them into the middle classes, as is explored in the following chapter. Victorian children's books are often as subtextually challenging as their adult counterparts and the prevalent ideologies of a period are inevitably reflected in its literature, whatever the age of the implied reader. But the realities of an era are ever-present too, and for many of the children's books discussed here, the transnormative family is representative of at least a part of the Victorian experience. While many children were born and grew up amongst conjugal kin, many others did not, and they too are part of the historical story that Davidoff, in the opening quote to this chapter, seeks to further investigate. By focussing on these children who stand apart from the ideological concept of the Victorian family and have therefore implicitly been marginalized, it may be possible, as Davidoff et al. also suggest, to "pull in from the margins of history the very different patterns of family life, practices and relationships which have existed in the past but which have been silenced or overshadowed" (1999: 269).

## PART TWO: TRANSNORMATIVE FAMILIES—CAUSES AND EFFECTS

### Children of the Empire

Elizabeth Buettner's research on the Talbot family, who were separated as a result of their father's colonial career in India, provides an often poignant glimpse into the emotions of a father, mother and four children as they attempt to maintain a semblance of an ideological family existence, while simultaneously experiencing the realities of separation and transnormative family life with relatives or at boarding school. Buettner writes:

> Adelbert and Agnes Talbot's years together in India . . . exemplified a form of family life made possible by a combination of middle-class professional opportunities in the empire and the promotion of white domesticity in colonial arenas. More significantly, methods of childrearing prevalent within the white colonial community resulted in long-term family division when children were sent back to Britain at early ages. Adelbert and Agnes had three daughters and one son born between 1873 and 1880, none of whom remained with them in India past the age of five. (1999: 117)

Buettner's more recent publication, *Empire Families: Britons and Late Imperial India* (2004), which also incorporates information about the Talbots, extends her work to include other individuals and provides some important data on families who left Britain for the Empire. As she records, in the 1891 census of India, the European community exceeded 165,000, with the military dominating (85,000 including wives and children). Civil employees and their families totaled approximately 10,5000, while the railway community amounted to 6,100 (p. 8). The remaining 65,000 men, women and children were supported by other work. There is no indication of how many children were sent "home" from what was generally perceived to be an unhealthy way of life, but their numbers were presumably substantial. Furthermore, as Buettner points out, although it was commonplace for British-based kin and sometimes family friends to play a role in child-rearing when parents were abroad, the children's experiences were not always happy ones, even among members of the same family. When they returned to England, the two eldest Talbot daughters, Guendolen and Muriel, initially stayed at the home of their aunt, Mary Coventry, and were evidently valued members of the household. Writing to Adelbert Talbot just prior to the girls' departure, Mary commented: "How strange it seems that the time is drawing to a close for the dear children to leave us! They have found Woolstone thoroughly a home and will always I think have a happy remembrance of these three years . . . they fret a good deal at the thought of leaving me . . . Muriel . . . scarcely remembers her mother, which must always be the case when separated before five years" (p. 118).

In contrast, the Talbot's youngest daughter, Esmé, was sent to stay with different relatives at the age of four and was regularly beaten by her aunt who falsely accused her of her cousins' misdeeds. Only when she was older did she learn that she had been visited during that time by a great-aunt, who found her both neglected and shabby (p. 119). Moreover, when Esmé finally left her aunt's care, she was moved into the home of a "gentleman farmer" and his wife, "who wanted to take in a girl of the same age as their daughter so that they might share the services (and costs) of a governess." The couple were kind to her, but, as Buettner points out, Esmé, her sisters and brother were seldom together (p. 119). Esmé Talbot's unhappy experiences would no doubt have been familiar to the young Rudyard Kipling, whom Buettner describes as "one of the best-known 'children of the Raj'" (p. 121). Kipling's artist father was employed in Bombay and Kipling and his sister Alice were both sent back to England in 1871 when Rudyard was six, becoming boarders with the Holloway family in Southsea, a fervently Evangelical group who, according to Kipling, behaved inhumanely to the young boy; as Buettner points out, Kipling discusses such issues in his short story "Baa, Baa Black Sheep" (2004: 122). Moreover, the sense of disenchantment with transnormative families experienced by ex-patriate children found its way into mainstream juvenile fiction. Frances Hodgson Burnett's *Sarah Crewe, or What Happened at Miss Minchin's* (1887), later dramatized as *A Little Princess* (1905), opens with the closing stages of a journey from Bombay to London where Sarah takes up residence at "a select seminary for young ladies" (p. 10). It proves no substitute "home"; when Sarah's young soldier father dies and she apparently becomes penniless, she is also forced to become a servant, although she is ultimately rescued and apparently happily located within a transnormative family by the ministrations of the kindly Mr Carrisford. For Sarah, as for Mary Lennox, the protagonist of Burnett's most famous, later novel, *The Secret Garden* (1911), England does not equate with home; in fact, although *The Secret Garden* concludes with what appears to be a portrait of family unity, a sub-textual reading suggests that Mary is ever the orphaned outsider. Interestingly, as Buettner points out, Burnett neither visited India nor came from a family with Indian connections (1999: 27) but, as Ariko Kawabata observes: "It is because Burnett was igno-rant of the reality, that her India has every imagined characteristic typified in Western discourse . . . Burnett's India is a vehicle through which to express colonial conventions" (2005: 40). Moreover, Burnett's portraits of what were fundamentally Anglo-Indian children are explorations not only of transnormative family experiences, but also of the cultural divide that confronted such children as they attempted to integrate into an essentially alien world.

Texts such as Burnett's *The Secret Garden* draw attention to the predicament of children from overseas who are transported to "home," but who may find their transnormative family situation a poor imitation of the domestic ideal, although in Mary Lennox's case, it might be argued that her transnormative family is ultimately a satisfactory and happy unit. Other writers offered a less ambiguous and generally positive view of assimilation into transnormative family spheres: Ismay Thorn's *Quite Unexpected* (1889), discussed in the next section, and Mary Louisa Molesworth's *Rosy* (1882), examined in Chapter Four, focus to varying degrees on the phenomenon of the Empire family with specific reference to dispossessed children and do so, overall, with apparent optimism. Yet neither Thorn nor Molesworth shy away from the problems inherent to such experiences; the Harrington children are initially unwelcome at their elderly relatives' home and in *Rosy*, Empire child Beata is subjected to the jealousies of her foster parents' daughter. Whether real or fictional, Empire children's experiences of transnormative family life were varied, as indeed they were for the many other children who found themselves within a transnormative family environment.

## A Variety of Arrangements

There were many reasons why a nineteenth-century child might have been located within a transnormative family. For children such as Kipling, it was parental commitment to work; for others it was perhaps illegitimacy, the death of a parent or the desire of relatives for social progeny that placed them within an alternative construct of home. Harriet Childe-Pemberton's "All My Doing or Red Riding Hood Over Again," from *The Fairy Tales of Every Day* (1882), a reinterpretation of fairy-tale themes, offers just such a scenario: protagonist Pussy, one of ten children, opts to live with her grandmother, lured by the prospect of a quiet home and lavish lifestyle.[7]

While this transference from the family home to one of luxury and riches was undoubtedly more likely for upper- and middle-class children, transnormative groupings affected children throughout the social strata. Anna Davin's study of daily life among the labouring poor of London asserts that within working-class communities, it was not at all unusual for children to join other households. It was, she says,

> sometimes as an arrangement of mutual convenience, often as a result of crisis or bereavement. Applications for the remission of school fees in 1870 reveal cases of orphaned children adopted by cousins, by older sisters and by grandmothers, themselves not in easy circumstances. Babies whose fathers did not acknowledge or support them were often taken in by the maternal grandparents or other relatives so that the mother could find work, especially if she was a servant. For other reasons too it could be desirable to farm a child out for a time at least; for example extreme overcrowding or illness at home, the need for a mother to earn, bad feelings between a child and a parent or a step-parent, or some other tension, perhaps between the parents. But where crisis was chronic and there were children, they would probably be dispersed, and some might end up in the workhouse. (1996: 40)

The workhouse was generally, and perhaps thankfully, not an option for middle-class orphans although Dickens' Oliver Twist, born illegitimately and eminently middle class, spends the first few years of his life in such an institution following the death of his mother. Children's fiction of the period is replete with offspring whose mother, father, or sometimes both, are absent or dead, and with quasi-adoptions by other relatives. Ismay Thorn, writing of the four Harrington children in *Quite Unexpected* (1889), relocates the children with their uncle and great-aunt when their mother dies traveling back to England from Bombay where her husband is stationed:

> Captain Harrington had been sending his wife and children home from India, and Mrs O'Leary, the wife of a soldier, had come with them as nurse to the children during the voyage. Mrs Harrington had taken a severe cold immediately after they had left Bombay, and as she neglected taking proper care of herself it had settled on her lungs.[8] Severe inflammation came on rapidly, and after a few days her strength had given way, and she had died from exhaustion (1889: 4).

Mamma is thus swiftly dispensed with, the transnormative family is created, and when the children's father arrives, the children continue to live with their surrogate parents. Dever's assertion that "the ideal mother is the ghost that haunts the Victorian novel" is largely unconvincing when applied to Thorn's texts; although the death of the children's mother *has* precipitated a major change that alters their concept of home, there is relatively little lamentation amongst her offspring. Nevertheless, the death of the mother was assuredly a traumatic event for many Victorian children, and although mothers must have died from a multitude of causes, the image of a mother dying in childbirth is one that often prevails in discussions of Victorian mortality. It is a supremely emotional event and instantly lends credibility to the notion of the mother as a martyr, a creature who relinquishes her own existence whilst striving to give life to another.

### The Death of the Parent

In Loving Memory of Eva
The Darling Wife of Arthur Beeney
Who fell asleep in Jesus May 15 1898
Also of her precious babe Arthur John
Who died May 16 aged 2 days

Inscription on memorial tablet: St. James' Churchyard,
Abinger Common, Surrey.

Maternal mortality rates during the nineteenth century have long been the subject of fierce debate, largely because of the lack of clarity surrounding the recording of causes of death, particularly from the mid- to late-Victorian period. What would clearly seem to be true, however, is that deaths as a result of childbirth were often under-reported. As Dever details, the debate surrounding such mis-reporting originated in an article by MD Robert Barnes in 1859, which argued for more skepticism over the reliability of childbed death statistics and asserted:

> It is stated in the Registrar General's Report for 1856 that the mortality in child-birth in England and Wales in 1847 was 1 in 167 and that it had fallen to 1 in 227 in 1856. Now, having applied to Dr. Elkington for the puerperal statistics of Birmingham, I learn that the Registrar of that town says that "no one ever specifies the deaths in child-birth or from puerperal fever". (1998: 14)

Although William Farr, compiler of abstracts at the General Register Office, was initially outraged by the report, stating that "there may be an indisposition in some cases to record the child-birth as cause, but there is no reason to believe that practitioners have generally shrunk from their duty" (cited in Dever 1998: 15), he was later to acknowledge that as many as 2,000 out of the over 4,000 maternal deaths a year were avoidable (Loudon 1992: 2). Furthermore, as Irvine Loudon reports in his 1992 publication, *Death in Childbirth: An International Study of Maternal Care and Maternal Mortality 1800–1950*, after 1,200 letters of enquiry were sent out in 1880 as a response to unsatisfactory medical certificates, a total of 330 "hidden" maternal deaths were discovered. A similar exercise, carried out from 1881 to 1890 revealed that nearly 3,000 deaths were found to be deaths in childbirth, although certifying practitioners had written "a vague cause of death." After corrections had been made, childbirth deaths for the decade in England and Wales amounted to 42,092 (pp. 518–19), although this figure, of course, may also have been subject to under-estimation.

Whether the intention was to protect the medical profession, or, as Dever suggests, to "market motherhood positively to young women" (1998: 17), truer figures, when they at last emerged, suggested that childbirth was sometimes a precarious business. As Pat Jalland comments in *Death in the Victorian Family* (1996):

> Puerperal fever was the disease dreaded by all pregnant women. Maternal mortality was high in the Victorian period and remained so even after the introduction of antisepsis in the 1880s . . . Puerperal fever caused between 33 and 38 per cent of maternal deaths in England and Wales from 1847 to 1874, though this was likely in reality to have been closer to the 50 per cent recorded for the last quarter of the century. (pp. 46, 47)

In addition, maternal mortality was, and remains, a highly emotive subject; Loudon describes it as "terrible in ways that other mortalities are not," adding:

Childbirth is a physiological process in which, as an American obstetrician said in the 1850s, death is a "sort of desecration." Few women died in pregnancy, fewer still in labour. Most lived long enough to see and hold their newborn before dying, often with brutal abruptness, leaving their newborn (and frequently other small children) without a mother, and their husbands without their wives. (1992: 2–3)

But if the image of the dying, recently delivered mother provided material for the nineteenth-century novelist, as with Dickens' *Oliver Twist*, for example,[9] its poignancy was undoubtedly based on fact. The inscription that introduces this section is typical of many others scattered through churchyards around the country as a gravestone in Mevagissey Old Cemetery in Cornwall confirms: "Erected in memory of Elizabeth . . . who departed this life on 7th September 1847 in the 28th year of her age. Husband and babe farewell" (Gorran-Haven.com 2003). The inscription suggests that the deceased Elizabeth was only recently a mother.

There were, of course, various other ailments that could affect and sometimes kill a parent. Walvin states that tuberculosis, though gradually declining as the century advanced, remained the worst of British urban killers, fatally infecting one Briton in six throughout the nineteenth century (1987: 28). In 1842, when Edwin Chadwick reported on the sanitary conditions of the laboring people, he remarked that "the deaths caused during one year in England and Wales by epidemic, endemic and contagious diseases" amounted to 56,461: "The effect is as if the whole county of Westmorland . . . or the whole county of Huntingdonshire, or any other equivalent district were entirely depopulated annually." Whooping cough killed 10,000 each year at mid-century and was virulent in towns, and typhus accounted for thousands of deaths—19,000 in 1837 and 17,000 ten years later (Walvin 1987: 28). If certain diseases privileged the overcrowded and unhealthy conditions of the inner cities, others were commonplace amongst all classes.

## Widows, Widowers and Stepfamilies

Jalland notes that "the high rates of mortality in the nineteenth-century produced high rates of widowed people," with the majority of those widowed individuals being women, primarily because of the mortality differential favoring the females (1996: 230). After 1850, the number of widows over thirty-five in England and Wales was over double that of widowers. Moreover, with marriage *the* most important institution for the vast majority of Victorian women, particularly those of the middle and upper classes, widowhood could prove a devastating experience because it destroyed a woman's role as wife. According to Michael Anderson, post-1850, 14 per cent of men aged fifty-five to sixty-four were widowed, compared with 30 per cent of women, a differential that increased with age and that resulted in a surplus of elderly widows (cited in Jalland 1996: 230).

For women who had lost a husband, the prospect of finding a new father for their children was fairly remote, although occasionally it proved equally difficult for a widower. In *Family Ties: English Families 1540–1920* (1993), Mary Abbott tells how Lord Lyttleton, under forty when his wife died in 1857, looked forward to thirty or forty years of solitary misery and was plunged further into depression three years later by the marriage of his eldest daughter who was also his companion and foster mother to the younger children. With twelve children—unrelieved childbearing had been the death of his first wife—and inadequate means, only a mature and childless woman with a fortune would consider him and he believed he "might as well think of the moon" (p. 67). However, other titled and presumably wealthier men fared more successfully. Sir Frederick Pollock, Attorney General in 1834, and the father of author Ismay Thorn, fathered eleven children with his first wife Frances and married his second, Sarah, Edith's mother, some seven years after Frances' death. The couple produced twelve more children.

But if many young and middle-aged widowers were encouraged by friends and relatives to remarry, and successfully did so, only younger widows could truly anticipate a new spouse to provide comfort, and presumably financial support, for themselves and their offspring. Jalland explains:

> Studies . . . have demonstrated that prospects of remarriage for widowed people varied greatly according to gender and age . . . [and] in the nineteenth-century, also, widows over 30 had far less hope of remarriage than widowers, and, after 40 their prospects were negligable, as William Farr's tables of marriage rates for 1851 and 1870–2 suggest. While the annual marriage rates for widows in 1851 per 1,000 of population sank from 19.649 at 20 years of age to 11.611 at 30, 4.333 at 40 and 1.298 at 50, for widowers the rates remained much higher—30.766 at 20, 28.627 at 30, 14.075 at 40 and 5.711 at 50. (1996: 253)

This imbalance in remarriage rates between men and women would seem to be mirrored in the children's literature of the period; there are noticeably fewer stepfathers than stepmothers, indeed, stepfathers are conspicuous by their absence.[10] Furthermore, there is often active encouragement for fictional widowers to remarry, sometimes even from their offspring, or at least from those who are considered mature. Fourteen-year-old Blanche, daughter of the widowed Mr Haviland in Harriet Childe-Pemberton's *Birdie: A Tale of Child Life* (1888), is described as possessing a "mind more awake to the real state of things than the minds of the younger children" (p. 66) and clearly welcomes her father's remarriage:

> She had watched and listened to some purpose. Furthermore, she had faced the fact that the time was not very far distant when she would need someone to take her into society . . . that, in short, a home, a house,

an establishment like that of Mr Haviland of Redcross, needed a mistress at its head. Blanche was a business-like, practical young person . . . she took her ideas from those around her and, unconsciously to herself, she had caught from her grandmother, from her uncle and her aunt, the idea that it would really be a good thing for her father to marry again. I do not think that Blanche meant more disloyalty to her mother's memory than did Birdie. Hers was only another way of viewing the question—that was all! (p. 66)

So pragmatic Blanche is hospitable to the new Mrs Haviland, although, and for some time, her younger sister Birdie resists the change. Such resistance to a new stepmother is commonplace in Victorian children's literature and will be discussed further in Chapter Three, but the majority of children's texts that deal with what is essentially a sensitive subject, and one that must have been experienced by many children, profess to offer the child reader a comforting resolution and often seem at pains to stress the kindliness of the stepmother. Only rarely is she portrayed as the evil being of fairy tale, and this characterization is evident primarily in those narratives that venture into the realm of fantasy.

However, the introduction of a stepmother into a home mourning the loss of a loved parent was clearly difficult, despite the fact that the outgoing mother, so to speak, may have publicly endorsed such an event. Jalland points out that "dying wives and their friends encouraged husbands to remarry in the interests of motherless children and to satisfy the assumed male need for sympathy and support," and cites the case of Elvira Horsley, who died of tuberculosis at the age of 31 in 1853, leaving three young sons under the age of five:

At her deathbed, husband and wife talked freely of the consequences of her death: "She spoke (having done so frequently before) of my marrying again, how she wished me to do so if it was for my and the children's comfort and good." Her husband, John Callcott Horsley, the artist, took his first wife at her word and, less than two years later, married Rose Haden, a friend of his sister's, to start a new family of seven. The engagement to Rose Haden was kept a secret for many months, but the Haden and Horsley families seem to have welcomed it. (1996: 255)

For a widower to marry a friend of the family or of his deceased wife undoubtedly eased the transition; the new Mrs Haviland in Childe-Pemberton's text is a friend of the children's mother. But for some widowers, their new relationship was altogether *much* closer. In *The Spectacle of Intimacy: A Public Life for the Victorian Family* (2000), Karen Chase and Michael Levenson provide an insight into the generally "taboo" subject of marriage to a deceased wife's sister. During the 1840s, those who sought to legalize such an arrangement proffered a persuasive argument:

> A man's wife falls ill; her sister arrives to support the family in its need. The children see their mother languish and come to depend on their aunt, much as the husband in his grief looks to the affection of his sister-in-law. After the death, this sister becomes more indispensable than ever. She is not only a source of emotional succour; she is a familiar face. When there might have been a cold stranger, there is instead a dear, well-known intimate, already a member of the domestic circle. In the hour of need, what could be more natural, more inevitable, indeed more beautiful, than that husband and children would transfer their love to this domestic redeemer? (p. 111)

Throughout the first half of the nineteenth century, the question of whether marriage to a deceased wife's sister was permissible or not was the subject of much campaigning, as Chase and Levenson explain. Rooted in the forbidden zones of marriage established during the reign of Henry VIII, such a union was allowed during the time of James I, but only if it remained unchallenged; if no action was taken against the couple during their lifetimes, the question could not be raised after their deaths. However, the emphasis here was financial: by allowing such a marriage, the legitimacy of children born within that second marriage and their right to inheritance were ensured. With the introduction of a Parliamentary Act in 1835, Lord Lyndhurst attempted to eradicate such ambiguity. His stated aim was to end the uncertainty of what had been termed "voidable" ties and the new Act "prohibited any new transgressions but legitimised all existing marriages within the prohibited degrees" (Chase and Levenson 2000: 107). Yet despite this prohibition and according to Chase and Levenson, marriages to dead wives' sisters continued to take place, with some couples taking their vows in Hamburg, Denmark, or simply lying to the authorities. Petitions, both for and against the legality of such a union, continued to flourish into the 1840s and it was not until 1907 that the Act was repealed. Paradoxically, the idea of a woman marrying her dead husband's brother was never truly considered, nor debated to any degree. Chase and Levenson offer an explanation:

> And the deceased husband's brother? Where was he in the cauldron of polemic? The logic of symmetry demanded that the husband consider-ing marriage with his dead wife's sister should be mirrored by the wife pondering a future with her brother-in-law. But no sooner was the issue raised than it was quickly set aside. Biology was definitive; the symmetry was an illusion. If the wife became the body in common between two men, then their blood would incestuously, immorally mingle, and this presumably because the wife was a vessel, while the husband was a dry stick, into which no fluids could dangerously penetrate. (p. 114)

Thus patriarchy, validated by scientific reasoning and morality, ensured that the privileges available to the male of the species were simultaneously denied to his female counterpart.

Whether the new stepmother was a relative or a friend of the family, children's responses to this new resident were clearly mixed, as many nineteenth-century texts for children indicate. Birdie in Childe-Pemberton's tale resists change because she feels disloyal to her dead mama; Judy, the central protagonist of Caroline Birley's *We Are Seven*, has assumed the role of her father's helpmeet and so is vehemently opposed to his remarriage.

Other than through detailed case histories it remains largely impossible to estimate the extent to which children resisted the introduction of a stepmother, but letters written to *The Girl's Own Paper* during the late Victorian period give some indication that a new mother in the home was sometimes a less-than-welcome intrusion. Tantalizingly, the publication never carried the letters that correspondents had written, merely providing answers, but there is nevertheless evidence enough to suppose that these particular writers were experiencing difficulties. In the 29 January 1881 edition, Bertie and Ethel—the names that correspondents used were frequently aliases—were told: "Your stepmother, as your father's wife, has the strongest claims on your respect and affection and you must remember that, unless you 'give all their due'—'honour to whom honour'—you cannot expect to receive the kindness and affection which belongs to you of right" (*TGOP* [1] 1881: 288). The editors, answering "Queenie" on 16 July 1881, stated: "To live with your stepmother on good terms should be one of your chief aims in life. But having begun so ill, the task will now be somewhat more difficult than it needed to have been" (*TGOP* [2] 1881: 672). As always, the tone of the paper's editors was morally upright and their responses uncompromising; the duty of a stepchild was an absolute prerequisite and any deviation was to be severely lamented, whatever the views of the subscriber.

## Entirely Alone

If life with a stepmother was difficult, those whose parents were both absent, either temporarily or permanently, faced even greater domestic disruption. As the Talbot family demonstrate, a transnormative family life with relatives was not always idyllic, but for those children who had been orphaned and subsequently adopted by relatives in a non-formalized fashion, there were few alternatives. Again, there is scant information on these groupings, but there are occasional glimpses into such lives, particularly when problems arise. "Boronia," whose reply appeared in *The Girl's Own Paper* on 7 November, 1896, was clearly experiencing conflict between what she perceived as her parents' wishes and those of the relative with whom she was living. In response to her letter, the editors wrote:

> We feel for your present position, as your relative is endeavouring to upset your deceased parents' teaching and wishes. But you are still very young and you are under her care; and it is your duty as a Christian to conduct

yourself humbly, and show respect to her, and endeavour not to aggravate her by saying all you think and acting as you feel. The little trinket-souvenir given you by your mother lay by carefully, and do not anger your relative by wearing it. You might place it in the care of some reliable friend. (*TGOP* [3] 1896: 96)

Moreover, a guardian was not always as dutiful in his or her care as a parent might have been, as a response from 3 June 1893, addressed to "Une Malheureuse," suggests. In this instance, as in many others in *The Girl's Own Paper*, the tone of the editor's reply is unmistakably parental. As guides for their young readers, such editors assume the role of transnormative family parent; in this case, the editor or editors proffer advice on propriety to a girl who lacks mother and father and whose behavior is governed by a careless guardian:

Your guardian has failed very seriously in his duty towards you. He should never have allowed you to walk out nor ride alone. It is highly improper, especially when a girl is so very young and inexperienced . . . a man who has so little honour as to take advantage of a young girl's loneliness and ignorance of the usages of society as to join her without an intro-duction and, worse still, dare to tempt her (a minor) to run away from her guardian and go abroad with him, is simply a scoundrel. At sixteen you ought to be in the schoolroom attending to your education. (*TGOP* [4] 1893: 575)

Home, then, for these children and others like them, bore little resemblance to the domestic ideal of loving, caring parents and offspring, yet for many middle-class children there was at least the refuge of a transnormative family that equated, in part, with more traditional images. But while poorer children might be assimilated into a neighboring home, as Davin has noted, others found themselves entirely alone and dependent on their own resources or on those of a charitable institution. Those children who relied on their wits might have lived in a tumbledown garret or on the streets, as many nineteenth-century texts for children suggest. It is difficult to accurately estimate their numbers or the conditions under which they lived, because only those who came to the notice of the police or charitable societies, for example, are recorded in detail. In the second half of the century, numerous and often successful movements to improve the lives of the poor, particularly those of children, initiated changes that gathered up many of the homeless and provided them with shelter and education, and it is largely through the records of such organizations that information about the lives of impoverished children can be gleaned.

For children under the auspices of the Poor Law Board, access to a transnor-mative family was often through fostering, which was essentially boarding-out in modest homes. Behlmer explains that both private charities and Poor Law authorities used fostering as a way to stimulate "the divine institution of the family" for abandoned children, an eloquent description by *The Times* of 7 November 1874 (1998: 285). In 1870 the Poor Law Board authorized guardians to place selected children with foster parents but, as Behlmer notes, this "liberalisation of policy stemmed largely from the pressure of middle-class women concerned about the plight of girls in workhouses" and their potential for sin (p. 285). Public response to boarding-out was mixed, but cases increased, and during the second half of the century a number of charitable organizations also evolved in response to demands for social reforms, among them the Ragged Schools Union, the Waifs and Strays Society and Barnardo's. Furthermore, as a report by journalist John Hollingshead suggests,[11] it was in such institutions that children often found a semblance of home and family. Writing of the George Yard Ragged School in Whitechapel, Hollingshead notes:

> They have gathered some four hundred children, of all ages, and of both sexes; and they give them every encouragement to consider the school as their home . . . and they have taken eight poor castaways—nobody's children—"into the house,"[12] and are endeavouring to train them into honest working boys. The stories of destitution, cruelty, and desertion which these outcasts have to tell are more harrowing than a thousand tragedies. One has lost all traces of his parents, another is a street beggar's orphan, and another owns no parent but a drunken prostitute, who kicked him, swore at him, stabbed him in the cheek and left a scar which he will carry to his grave. He can now find no traces of such a mother, except in the cruel mark upon his face; and is more happy, perhaps, in calling his schoolmaster father than he ever was before in his life. (1861: 24–5)

The idyllic family unit clearly bears no resemblance to the lived experiences of such children; the physically abused child, scarred forever by his "drunken prostitute" carer, is described as owning "no parent" other than the violent woman of the streets, although in nineteenth-century ideological parlance, she is no parent at all.

Today, the records of nineteenth-century philanthropic organizations offer numerous insights into the conditions of British children seeking a new "home" beyond the parental domicile. "Hidden Lives Revealed," an online archive published by The Children's Society (www.hiddenlives.org.uk), formerly The Waifs and Strays Society, contains hundreds of entries about children passing through its care and although each individual is anonymous, there are sufficient details to establish what frequently must have been an emotive tale. "G," a boy born in 1885 (case 6135), had lost his mother at the age of five and his father was described as "a very unnatural parent." The boy and his siblings had gone to live with their grandparents but eventually, having been "put to endless expense through the evil doings of the boy's father," the grandparents believed that they could do no more and that they would be forced to send the boy, now aged thirteen, back to his father unless he could be placed in an institution. He was admitted to the Rochdale home and two years later went into service with a barber in Lancashire. Orphan "I" (case 4166) and some of her siblings had been cared for by an aunt following their father's death, but when the aunt returned to her own family in Suffolk, "I" and two of her siblings were placed in a workhouse. Prior to this, the children "had been much neglected"; they had been living at their grandfather's house under the care of their fifteen-year-old sister, but both their grandfather and father drank. At the time of their application to The Waifs and Strays Society, the children were destitute and "I" "was received" into the Society's Brighton home in 1894 at the age of ten. At seventeen she went into service in Bournemouth. There are fewer details on orphan "A" (case 499), but she was clearly still a young child when she joined the Kilburn orphanage in 1882. Her father, a platemaker with the North London Railway, was killed on the railway that same year and two months after his death her mother died of tuberculosis. Among the paperwork on the child is a letter from "a lady" seeking an eight or nine-year-old who could be sent to Natal as a servant for her daughter, but there is no evidence that "A," or indeed any other child, was sent.

These various case histories indicate the variety of events that culminated in a child entering a children's institution and the emotional and physical hardship that many of them undoubtedly endured. To be placed, finally, in a "home"—a name which, in itself, implicitly endorses the Victorian predilection for domesticity—was inevitably something of a lifeline; the earlier "homes" from which most of these children would have emerged were clearly far removed from perceived "normality." Their later years might have seen them once more in transnormative family groupings, perhaps as servants in houses where more senior staff assumed the responsibility of mother and father to these surrogate "offspring," or in humbler homes where they might be guided, morally and spiritually, by the master and his wife. Whatever their backgrounds, these children, some of whom had lived on the streets or with inadequate parents, were a popular choice of subject for writers in the mid- to late-nineteenth century. The chapter that follows examines Victorian texts for children that focus on those who were popularly termed street arabs and explores the ways in which authors strove to underwrite middle-class ideology, even for those whose experiences of family life were shadowy imitations of the domestic ideal.

# Chapter Two
## Snatched from "The Seed-plot"[1] of Degeneracy: The "rescue" of the destitute child in tales of street-arab life

Take them away! Take them away!
Out of the gutter, the ooze and the slime,
Where the little vermin paddle and crawl,
Till they grow and ripen into crime.

Take them away from the jaws of death,
And the coils of evil that swaddle them round
And stifle their souls in every breath
They draw on the foul and fetid ground.

Take them away! Away! Away!
The bountiful earth is wide and free,
The New shall repair the wrongs of the Old—
Take them away o'er the rolling sea!
"The Departure of the Innocents," *Our Waifs and Strays*, 1887
(cited in Horn 1997: n.p.)

Although the above verses were written primarily to endorse the Victorian child emigration programme—a scheme that reached its zenith in the mid- to late-years of the century—they also encapsulated the anxieties of a middle-class world that lived closely with destitution and frequently perceived the poor as an entirely different race that needed to be governed. While thousands of pauper children were "managed" through transportation to new lives overseas as farm labourers and domestic servants,[2] the colonial enterprise simultaneously strove

43

to take control of the remaining ragged masses that threatened to wreak havoc on English soil. The destitute poor of the cities, reportedly breeding unchecked in their disease-ridden rookeries, posed a danger to social stability generally, but it was their "vermin" offspring, "swaddled" in evil and genetically destined for crime and depravity, that were viewed as the potential contaminants of the future.

Yet many Victorians believed that such children *could* ultimately be saved, though their parents might be past redemption. The stories of street-arab children[3] that flourished in the mid- to late-nineteenth century took the salvation of the poor child as their theme and were seemingly genuinely philanthropic in their desire to elicit sympathy for such children and raise funds for the numerous charities that homed and educated street waifs. But they also perpetuated the notion that destitute children must be wrested from the gutter, and, by implication, from their families, both for their own moral and spiritual benefit and for the overall good of society. Poor parents, such texts generally asserted, were incapable of rearing "acceptable" adults because they were inevitably afflicted by physical or mental weakness or bestial tendencies; their offspring would assuredly weaken and die, be abandoned, or find themselves consigned to a worse fate. Furthermore, street-arab tales sometimes suggested that such parents did not love their children or that they expected them to die. Overall, the message that arose from such books was stark: while the offspring of the middle and upper classes were nurtured and consequently flourished, those of the destitute withered and perished. Indeed, the destitute family was clearly no family at all, but a perversion of the middle-class domestic ideal, itself a concept that was enhanced by the very existence of the impoverished masses. As Anne McClintock suggests, the degenerate classes, defined as departures from the "'normal' human type," were necessary to the self-definition of the middle classes (1995: 46). In the same way, the destitute family, redolent with poverty and corruption, whose dwelling was considered "the seed-plot of . . . future criminals," and who produced needy, often disreputable individuals, further defined the idealized middle-class home and its professed identity as the site of domestic bliss. Significantly, in street-arab tales, the child protagonist is invariably relocated to a middle-class environment, or one that at least displays middle-class conventions. The ability to create a domestic idyll was thus shown to lie primarily with the middle classes.

The novels discussed in this chapter are representative of the street-arab genre inasmuch as each is, to some degree, loyal to the formulaic structure peculiar to the street-arab tale; the archetypal story is redolent with pathos, commonly focusing on a child who is rescued from destitution and relocated to a caring, moral, and religious transnormative family environment where a "safe" future is assured. Often replete with didacticism, such stories proliferated during the mid- to late-nineteenth century and were bought by schools and religious institutions as prizes for good behaviour or attendance.[4] However, although the street-arab tale, with its emphasis on religious conviction and its happy-ever-after finale was seemingly the perfect vehicle for the education and edification of the young, its emphasis on the social obligations of the wealthier classes also drew attention to social inequalities (Bratton 1981: 101) and, according to Mary Davidson, resulted in "a resounding clash of ethics and class" (2000: 87). For the first time, middle-class children were invited to be instruments of change through literature specifically addressed to them, but they were encouraged to do so at a distance. As Davidson points out:

> Children were taught that the poor could never be the same as themselves. In some ways, of course, waifs were visibly different. Mayhew describes them as weary crones, old beyond their years . . . *The Pall Mall Gazette* of 1874 perceived a physical and mental difference: "For the most part they come of a stock that has been degenerating . . . the very infants at the breast imbibe tainted nourishment." Class difference was rammed home. A Religious Tract Society pamphlet *If I Was a Lady* (n.d.), a moral tale about two poor little girls, stresses, "Time passed, and these children grew up, not to be *ladies*, for that they could not be." An engraved photograph in Dr Barnardo's children's magazine *The Children's Treasury* in 1873, shows first, Martha in rags begging for admission in the Home and second, Martha as a nice neat little maid, sweeping the floor. Religion, morality, class and expediency demanded that poor children *must* be helped as much as they *must* be kept in their place. (p. 90)

Moreover, poverty and an obvious need for charitable assistance were insufficient to validate the street arab as a worthy cause. It was imperative that he was also characterized as morally sound, or potentially capable of becoming so, and, more importantly perhaps, as spiritually pure if he was to be deemed deserving of charity. The scrubbed and polished representations of waifs that appear in magazines of the period, ranging from the children's publication *Aunt Judy's Magazine* (1866–85) to the family magazine *The Quiver* (1861–1926), display a physical purity that, by association, imbues the child with a saintly hue. Mary Jane, a seven-year-old "adopted" in 1888 as a *Quiver* waif, and funded by the publication and its readers, is destined for emigration to Canada and "a cheerful and useful life." The editorial describes Mary Jane as a bright, interesting child whose mother had abused her: "when the lady at Miss Rye's Home undressed the little one to wash her, she found great wales (*sic*) and lashes scored into her back—the work of a mother's hand!" (Author Unknown [1] 1888: 3). However, Mary Jane is pictured in Figure 2.1 looking bright and happy; indeed, says the writer, "she looked so sweet and clean in the brown dress and large white pinafore . . . that we could not refrain from giving her a kiss" (p. 2). Saved from degeneracy, she will be transported overseas, although it will probably be as a domestic servant, rather than as a cherished family member, that her new life in Canada will begin.

MARY JANE.
(THE QUIVER *Girl Waif.*)

Figure 2.1

**An Ambiguous Figure**

Davidson suggests that fact and fiction intertwine in such articles (2000: 91) and it is certainly feasible that Mary Jane and others like her were imaginative representations of charity cases, rather than authentic children. Sanitized and packaged as victimized, but essentially worthy and pure, recreated in accordance with ideological expectations of childhood, from their demure behavior to their characterization as pets to be kissed, these images of children bear little resemblance to Henry Mayhew's 1861 portraits of the London's lowlife, among them the child pickpocket who "cre[eps] up behind [his victims] much like a cat with his claws out" (n.p.), although a philanthropic interpretation might well ascribe the child's criminality to disreputable parenting. There is clearly an ambiguity in nineteenth-century perceptions of the street child; on one hand she is a charming innocent, prey to corruption by an evil environment and, on the other, a creature capable of wickedness and guile. Moreover, the ragged urchin is not always presented as wretched, although such a perception is seemingly a rarity. In 1890, Mrs H.M. Stanley (Margaret Tennant), wife of Henry Morton Stanley the explorer, depicted the street arab as an altogether more carefree creature, commenting:

> Most of the pictures I had seen of ragged life appeared to me false and made up. They were all so deplorably piteous . . . how was it that the other side is so seldom represented? The merry, reckless, happy-go-lucky urchin; the tomboy girl; the plump untidy mother dancing and tossing her ragged baby? (1890: 5)

Mrs Stanley's publication, *London Street Arabs*, is essentially a handbook on how to draw street children and provides a fascinating insight into an alternative view of the impoverished child. In her introduction, Mrs Stanley advises her would-be artist readers to bribe children to pose for them and, because such children *will* come brushed and groomed, to keep "a good supply of rags . . . (carefully fumigated, camphored and peppered) . . . to dress up your too respectable ragamuffin till he looks as disreputable as you wish" (p. 7). Despite her enthusiasm for "the other side" of street life, there is an ambiguity in Mrs Stanley's sentiments that reveals a distinct tension between her depiction of the "merry" street arab and his characterization as an undesirable individual. While she may urge recognition of the happy, implicitly child-like urchin, she also acknowledges his reputation as "disreputable."

Commenting directly on Mrs Stanley's art works, Edmund Spearman, writing in *The Poor in Great Cities* in 1896, emphasized this latter interpretation of the street child:

> Street Arabs are often picturesque to look at, especially on the canvases of the fair bride of an African explorer. They are also amusing in their

"cheek" and their "lingo," especially in the pages of Dickens. But they are also highly dangerous to the public peace if allowed to "run to seed," the seed being often robbery, outrage and even murder. The street Arab battalions of London during recent years have kept whole districts under a reign of terror, and one notorious murder in Marylebone, connected with the wild excesses of the London urchins . . . set all tongues to wagging over the necessity of some sweeping reform. (p. 275)

Both Mrs Stanley and Spearman were writing towards the close of the century, but Spearman's considerable anxiety about the children of the streets echoes that expressed some twenty-five years earlier by James Greenwood in *The Seven Curses of London* and suggests that little had changed in the intervening years. Greenwood, publishing in 1869, claimed that although some 350,000 children were dependent on "parochial authorities" and so had at least some form of guardianship, there were 100,000 destitute boys and girls wandering the streets of London.[5] They were, he said, "in fair training for the treadmill and the oakum shed, and finally for Portland and the convict's mark" (p. 3).[6] He continued:

There is no present fear of the noble annual crop of a hundred thousand diminishing. They are so plentifully propagated that a savage preaching "civilisation" might regard it as a mercy that the localities of their infant nurture are such as suit the ravening appetites of cholera and typhus. Otherwise they would breed like rabbits in an undisturbed warren, and presently swarm so abundantly that the highways would be over-run, making it necessary to pass an Act of Parliament, improving on the latest enacted for dogs, against the roaming at large of unmuzzled children of the gutter. (p. 5)

Although Spearman and Greenwood's perceptions appear similar, it is perhaps Greenwood's article that is most relevant to this chapter in terms of its chronology; the street-arab stories discussed here are drawn mainly from the 1860s and 1870s. Paradoxically, however, Greenwood-like sentiments are conspicuously absent from these tales, although the middle- and upper-class writers of the period would have assuredly been aware that the poor classes were a potential threat. As Gareth Stedman Jones discusses in *Outcast London* (1971), bread riots, collapsing industry, the cholera epidemic, a bad harvest and severe weather conditions in 1866 to 1867 were followed by rises in pauperism; London was visited by "a plague of beggars" (pp. 241–2). According to Thomas Beggs, writing in *The National Association for the Promotion of Social Science* (1867–8): "No one who lived in the suburbs could help feeling that they were in circumstances of considerable peril" (cited in Stedman Jones 1971: 242). The gulf between rich and impoverished was becoming more visible and, despite the emergence of a wealth of charitable organizations, the problem of the poor was significant. Yet the poor child herself remained an ambiguous figure; street arabs might well be breeding like rabbits, but for many individuals, particularly the authors of street-arab tales, the image of the innocent child was the predominant paradigm.

In many ways, the notion that the street child was a blameless victim was an attractive proposition. To perceive street arabs as innocent and prey to the vagaries of circumstance was certainly a more palatable option than conceptualizing them as rampaging hordes of savages, and it was with the former image that many writers of fiction for children chose to align their work. In doing so they complied with and validated the philanthropic work of the charitable organizations that existed to "rescue" destitute children, and implicitly calmed fears that the child could ever be a threat. For the authors of street-arab tales, the child was inherently innocent and both needed and deserved to find a better life beyond the slime, ooze, and depravity of the slums.

This image of the child as intrinsically innocent, rooted in Rousseau and Romanticism, found its zenith in Wordsworth's ode on *Intimations of Immortality from Recollections of Early Childhood* (1807) in which the child was inextricably allied to God. The Romantic child represented not only that which the adult had lost, but, and more vitally, possessed the natural and God-given ability to achieve an adult state of grace inaccessible to those who were no longer childlike. The role of the adult was to assist the child toward a maturity of goodness, and although the child might fall along the way, his intuitive innocence would ensure that he could always be restored. The child's capabilities were such that he could also bring others to God and to a righteous way of life, and both children and adults were within his aegis. Newly orphaned Susie of Emma Leslie's *Saved by Love: A Story of London Streets* (1889), guides streetchild, Elfie, toward God and a moral way of life, while Jessica, the central protagonist of Stretton's *Jessica's First Prayer* (1867), frequently cited as one of the original street-arab tales, is converted to Christianity and, in turn, brings churchwarden, Daniel Standring, to a new understanding of himself and of God. Peter Coveney comments that in Dickens' novels, the child "lives at the point of impact between the world of innocent awareness and the world of man's insensitivity to man" (1969: 112), and many of the more successful streetarab novels would appear to subscribe to a similar notion. An amalgamation, in Blakean terms, of the dialectic between innocence and experience, the street arab is portrayed as a young creature whose life on the streets has provided her with knowledge of the world and its evils, but who, despite temptation, remains unsullied. Her greatest enemy is her environment and her absent, depraved, irresponsible, or merely inept parents who cannot ensure that she will be nurtured, as she deserves to be, within the bosom of a loving, secure domestic sphere.

**Parental Responsibilities**

For the Victorians, parental duty lay at the very heart of the happy and successful family. From the pre-Victorian Janeway and Edgeworth, to popular nineteenth-century authors, Sherwood and Yonge, children's writers had long emphasized the necessity of good parenting in order that children should grow into responsible and implicitly respectable adults. If the neglectful parent was an anathema to moral convention and a blasphemous affront to the divine institution of the family, the parent who encouraged a child to descend into crime or beggary was perceived as entirely unnatural. In early 1871, the *North British Daily Mail*, in its series of articles about "The Dark Side of Glasgow," reported on youthful begging and described how slum children, who had been raised in the midst of drunkenness and vice, were turned out in freezing temperatures to sing, beg, or sell newspapers and were despatched with parental threats in case they should return with insufficient money. The investigator gave one ragged six-year-old girl some money in response to her begging to buy a scone, and then watched and listened to the conversation as the girl returned to her mother:

> "What did he gie ye?"
> The child mentioned the sum which was correct.
> "It is a lie," said the women, "he gied ye mair."
> "No he didna," said the little one with child-like earnestness—"as sure as dathe."
> The mother shook the child violently, warning her with strong language to "see and get mair next time," then went across to the whisky shop opposite, to spend the child's earnings. (cited in Rose 1988: 38)

In such scenarios, whether fact or fiction, it is invariably the mother figure who is deemed to be the most unnatural of all in a household where drink and vice are in evidence. Alcoholic fathers may be brutes, but drunken mothers are despicable; as Needham comments: "That a *man* should become a vicious monster does not alarm us with such surprise, as that a woman should become a frenzied demon" (1884: 76). The Victorian idealization of womanhood largely disallows such women a significant voice in children's fiction, although they may briefly be heard if they convert to Christianity, but, overall, the negligent mother is effectively silenced; to allow her a voice would be to acknowledge her existence as an individual and, perhaps, permit her to challenge the concept of the "natural" maternal impulse. Moreover, there is little compromise in portraits of maternal failure amongst the lower classes. For example, the narrator of Florence Montgomery's *Wild Mike and His Victim* (1875),[7] the story of Tim, an impoverished invalid boy, and his bullying tormentor, Mike, firmly indicates who is culpable for Mike's behavior:

> [Mike's mother] is violent-tempered and seldom sober, and her way of treating her own children often makes Tim tremble at her approach . . .

But he is more in awe of the children still; or, rather, of one of them—the eldest, a big, tawny-haired boy who goes by the name Wild Mike. No one can manage Wild Mike. His mother's hard words and harder blows have no effect upon him. He is the terror of all the children in the street; a born bully, reckless and cruel. (p. 6)

Mike may have been "born" a bully, but his temperament is inherited from his violent mother and father who are raising a brood of abused and abusive children.[8] In this instance, Wild Mike is saved prior to the end of the tale and is spared a life of degeneracy; ill and dying, he is "converted" by Mrs Collins, an angelic maternal being, and is forgiven by Tim before going to his beautiful death in peace: "And when the hospital awoke to life next morning, one little bed was empty; for the angels had come in the darkness and carried Wild Mike away" (p. 130). In contrast to the saintly Mrs Collins, Mike's violent mother, frustrated because she cannot secure a bed in the Children's Hospital for her son, "we[eps] and wails over him in loud and violent grief . . . [and] then, to drown her despair, [takes] to drinking more deeply than ever, and so render[s] herself useless, and worse than useless, to her unfortunate boy" (p. 78). Her maternal impulse may surface temporarily, but her inherent weakness of character and alcoholism serve to eradicate her natural feelings, while her violent lamentations characterize her as entirely alien to the maternal ideal.

Neglectful parents such as Mike's mother have only a limited role in street-arab narratives, but they serve to justify the removal of the child to a "safer" environment. The intervention of the angelic Mrs Collins is representative of a commonplace technique; a mother who is portrayed as negligent and failing in her duty is inevitably succeeded by an ideologically commendable character who, through a blending of religious instruction and careful nurturing, can ensure the spiritual well-being of the child and frequently endows him or her with a secure future. Similarly, sickly or weak parents are replaced with more physically able individuals to ensure the salvation of the protagonist. In order for the child to thrive, it is essential that he be removed from the family home and relocated to more wholesome surroundings that implicitly, and sometimes explicitly, replicate at least some aspects of the middle-class family ideal. The viability of the impoverished family as a support network is thus denied and the transnormative family, for that is essentially what these alternative environments tend to provide, is ultimately depicted as preferable. Poor parents are presented as deceased, frail, and incapable, or as corrupt and uncaring, and so represent the very antithesis of the ideological middle-class family.[9] Moreover, the child himself is conceptualized in relation to those who "care" or once cared for him. Identifiable primarily as the offspring of a drunken mother, a brutal father, or a weak, dying, or dead parent, he is not so much an individual as a representation of childhood that must strive to exist beyond the destructive influence of parental ineptitude or neglect.

## DRUNK AND DISORDERLY: THE NEGLIGENT MOTHER IN HESBA STRETTON'S *Jessica's First Prayer* (1867), *Jessica's Mother* (1867) and *Lost Gip* (1873)

Hesba Stretton's *Jessica's First Prayer* is perhaps one of the most successful of the street-arab genre, particularly in terms of its commercial success. As Nancy Cutt reports, two million copies of the book were said to have been printed prior to Stretton's death in 1911 and within five years of publication it was in translation all over the world (1979: 101). Stretton, who wrote under a pseudonym —her real name was Sarah Smith—published some sixty stories in all, many of which followed the successful formula of *Jessica's First Prayer*. Parental drunkenness and negligence feature strongly in a number of these texts and, in many a denouement parentless children are relocated to a family environment that is clearly preferable to their first, often squalid, home.

*Jessica's First Prayer* and its sequel, *Jessica's Mother*, follow the fortunes of a young girl as she learns about Christianity, achieves an improved way of life as surrogate daughter to an elderly churchwarden and is finally taken into the care of a much-admired minister possessed of an inherent holiness that allies him closely with God.[10] It is clear from the outset of the narrative that Jessica must be extricated from her wretched mother if she is to attain a respectable adulthood; within the first three pages of the book the reader has been presented with an acute image of parental neglect:

> [T]he owner [of the coffee stall] became suddenly aware of a pair of very bright dark eyes being fastened upon him and the slices of bread and butter on his board, with a gaze as hungry as that of a mouse which has been driven by famine into a trap. A thin and meagre face belonged to the eyes, which was half hidden by a mass of matted hair hanging over the forehead and down the neck—the only covering which the head or neck had, for a tattered frock, scarcely fastened together with broken strings, was slipping down over the shivering shoulders of the little girl. Stooping down . . . he caught sight of two bare little feet curling up from the damp pavement. (*Jessica's First Prayer*: 8)

Stretton's portrait of Jessica is that of a child whose mother has entirely failed in her duties. Allowed to wander alone in the city streets, Jessica is thin, barefoot, shivering, and implicitly asking for food; she has been driven to beggary because of her mother's neglect. Moreover, with her unkempt hair and tattered dress, she is less an image of childhood than of adult female sluttishness; in many ways she replicates the figure of her mother, who has yet to be introduced but is later exposed as a former prostitute. There are further sexual implications in the image of Jessica's bared shoulders; the child's dress is "scarcely fastened together," its strings are broken and the neck is slipping down, exposing Jessica's body to the public gaze. Under her mother's guardianship, Jessica has not only been neglected, but has been denied a traditional childhood; instead, she has become a sexualized creature who scavenges on the city streets.

However, her efforts to temporarily stave off hunger are successful. Jessica is chastized by Daniel, the coffee stall owner, who is sympathetic, although fearful that other beggars will approach his stall. But when Jessica tells him that "it's raining cats and dogs outside; and mother's been away all night, and she took the key with her" (p. 9), Daniel softens, and gives Jessica a cup of coffee. Jessica is evidently an abused child; she tells Daniel that people "think nothing of giving [her] smacks, and kicks and pinches" (p. 12) and shows him her arms, which are black and blue, although Daniel cannot tell whether the marks are from the cold or ill-usage. A relationship eventually develops between the old man and the child in which Daniel, a churchwarden, becomes aware of his lack of true religiosity and is converted, through Jessica's innocence, to a new spiritual understanding.

## A Potential for Degeneracy

Although Jessica is the central protagonist of Stretton's text, her often-intoxicated mother is a compelling character, despite the fact that she never actually appears in *Jessica's First Prayer*. Stretton unashamedly faces the less palatable truths of destitute life in her texts: in *Little Meg's Children* (1868), neighbor's daughter Kitty is obviously a prostitute; and in *Jessica's First Prayer*, Jessica's mother is a former actress known as "the Vixen" in the theatre, who "always gets drunk of a Sunday," nearly killed a missionary and would pawn her child's new clothes for gin (*Jessica's First Prayer*: 55–6). Furthermore, her former profession is evidently euphemistic for prostitution: in *Jessica's Mother*, the woman declares that she "rode in [her] carriage once" (*Jessica's Mother*: 13) and, as Cutt points out, "[t]he Victorian reader above nursery level would grasp the significance; she had been the kept mistress of a wealthy man; she is now on the streets." Indeed, Cutt also reports that Mayhew quotes several women at various stages in their careers of vice using this selfsame phrase (1979: 138). Jessica's "rescue" from the dubious ministrations of such a woman and her introduction to church and middle-class morality, as displayed by the minister and his family, is therefore her salvation from what might ultimately be a life of sin and debauchery; she used to play a fairy in the pantomime "till [she] grew too tall and ugly," she tells the minister, adding: "If I'm pretty when I grow up, mother says I shall play too; but I've a long time to wait" (*Jessica's First Prayer*: 48) and, taken in such a context, the term "play" is highly ambiguous. Fatherless —"I never had any father" (p. 54)—Jessica falls ill, is deserted by her mother and is found lying in darkness in her dismal room by Daniel, who takes Jessica to his own home where she eventually recovers. Daniel is unable to trace the errant mother and so informally adopts Jessica, establishing a new home in "a little house" that he rents for them (p. 93). The text closes with Jessica as

Daniel's helpmeet, assisting on his coffee stall and working in the chapel where she was first introduced to God.

Notions of home and domesticity reverberate throughout Stretton's first Jessica text, and Jessica's slum residence is shown to be in complete contrast to the ideological norm. Her "home" is a single room that was once a hayloft and although there are Christian resonances in its identity as a stable building, it is also a hovel:

> [A]s desolate and comfortless [an interior] as that of the stable below, with only a litter of straw for the bedding, and a few bricks and boards for the furniture. Everything that could be pawned had disappeared long ago, and Jessica's mother often lamented that she could not thus dispose of her child. (pp. 25–6)

The idea of a mother fleeing her sick child would undoubtedly have been shocking to a Victorian reader, but the prospect of a woman wishing to *sell* her daughter would assuredly have been more horrifying. Although Jessica's mother has apparently sold herself as a prostitute, Stretton's depiction of the child as an object of financial exchange once again hints at a link between Jessica and her potential fate. Jessica cannot literally be pawned, but she can nevertheless be sold for cash; her childhood and innate innocence might thus be stripped away. Already the "drudge and errand girl" (p. 26) of the court in which the slum is situated, Jessica has to earn or beg for herself in order to eat, but as she begins to experience more of Daniel's world, she encounters images of home that expose the inadequacies of her own poor dwelling. The coffee stall becomes a once-weekly refuge where, sitting on an upturned basket with her feet toward the fire, she is welcomed and fed, but it is the chapel building with its "light and warmth and music" (p. 36) for which she yearns[11] and it is there that she creeps to watch and listen and where, eventually, she meets those who lead her to Christianity and whose family life is in most contrast to her own.

The minister and his young daughters, Winny and Jane, are the products of a nurturing domestic sphere and Jessica is swift to evaluate the difference between the girls and herself: "The younger one was fair and the elder was about as tall as herself, and had eyes and hair as dark; but oh, how cared for, how plainly waited on by tender hands!" (p. 38). Spied by the sisters as they come early to chapel, Jessica begs to remain, but while Winny, the younger child, impulsively invites Jessica into the family pew, Jane is more perplexed: "The little outcast was plainly too dirty and neglected for them to invite her to sit side by side with them in their crimson-lined pew, and no poor people attended the chapel with whom she could have a seat" (p. 48). However, when her younger sister cites a biblical quotation concerning charity to the poor, Jane suggests that they ask their father what must be done and he speaks to Jessica of God before inviting her to sit, not in the pews, but in front of them, "close under" his pulpit

(p. 52). Her appearance in the chapel becomes a regular Sunday event. Literally clothed in respectability—she is given a cloak and bonnet which once belonged to Jane—Jessica is bathed in the influence of the minister and his family; she spends "many a happy day . . . in helping to sweep and dust the chapel" and her great delight is to attend to the pulpit, the vestry and the pew where the minister's children sit (p. 4). Content to sit at the minister's feet, Jessica's role is that of domestic and disciple to the family; the narrative proposes that although she is clearly not their equal, she is grateful for their patronage and is happy to adopt a subservient stance.

Stretton's emphasis on Jessica's "worship" of the minister's family not only highlights its evident worthiness as a religious and caring familial unit, but simultaneously encourages the reader's admiration for such a group. In ideological terms, the minister and his children exemplify much of the middle-class domestic ideal; the minister is a loving parent at all times and his children are respectful and devoted. In addition, the minister enthusiastically expands his role as father to his "flock" by tending to Jessica; as a caring, nurturing character, he might be perceived as fusing male and female characteristics and so implicitly compensates for his absent wife. His family is transnormative inasmuch as it lacks a mother figure, but it is nevertheless portrayed as united and supportive. When Jane and Winny find Jessica in the chapel, they take her to their father and he is immediately welcoming: "The minister was sitting in an easy chair before a comfortable fire, with a hymn book in his hand, which he closed as the three children appeared in the open doorway . . . His children ran to him . . . and with eager voices and gestures told him the difficulty they were in" (p. 47). Jessica delights in the company of the minister and his children and immerses herself in their world as far as is appropriate to her class and position and the reader is thus invited to join with her in worshipping this particular image of the family.

Although Jessica remains largely "other" to the minister's family, the narrator hints at the possibility of a more inclusive relationship in the sequel text, *Jessica's Mother*. Time has moved forward three years, and Jessica's mother reappears to claim her daughter and to impose herself on both Jessica and Daniel: "Jessica's home is my home. If you turn me out, out she goes with me," she tells the churchwarden (*Jessica's Mother*. 13). Conveniently perhaps, the wayward woman finally commits suicide, despite Jessica's most Christian and caring behavior, and Daniel too dies at the end of the tale, leaving Jessica with only the minister and his family as allies. However, the narrator has already laid the seeds of a potentially close relationship between the formerly outcast child and the minister's family. In the course of the story, the minister suffers a non-fatal stroke and Jessica stays the night with his children who look to her "as one who could help and counsel them" (p. 8). The relationship between the minister's family and Jessica is further enhanced by the minister's declaration to Jessica's mother that he "loves [the child] almost like one of his own little girls" (p. 26). Despite the fact that the "almost" of this sentence implies a distance between Jessica and the middle-class family that she so admires, the conclusion of the story, as Cutt says (1979: 140), implies that Jessica will join the family as companion or adopted daughter. As Daniel lays dying, the minister pledges, "Jessica shall come home to me" (*Jessica's Mother*: 30). However, and ambiguously, the narrative forbears to detail the precise role that Jessica will play. It may be that Jessica has found a refuge in a transnormative family that in many ways represents the middle-class ideal, but it may also be that she will, in common with many other street-arab protagonists, continue her place in that family as servant, rather than equal. As Davidson (2000) has commented, poor children can never be the same as the offspring of the middle classes.

## The Abdication of the Maternal Role

Although Jessica's future within a middle-class family remains a matter for speculation, the adoption of a waif into a working-class home with middle-class values was seen as eminently possible, according to Stretton, and her *Lost Gip*, published six years after *Jessica's First Prayer*, features just such a scenario. Sandy and his baby sister Gip leave destitution behind to find a new home in Canada as surrogate offspring to Mr and Mrs Shafto, whose only son, the crippled John, dies a beautiful death. Family dynamics inform much of the tale, from the characterization of Sandy, whose role is to save his sister from a negligent mother, to undertaker Mr Shafto, whose pride and delusions render him idle, but who is ultimately redeemed. There is a positive characterization of working-class motherhood in the form of the respectable and maternal Mrs Shafto, who nurses her dying last child and is kindly to both Sandy and his sister. But there is also vivid characterization of bad and negligent mothering, primarily in the depiction of Nancy Carroll, the mother of Sandy and Gip, a degenerate creature who is so blatantly irresponsible and negligent that Jessica's parent might be deemed a mediocre mother by contrast.

The slum dwelling where the Carroll family live is in the East End of London and in this labyrinth of alleys and courts, "there is a dead level of misery and degradation. The dirt becomes more loathsome and the diseases bred by it more deadly. Half the children born [there] die before they have lived out their twelve months of misery" (*Gip*: 8). In this hellish location, babies' funerals are frequent and any semblance of maternal care has apparently been eradicated: "As for the mothers, the greater portion of them seems to have lost their natural love for their little ones, and are glad to be rid of a care which would have made their lives a still heavier burden to them" (p. 9). The narrator's generalization implies that the children are burdensome to their parents and that mothers have no love for their offspring which, in turn, validates the removal of such children from their homes. In these unhappy circumstances, unnatural surroundings, unfit for human habitation, breed unnatural mothers and because Nancy is not to be trusted as a parent, Sandy assumes the role of protector in cherishing his latest sibling:

He had a passion for young helpless creatures, and he had nursed and tended two other babies before this one, and had seen them both fade away slowly, and die in this unwholesome air. He did not care much for his mother; how could he, when he seldom saw her sober?[12] But the babies were very precious to him. (p. 10)

There is no mention of a father figure in Sandy's life and his mother is overly fecund—the narrator refers to Sandy's absences "when there was no baby at home" (p. 14), implying that illegitimate babies randomly and frequently appear in the family dwelling.[13] Baby Gip is "a new treasure" to Sandy, but patently not to his mother: it is Sandy who takes the newborn child within moments of her birth and sits quietly down to peep at her, but he is crying as he does so because he can recall earlier siblings, Tom and Vic, "now in their tiny coffins deep down in the ground" (p. 12). As he looks down at the black-eyed child, Sandy wishes that someone could keep her alive:

He had a vague notion that there was someone, somewhere, who could save the new-born baby from dying, as Tom and little Vic had died. In the streets he had seen numbers of rich babies, who did not want for anything, and whose cheeks were fat and rosy . . . But how it happened, whether it was simply because they were rich, or because there was somebody who could keep them alive, and cared more for them than the poor, he could not tell. (p. 13)

Stretton's narrative explicitly proposes that poor parents care little for their children; unlike the rich, they allow their offspring to decay. Within days of birthing, Sandy's mother is up and "about her business again" (p. 13) with little thought for her new-born. Earning her living some of the time by "going about as a costermonger," she buys fruit and vegetables if she can display the strength of mind to stay away from the spirit-vault, although, as the narrator states, "it was seldom that her strength of mind did not fail before the temptation of another and another dram" (p. 14). Weak-minded and degenerate, she has neither strength nor inclination to tend her child. If there is no baby to look after, Sandy stays away from the tenement house and survives by selling fusees (matches) on the streets and sleeping wherever he can find shelter. But if his mother encounters him "during these spells of wandering" (p. 14), she shows no proof of relationship other than demanding any or all of the money he might have, and searching his clothes for coins. In a reversal of the ideological parenting role, Sandy's mother seeks to deprive her son of his means of sustenance in order to fund her own illicit desires. In ideological terms, and in common with many other fictional destitute parents, she is evidently no parent at all.

Sandy is Gip's carer as she grows; his mother becomes too much of a drunk to be much interested in her new daughter, although she occasionally takes the baby with her on her visits to the spirit-vaults from where she comes reeling home. With an instinct more traditionally associated with the maternal ideal, Sandy takes the baby away from the foul air of the slums and into more open areas,[14] watches carefully as Gip teethes, teaches her tricks and, despite the fact that Gip has been "fed with more gin than milk" (p. 17), she is still alive at the end of her first year, although, by now, she has learned the route to the spirit-vault. However, one night she is missing and Sandy begins a frantic and lengthy search for his sibling. His mother, "lying [on the floor] in a dead sleep, her face swollen and red and her ragged gown drawn over her" (p. 23), is of no use. Sandy attempts to wake her, but "she [is] almost like one dead" and when she does wake she strikes at him and tells him "in her thick, drunken voice" that she couldn't find Gip anywhere, before falling asleep again (p. 24). Depicted by Stretton as the epitome of the negligent mother, Nancy has submitted entirely to her own physical pleasures and has finally and fully abdicated the maternal role as decreed by domestic ideology.

Gip is eventually found; gathered in by a welfare organization, she is due to emigrate to Canada the following day, but Sandy takes her back to the Shaftos just prior to John's death and it is the dying boy who facilitates the birth of the transnormative family into which Sandy and Gip are subsequently incorporated. John encourages his mother to "take" Sandy as a new son, echoing a biblical tale as he does so:

> I'll promise for him . . . he'll be a good son to you and some day you'll wear the blue ribbons for him and be very happy again. Look at him mother. Why! Isn't it something like what Jesus said upon the cross to John? "Behold thy mother!" and to His mother, "Behold thy son!" . . . It is something like that . . . Sandy's sure to be a good son to you, mother. (pp. 126–7)

Stretton characterizes John's mother as the ideologically perfect maternal figure. With her rosy cheeks and her beaming expression, Mrs Shafto makes a home of the old and shabby house in which the family live; the kitchen is bright, shining and cosy and she nurtures her family within an organized environment: "Eating before talking is my rule," she says, as she cuts slices of bread and treacle for Sandy and John (p. 49). In the wake of John's death, she ostensibly comforts little Gip, but the intensity of her emotion as she clasps the child and rocks to and fro emphasizes her need for another child; her "natural" role as a mother and nurturer, a role that accords precisely with Victorian ideology, demands a replacement child to fill the void, and she is depicted as a most worthy recipient of Sandy and Gip.

Little by little, the transnormative family begins to establish itself. Gip's "funny ways" bring a smile to Mrs Shafto's sad eyes and even the "grave and solemn" Mr Shafto learns to play with the child who calls him "father" (p. 146). Finally, Mr Shafto is offered a sum of money by a railway company planning to lay tracks through his home, the chapel, and churchyard, and decides to buy a farm in Canada for himself and his family. Although Stretton would seem to be advocating the benefits of emigration in this final section of the book, there is no suggestion that England is, overall, a less viable proposition for the Shaftos. Stretton's use of the emigration motif may be a deliberate ratification of such programmes, or simply a structural maneuver that enhances the tale; the Shaftos, reconstituted as a "new" family, are making a new home in a "new" country.

On the last day before departure, Sandy discovers his natural mother in the graveyard, "half lying and half sitting on the rank grass" (p. 153). Believing her to be drunk and fearful that she will drag both himself and Gip back to poverty, he attempts to ignore her presence, but eventually confesses to Mrs Shafto, who discovers that the woman is dead. Although Sandy's heart gives "a great bound of relief" when he hears the news (p. 157), he is characterized throughout Stretton's text as a "good" child, and so genuinely laments for his deceased mother:

> Yet the next minute he felt a sort of sorrow, very faint and fleeting, as if, after all her wickedness, there was a little natural love for his mother lingering in his heart. He knelt down by her, and drew the old shawl more closely round her, as though she could even yet feel the east wind blowing coldly. (p. 157)

Sandy has already wished that his own mother had been more like John Shafto's and believes that had she been so, he would have loved her and worked for her (p. 154). But in this instance, as in the majority of street-arab tales, the transnormative family has proved itself infinitely superior to the natural, but destitute and incompetent parent. Although Sandy and Gip have not entirely transferred their allegiance to the middle classes, as do many of their street-arab contemporaries, they have been "saved" and transported to a working-class home that in many ways epitomizes the middle-class domestic ideal.

Stretton's emphasis throughout the "Jessica" books and *Lost Gip* is one that denies the viability of the truly impoverished family and subscribes to the notion that the domestic ideal can only be found within the respectable, middle-class domicile or, as in *Lost Gip*, in a home that replicates middle-class ideologies. For the child to survive, he or she must be removed from the sinful, corrupt environment provided by the natural parent and placed with those who are capable of raising children in accordance with social dictate. Without such intervention, Jessica is destined to become a prostitute, while Gip, familiar with the spirit-vaults at an early age, is assuredly similarly doomed. The transnormative family is, in both instances, a moral and religious sanctuary that far outweighs life with natural kin.

"MOTHERLESS, FATHERLESS AND FRIENDLESS!":
PORTRAITS OF THE ORPHAN IN BRENDA'S *Nothing to Nobody* (1873) and *Froggy's Little Brother* (1875)

For Brenda (Georgina Castle Smith), it was also necessary for the destitute child to be removed from the scene of his poverty and relocated to the sanctuary of the middle classes. A popular children's author whose oeuvre included a number of tales about middle-class Victorian family life, Brenda is nevertheless consistently remembered as a writer of street-arab stories. Her first novel, *Nothing to Nobody*, the story of an orphaned child, was described as "a little tale . . . admirably told and . . . replete with pathos" by *The English Churchman and Clerical Journal* of 5 February 1874, whose reviewer also praised the author's "art of appealing with great power, in natural and unaffected language, to the best sympathies and kindliest emotions of the human heart" (n.p.). Brenda continued to write and produced several street-arab tales, of which *Froggy's Little Brother* is perhaps the most renowned, but despite her reputation as a street-arab author, only three of her texts, *Nothing to Nobody*, *Froggy's Little Brother* and *Wonderful Mates* (1900), truly conform to the genre.

*Nothing to Nobody* is clearly of the street-arab genre, although its emphases extend beyond the children of the streets to consider a variety of individuals and family structures. Taking as its protagonist thirteen-year-old orphan Mary Sulivan, nicknamed "Daddy Long-legs" because she is so tall, it focuses not only on Mary's plight but on the trials and tribulations of seamstress spinster Maria Loveday, or "Psalm singing Maria," as she is called by the tenement residents, who tends her elderly mother in the garret of the house where Daddy lodges. Daddy is the central protagonist of the tale and is also responsible for engineering its happy-ever-after closure through a coincidental meeting that reunites Maria, her mother and their presumed-lost soldier brother and son. Daddy does not bring them to religion because all are already pious, but she is nevertheless proactive in ensuring the happiness of those around her.

Daddy, like Stretton's Jessica, epitomizes the street-arab child of nineteenth-century children's fiction. Portrayed at the outset as honest[15]—she meets her "saviour," Barbara Russel, a Sunday School teacher and clergyman's daughter, because she points out that the woman has dropped her handkerchief (*Nothing to Nobody*: 3)—she is also stereotypically waif-like in her appearance when she is first introduced to the reader: "It was a ragged child, with only half a bonnet on and no shawl, and she was cowering down with the chin of her pale wretched face almost touching her knees, as if she were trying to keep warm" (p. 3). Her vulnerability is evident: long-limbed, she appears older than her age and tells Barbara, "I am only thirteen, and I'm taller than Punchy, who's past fifteen" (p. 6), yet she is out on her own in London on "a cold, dark, miserable afternoon late in November," sitting in thickening yellow fog in the doorway of a tobacconist's shop. At thirteen, Daddy has reached the age of sexual consent and there is, in the narrator's description of her protagonist, a suggestion of the embryonic prostitute, a resemblance which an adult reader might well have identified.[16] Furthermore, Daddy's brusqueness during her initial conversation with Barbara is that of a world-weary woman, rather than a child, and intimates that she already lacks the enthusiasm for life that might conventionally be expected to characterize a child:

> "Was it you who spoke?" [asked Miss Barbara]
> "Yes"—The answer was given in not an encouraging tone at all, rather doggedly, as if the poor thin creature did not care to enter into conversation, but Miss Barbara, full of loving charity, went on.
> "Why are you here?" she asked.
> "Because I am, I suppose!" This very uncivil answer was given without the head being raised in the least. But still Miss Barbara went on.
> "Have you no home?—where do you live?"
> "On this doorstep a good part of the time," said the child; then after a pause she added, "I've no other home; at least, what *I* call *home!*" This was said rather vehemently.
> "Have you no father, no mother, no one who takes care of you?" inquired Miss Barbara.
> "No, not any one—I'm *nothing to nobody!*" (p. 4)[17]

"Home" to Daddy is obviously far removed from the ideological norm, although she displays some knowledge, whether gleaned through experience or instinct, of what a "true" home should be like. Moreover, while she denies that she has a mother, the reader later learns that she refers to her aunt in this manner, despite the fact that the woman demonstrates no maternal tenderness toward her fostered child. The narrative positioning within the above excerpt is perplexing; Daddy is depicted as a child to be pitied, whilst simultaneously she is shown to be an abrasive individual who implicitly alienates her interrogator. However, it may be that Brenda was aware of the psychological complexities of the street-arab child and that in this passage she was striving to achieve a realism absent from the work of many of her contemporaries. For example, Daddy is an inherently good child, but also displays what might be interpreted as greedy behavior. Initially resistant to Miss Barbara, Daddy refuses to accompany her to the Sunday School—"I should *hate* to go to school; I don't even know my A B C and don't want to!" (p. 7), she declares—but when Miss Barbara says that she may come and see Daddy and bring her something, Daddy's eyes brighten at the promise of a gift, and she divulges her address. Unused to treats, Daddy nevertheless expresses child-like excitement at the prospect of a present. Precocious, yet inherently youthful, Daddy is the product of an uncaring familial environment that has denied her a traditional carefree childhood, whilst propelling her prematurely towards a potentially precarious adulthood.

### In Search of a Mother

The young Miss Barbara is not presented as a mother figure for Daddy, although she does initiate her academic and religious education and eventually facilitates Daddy's admission to a middle-class transnormative family, but Daddy, in common with many other street-arab protagonists, is evidently in need of maternal care.

Re-homed with her Aunt Sharpe on her mother's death, Daddy is poorly treated by the relatives who have been paid to foster her, but who mercilessly abuse her in the tenement house that they share with cobbler Michael, Maria Loveday and her mother, and various other unidentified occupants: "[B]eneath this roof there slept at least forty persons every night, some very poor, and others better off" (p. 18). Returning to the building after her meeting with Barbara, Daddy is dismayed to find that she is locked out. When she does gain admission, she is thoroughly beaten:

> She was just stooping down to take off her ragged boots to ascend the creaking stairs more quietly, when suddenly the door of the back-room opened noisily, and before she had time to speak or say a word, a tall ill-favoured woman had marched out upon her, given her a sounding cuff on the cheek, and with a violent push at the back, drove her in front of her, and with another push, yet more sharply administered, the woman sent her reeling head-foremost into the room from which she had come. (p. 15)

Mrs Sharpe, her "ill-tempered looking" husband and their brood live well enough in a material sense; the table is "spread for supper with bread, and treacle and meat in abundance" (p. 15), but the children are devoid of moral guidance and are noisy and aggressive like their parents. Daddy is bullied and denied sustenance, although she declares herself to be hungry; she is told that want must be her master and she weeps as she climbs the steep, dark stairway to the cupboard where she sleeps, although she is eventually hushed by the sound of Maria's hymn singing. Her identity as a good child who finds comfort in religion is established; Daddy is declared a worthy cause and her salvation is assured, although not within the bounds of her tenement-dwelling, transnormative family.

Paradoxically, despite the appalling treatment meted out to Daddy by her relatives, she yearns for a familial relationship; the hunger that she suffers is both physical and psychological. Daddy's desperation for a parent, emphasized by the child's persistence in calling Mrs Sharpe "mother," suggests that her yearning is instinctive and, in this way, Brenda foregrounds the child's "natural" psychological need for adequate parental care. However, Daddy's excessive use of such an epithet also suggests a certain irony that may be a deliberate authorial comment. Although the term "mother" might have commonly been employed

**Figure 2.2** Illustrator Unknown. "Nothing-to-Nobody was shut out for the night" (n.p.)

in such households, it appears to be highly inappropriate when applied to an individual who bears little resemblance to the maternal ideal.

Beaten by her aunt, Daddy cries out, "O mother, mother! . . . don't hit me so!" but is told, "Mother! . . . I'm not your mother. Don't call me mother. You haven't a mother, or a father, or a sister, or a relation belonging to you, and you ought to be in the workhouse, you who are 'nothing to nobody!'" (p. 16). When Daddy finally leaves the tenement to become "a little servant" in the Russels' London home, she rushes to tell Mrs Sharpe: "O mother! I'm going away. You'll never have to feed me any more—never, never, never!" (p. 139). Mrs Sharpe, typified by Brenda as a low-class, uncaring surrogate mother, responds in predictable fashion—"A good thing too, if it is true"—although the narrative then moderates Mrs Sharpe's characterization by stating that the woman feels "a terrible prick at the same time as she thought of her sister's death-bed, and that money she had taken" (p. 139). This emphasis on Mrs Sharpe's guilty conscience suggests authorial ambivalence; having constructed her character as a heartless bully, Brenda then moderates her portrait. It may be that Brenda's emphasis on the financial transaction between Daddy's dying mother and Mrs Sharpe is indicative of authorial sympathy; Mrs Sharpe, the mother of a poor family living in a tenement, has acceded to death-bed demands and accepted payment for an unwelcome child that she has then been obliged to raise. While the transnormative family that fosters a child for money is depicted as less than ideal, the ambiguity of Brenda's characterization suggests, at some level, that the lower-class transnormative family has the potential to become successful—an authorial position that clearly challenges classist prejudice.

As a surrogate family, the Sharpes may appear distinctly distant from the concept of the domestic ideal, although their own children are well fed, but the families that live beyond the tenement house whom Daddy encounters on her journey to physical and spiritual redemption are representative of the ideologically conformist Victorian family in its various guises. Dr. Russel loses son Jem and, later a much-loved wife, but Barbara remains a dutiful daughter and her marriage to Captain Norman in the closing stages of the book is celebrated by all. Maria and her mother, reunited with a brother and son, have further joy with Maria's marriage to Michael the cobbler and eventually, through unexpected inheritance, move from urban to pastoral life in the "sweet, fresh country, which they all love" (p. 175). Finally, Daddy herself is relocated within a second transnormative family that, this time, requires neither financial nor emotional bribery and that promises to be thoroughly nurturing and secure. Daddy is favored by Mrs Bush, the old housekeeper to the Russels and formerly the children's nurse, "a very kind, dear old person" (p. 135), who visits Daddy at the Sharpe home and promises to "teach her her place, and get her on, and in fact take Daddy under her wing" (p. 135). Part supervisor, part maternal figure, Mrs Bush is the nurturer that Daddy has been denied, and the child subsequently flourishes under her care. Daddy's transformation is evident in the closing pages of the text as the Russel household prepares for Miss Barbara's wedding and the reader is invited to celebrate Daddy's "re-birth" and to acknowledge the Russels' role in facilitating such a change:

> Is that Daddy—can that be Daddy, I wonder, with such a bright face, and looking so clean and neat, bustling about and helping everybody, and making herself so useful? She has been up ever since six o'clock, working hard and lending a willing hand to anybody and everybody who asks her . . . [and] setting to anything that comes in her way with her whole heart, whatever it may be, and in such a spirit of cheerfulness and good temper, that it must be quite pleasant to work with her. Who could call her Nothing-to-Nobody *now*? (p. 169)

Daddy has found her place in a home that in many ways perpetuates the Victorian ideal and the reader is encouraged to applaud the event. Daddy's role is not precisely that of daughter, although she is ostensibly "adopted" by Mrs Bush, and she is strictly a servant to the middle-class members of the household. Nevertheless, she is "something to somebody" (p. 176) at last, and while she may not be fully integrated into the domestic ideal on earth, she can at least anticipate joining the family of God in heaven as she "tread[s] onward to the Golden Gate" (p. 177).

**Struggling to Survive**

Brenda's second published text, *Froggy's Little Brother*, again focuses on the plight of the orphan, but does so through the story of two young brothers who lose both parents and must survive alone within their small transnormative family group. Froggy, nicknamed by his father because he "croaked sometimes when he had a cough, like those little creatures who live in the ditches" (*Froggy*: 8), is the protagonist of the tale and the narrative traces the death of the children's parents and the increasing hopelessness of the boys' situation as Froggy struggles, in vain, to provide a home for his younger sibling Benny. It is a tale that is rich in misery and sentimentality; parental demise is followed by the death of a neighboring child, the slaughter of Benny's pet mouse by a cat and, finally, by Benny's own death, an episode that extends over some fifty pages.

Overall, however, *Froggy's Little Brother* seeks social assistance for the Froggys and Bennys of the cities; it concludes with a direct address to parents and children, "especially those who are rich" (p. 222), asking them to remember destitute children when their clergyman appeals for money and relief for the East End. In many ways it is a highly manipulative text and often overtly so, and it proved successful; for example, Lord Arran, later to be an influential figure in the Children's Country Holiday Fund, read the text as a boy and ardently admired its sentiments (Thiel 2002: 19). But if *Froggy's Little Brother* engaged the attention and the wallets of those who read it, it did so not merely by detailing the wretchedness of Froggy and his sibling, but by emphasizing their inability to function without adequate adult care. Only in the home for children does Froggy finally locate a family group, albeit a transnormative family, that purports to resemble the ideal; the destitute parents and offspring that surround him in Shoreditch thoroughly challenge the notion of the family as the site of domestic bliss.

The portrait of Froggy's family that is presented in the opening pages of the text is one of poverty and hopelessness:

> It was a sad sight sometimes to see the family returning home after the day's work was done;—the father in front, carrying the Punch show, now and then walking, alas! very unsteadily, from the effects of a visit to the public-house;—and behind—saddest of all—the poor mother, with her thin face and consumptive cough, carrying little Benny, and cheering on Froggy at her side, who would often look up into her face and say—"I are so tired, Mudder! I wish I was little, like Benny, to be carried!" (*Froggy*: 9)

It is a scene that contrasts vividly with the portrait of middle-class family life that surrounds the destitute family and that is depicted in the novel's earlier pages. The narrator, speaking of the districts that Froggy's family and their Punch and Judy show visit in order to earn money, describes them as "wealthier neighbourhoods, where people could afford the luxury of Punch" (p. 8). In these more affluent districts, particularly on wet days when the young residents are incarcerated indoors, Froggy and his family are likely to increase their earnings:

> On rainy bad days, when the little children living in the squares and terraces towards the rich West End could not go out, as soon as they heard the familiar sound of the drum, and the shrill "Oy! Oy!" coming round the corner, they would run off and entreat mammas and papas and indulgent grandmammas, to let them set up Punch *just* this once, as it was so dull indoors and they had nothing to amuse them! (p. 8)

In this way, the narrator establishes a theme that is an essential feature of her message—the stark contrast between the spartan family life of those who are poor and the luxurious existence of the financially secure. The rich child with mother, father and grandmother, suffers from overindulgence; the poor child, burdened with sickly parents, is forever hungry and earns a living largely through the patronage of the wealthy. Throughout the tale, the narrative voice intervenes to emphasize the plight of the poor and to give it relevance to the middle-class reader's life. When Froggy's father dies as the result of a collision with a carriage full of drunk Derby-day revellers and Froggy and Benny become orphaned, their friendless state is emphasized and linked to the reader's everyday reality:

What a sad reflection—motherless, fatherless and friendless! But so it was; and this is the condition of hundreds of our poor little brothers and sisters[18] in great London. Let us think of this next Sunday when the petition comes in our beautiful Litany, "That it may please Thee to defend and provide for the fatherless children and widows, and all that are desolate and oppressed!" (p. 37)

And this same voice intrudes into the narrative to contrast the children of the slums with traditional visions of childhood:

Froggy was but eleven, and he should not have been feeling like a tired old man . . . London has nothing more sorrowful to show us, I think . . . than its old children, with their shrewd, anxious faces, and knitted brows, on which hard Care is stamped, instead of the glad expectancy and joyous carelessness which we generally associate with childhood. (p. 99)

## Inadequate Parents

Throughout *Froggy's Little Brother*, the failure of a parent through death, misadventure or negligence is the catalyst for the failure of the child, physically and/or psychologically, and it is most often the maternal figure who is implicated in his or her downfall. Froggy's mother, as she lies on her death-bed, tells her sobbing husband to send Froggy to night school,[19] although her final conversation is one preoccupied with "the Better Land" (p. 19). A religious and "simple-minded, loving . . . woman" (p. 15), she prays that the entire family will, one day, be brought home to God, but her prayer, while it may be satisfyingly sentimental to the reader, resonates with childish naivety. Her husband, "'Arry" (p. 14), becomes teetotal in the wake of his wife's death and attempts to support his children, but the Punch show is shattered in the accident that eventually kills him, and he bequeaths nothing of practical value to Froggy and Benny. Without parental support or the means to an income, the boys' future is bleak, but if Froggy and Benny are depicted as incapable of survival without parental support, those impoverished children who *do* have parents are also shown to be disadvantaged. According to Brenda's narrative, poor parents are aware of the fragility of their children's existence and consequently adopt a laissez-faire attitude. Tenement neighbor Mrs Blunt, mother-of-six and wife of a drunken husband, who "feels kindly towards the two little boys above her" (p. 106), loses her daughter Debbie, Benny's playmate, and when Benny joins the local women gathered by Deb's corpse, their advice to Mrs Blunt is blindly and passively fatalistic:

"Oh my dear, I wouldn't fret about it overmuch if I was you," said one poor woman, who looked as if she had found the waves of this world very troublesome. "Life's a sad business, take it altogether from cradle to grave, and it's worse I ses for women than for men. We don't likes to lose 'em when we've got 'em; no more we does, bless their innocent hearts, but depend upon it children's best out of it all!"

"Yes, that they be," said an older neighbour mournfully. "Robert and me, we've had seven, and we've buried 'em all, and we thank the Lord for it now, though we grieved terrible at first!" (pp. 138–9)

Such fatalism further endorses the "rescue" of children from an environment where they will assuredly perish—or where they will become the victims of parental assault. The passivity of Mrs Blunt's neighbors is contrasted with the more active parenting of landlady Mrs Ragbon, who is rumored to "thump . . . her own brats about awful" when she takes too much to drink (p. 22). Mrs Ragbon, sometime babysitter for Benny, is most notably mother of Mac, "a ragged boy of stunted growth, with yellow hair, that looked as if it had never been combed . . . and with a red dissipated countenance, sadly suggestive of unlimited beer-drinking and low companions" (p. 72) who has been "turned out of doors" by his mother "because he would not work" (p. 49). Mac is a thief, as Froggy later discovers, and is eventually taken by the police, but although the narrator stresses that it is Mac's duty, as a son, to "win his mother back again by leading a good life himself, and being kind" (p. 81), it is clearly Mrs Ragbon, whose "passion for drink . . . [has] drowned all her better feelings, her love for her husband and the duty she owe[s] her children," who is also responsible for his behavior.

The trope of the mother as failure and her contribution to the subsequent failure of the child is echoed finally and subtextually in the depiction of Queen Victoria, ostensibly mother of the Empire, who visits the East End and whom Froggy petitions in an attempt to gain assistance for himself and his brother. In her educational publication, *Old England's Story in Little Words for Little Children* (1884), Brenda praises the Queen as "great and good" (p. 227), but although she would appear to have been a Royalist, there is a certain ambiguity in *Froggy's Little Brother* that characterizes it as an overtly political text. The narrator praises Victoria for "her act of kindness" in "coming amongst" her people (*Froggy*: 84), but Froggy is sent reeling onto the pavement by a policeman clearing the road (p. 96) and the Queen passes swiftly by without stopping, leaving confusion behind her; old people are left dazed and bewildered to be pushed around by the crowd (p. 97). The letter that Froggy writes to the Queen is never acknowledged; he walks miles to Buckingham Palace in search of an answer, but the Queen is away and a soldier tells Froggy to try again: "[P]'r'aps you'll have better luck next time" (p. 154). Even the matriarch of England has failed to nurture her most needy subjects, and so the ultimate paradigm of the domestic ideal, featuring caring mother and tended nation, is exposed as nothing more than a sham.

## A Middle-Class Sanctuary

Froggy's survival is ensured only when he finally comes under the care of the philanthropist-as-parent and is welcomed into what is essentially a representation of the ideologically conformist, middle-class, family group. Clergyman Mr Wallace, summoned by the doctor to Benny's death-bed, is entirely empathetic to Froggy's situation and his manner is that of a kindly, fatherly figure: "'There, there,' said Mr Wallace soothingly, laying his small, gentleman-like hand on Froggy's little shoulder. 'I've been through a perfect furnace of trouble myself, so I can feel for you'" (p. 188). Mr Wallace tells Froggy that he will send "a lady" to look after Froggy and nurse Benny: "'she is a very kind, good lady . . . accustomed to nursing and sickness, and she will do for your brother all that his mother would have done, if she had been alive'" (p. 195). Miss Goff, under-matron at the orphanage where Froggy is eventually relocated, arrives after Benny's death, although she has previously slipped in to cover the sleeping boys with warm wraps. A "tall and gentle-looking [woman] dressed in quiet black clothes" with a "basket full of the food and necessaries which she had discovered were so sadly wanting" (p. 207), she offers Froggy religious consolation and motherly comfort and tells him: "You will not be left to live here alone . . . you must come home with me" (p. 209). "Home" is a children's institution, not a traditional family domicile, but it nevertheless signifies a warm, welcoming environment and successfully, if deceptively, suggests that Froggy will be assimilated into a familial sphere.

Froggy is transported to Miss Goff's "home" and from there, through "the kindness of Mr Wallace" and his friend, Dr Brown, to "a home for little boys in the city where he . . . [will learn] the trade of a carpenter" (p. 212) and where he is cared for by Mrs Holt, the matron, "a kind, motherly person" (p. 217). With Mr Wallace and Mrs Holt as substitute parents, Froggy's transnormative family is completed by the arrival of Billy, "the tiniest thing in the shape of a boy you ever saw" (p. 216), who reminds Froggy of his lost brother and whom Froggy is asked to befriend. The closure of the story finds Froggy and Billy together and still in the home, worrying only about whether or not there will be sufficient funds for a day out in the countryside. While their desires for a day trip might echo those of middle-class children, their dependence on philanthropic contributions still separates them from their supposed "brothers and sisters" who may, unlike their "siblings," reside in a "natural" family home.

*Froggy's Little Brother*, like *Nothing to Nobody*, focuses primarily on society's failure to nurture its destitute children, but it also emphasizes the ineptitude of impoverished parents and the inability of children to function successfully without the support of a competent and caring guardian. The transnormative, middle-class family may be represented by members of welfare organizations or employers, but, for Brenda, such a unit offers children the opportunity to survive and to exceed prior expectations; Froggy will become a carpenter and Daddy a trained servant, and both will escape destitution. Moreover, in *Froggy's*

*Little Brother*, as in *Lost Gip*, the child as substitute parent is shown to be an impractical and largely unworkable solution. Despite valiant efforts, Froggy cannot sustain his younger brother any more than can the various inadequate parents that share his tenement building. Adult intervention from respectable, God-fearing members of society and a transnormative family that replicates the domestic ideal by offering the child reliable parental figures in some guise is ultimately his only route to salvation. Yet these representations of family are frequently only metaphorical, as in *Nothing to Nobody* and *Froggy's Little Brother*, despite the fact that authors inculcate their portraits of such groups with familial terminology.

Intervention by respectable and philanthropic individuals, some clothed in familial personae, is a common characteristic of the five texts discussed here; indeed, there are numerous similarities overall, as befits a genre that is essentially formulaic. Each story, *Jessica's First Prayer, Jessica's Mother, Lost Gip, Nothing to Nobody*, and *Froggy's Little Brother*, attempts to engender social change and to do so through the transmission of religious and domestic ideologies that have implicitly evolved from and been perpetuated through the middle-class consciousness. It is inevitable that within such texts, the poverty-stricken family will be depicted as unable to care for its offspring; without such destitution there would be no story and the endemic poverty of some Londoners in the mid- to late-nineteenth century is undoubtedly often accurately portrayed. Yet, for a twenty-first-century reader, there is a certain discomfort and a suggestion of dishonesty in stories that deliberately orchestrate the transition of a child from an impoverished background to a middle-class representation of the domestic ideal. Poor parents are inevitably characterized as inept while only one of the five texts discussed, *Lost Gip*, fully acknowledges that a working-class family can be respectable and potentially successful.[20] Jessica, Daddy and Froggy are victims of parental incompetence, neglect and misadventure and their future can be assured only within the safety of the middle classes.

The street-arab tale would thus appear to reinscribe middle-class ideology by insisting that its protagonists can achieve happiness only within a setting that attempts to mirror the domestic ideal. It is solely within such locations that these essentially innocent characters can become fully cherished and nurtured in accordance with the Romantic notion of childhood and can develop into useful adult members of society. Furthermore, those who have actively denied them their youth are often punished. The maternal drunkards who feature so prominently in the texts above are apparently too despicable to be redeemed; the mothers of Jessica and Sandy die prior to conversion, and although Jessica's mother might be pitied for the wretchedness of her condition, the "sullenness and stupidity" stamped on her features (*Jessica's Mother*: 27) expose her as inherently brutish and so discourage the reader's sympathy. These are creatures who appear to live outside of God's grace; their disregard for the divine institution of family, coupled with their rejection of their "natural" maternal role, seemingly renders them beyond salvation. Indeed, as Stretton emphasizes,

Jessica's mother has chosen to entirely forsake God; when Jessica attempts to instruct her mother in religion, she discovers what the woman has already been told. Jessica tells Daniel:

> [S]he knew about. . . . [Jesus Christ, and God, and Heaven] . . . and she never told me, never! She never spoke of God at all, only when she was cursing. I don't know now anything that'll make her a good woman. I thought that if she only heard what I said she'd love God, but she only laughed at me, and said it's an old story. I don't know what can be done for her now. (*Jessica's Mother*. 21)

To live in contravention of religious dictate is sinful, according to Stretton's text, but for a mother to deny a child knowledge of Jesus, God and eternal life would seem to be supremely transgressive. The contrast between Jessica's mother and the minister's family is finally and effectively exposed.

However, if the street-arab tale proposed that the transnormative family could be preferable to the "natural" family for those of the destitute classes, the domestic ideology at play in texts that focus on the middle classes would appear to promote a different agenda. The actualities of stepmothering, which was a relatively commonplace occurrence and which is the subject of the subsequent chapter, necessarily demanded that child readers should be encouraged to embrace the idea of a new mama and the viability of the reconstructed family group. While texts focusing on stepmothering may reinscribe domestic ideology and strive to insist that this alternative paradigm of the family is sustainable, there are moments within such tales in which *aporia* betray the overall feasibility of such an assertion. In fact, these mismatches between rhetoric and thought would appear to suggest that, even for the middle classes, the domestic ideal is largely untenable without compromise and that the successful transnormative family can rarely be anything more than a myth.

# Chapter Three
## Forever Cursed: Stepmothers, "otherness," and the re-inscription of myth in transnormative family narratives

The Step- in Stepmother derives from the Middle English *steif*, meaning bereaved, and was originally applied to orphaned children. A Stepmother, then is the mother of a bereaved child. Loss and grief are her milieu, her *raison d'etre* . . . she is a *creature* of the grief in which she moves, a shadow figure rising not *ex nihilo*, but out of wrenching loss. (Schectman 1993: xvi)

In her 1993 study *The Stepmother in Fairy Tales: Bereavement and the Feminine Shadow*, Jungian analyst Jacqueline Schectman asserts that fairy tales allow for a distancing of what might otherwise be unpalatable: "cannibalistic giants and ogres stand in for bad fathers, and, more frequently, the Wicked Stepmother carries the role of the dark, envious, vengeful mother. Natural parents, the tales seem to say, would never treat their children in that way" (p. xiv).[1] Moreover, suggests Schectman, the presence of the bad or monstrous mother implicitly ratifies the unimpeachable status of the good, but absent, maternal figure; she points out that the Grimm Brothers substituted "stepmother" for "mother" in their tales of "child abuse" to protect and preserve the image of good mother-hood (p. xiv). Yet neither good nor monstrous mother can exist in isolation; each requires the other to give it form, and as Christina Hughes asserts, while the contradictory nature of myths about women is highlighted in the opposition between the Virgin Mary and Eve, myths of motherhood are similarly counter-posing (1991: 15).[2] For Hughes, the "counterveiling themes of perfection and fear exist side by side but are not allowed to be directly confronted," and because the myth of perfection is predominant, it inhibits any opposing image which may threaten it (p. 15).

To apply the theories of Schectman and Hughes to the figure of the step-mother in nineteenth-century children's literature is to begin to expose the complexities of a character who is essentially problematic, whether she is a creature of fairy tale or of more naturalistic fiction. Arising from the negativity of death and "wrenching loss," she exemplifies the otherness that stands in opposition to the perfect mother and, by implication, is a threat to the domestic ideal. The deceased mother of nineteenth-century children's fiction, specifically of middle- and upper-class families, is invariably portrayed as saint-like; she is, as Dever points out, "the ghost that haunts the Victorian novel" (1998: xi). Thus the stepmother of such fiction is cursed by the spectral presence of maternal perfection and lost domestic bliss before her task begins and, in addition, carries with her the echoes of her wicked fictional predecessors. In Lucy Lane Clifford's "The New Mother" (1882), the glass-eyed, wooden-tailed, substitute parent is allied to the myth of the monstrous stepmother, although it is the children's perception of the newcomer, gleaned from hearsay, that fully characterizes her as a fiendish being. Other children's authors are less explicit, but the relation-ship between stepmother and monster is nevertheless in evidence, although admittedly to varying degrees. The stepmothers in Caroline Birley's *We are Seven* (1880) and Harriet Childe-Pemberton's *Birdie: A Tale of Child-Life* (1888) are ostensibly kindly and religious beings, but it is largely through death or injury and emotional manipulation that their rule is established. Conversely, in Charlotte M. Yonge's *The Young Step-mother* (1861), it is the protagonist's *inability* to resemble her tyrannical, mythical counterpart in any way that results in the overall failure of her unruly transnormative family. Although it may initially appear that authors such as Childe-Pemberton, Birley, and Yonge seek to critique mythical representations of motherhood and to distance the contemporary stepmother from the creature of myth, their texts ultimately serve to re-affirm the existence of a close association. As Hughes points out, tales of wicked stepmothers permeate every culture and pervade consciousness from early childhood (1991: 53). For the Victorians, immersed in the tales of the Brothers Grimm, the wicked stepmother was evidently something of a potent image.

## Handbooks for the Happy Home

Although the image of the wicked stepmother may have lurked within the common consciousness of the Victorians, she was at least abjected,[3] or seemingly so, for those authors who chose to present stepmothering as a viable proposi-tion. There was clearly a social purpose in such work; as discussed in Chapter One, maternal mortality figures were significant and women were undoubtedly encouraged to consider stepmotherhood as an option, while children bereft of a mother could learn, through fiction, that domestic happiness could once more be gained through the love and affection of a surrogate parent. Indeed, the child reader is frequently a priority in such texts; the narrative voice often privileges the child's point of view as it details the problems inherent to offspring when a new mother enters the domestic sphere, and offers solutions to the resentment and general unease that many children assuredly felt. Writers of non-fiction were also swift to encourage a smooth transition as the new matriarch took her place. The *Girl's Own Paper* preached loyalty and obedience to step-mothers (see Chapter One), while other women writers discussed the potential pitfalls and pleasures of stepmothering, presumably for the benefit of their female readers.

Mrs J. Bakewell, contributor to and editor of *The British Mother's Magazine*, later retitled *The British Mothers' Journal and Domestic Magazine*, who was also author of *The Mother's Practical Guide in the Physical, Intellectual and Moral Training of her Children* (1843),[4] incorporated articles on stepmothering in her journal and included a chapter "On the Claims and Responsibilities of Stepmothers" in her manual.[5] For Bakewell, the role of surrogate mother was potentially difficult, although these problems could be overcome. In her introductory paragraph to the stepmother section of her book, she warns:

> The position in which a second wife is placed with respect to the children of her husband by a former marriage, is one of peculiar difficulty. It is deeply to be regretted that the relative claims of parties so circumstanced are not better understood, as until this is the case, we cannot expect that the stigma, so often unjustly, attached to stepmothers will be entirely removed. (p. 268)

She acknowledges that children may be encouraged to feel prejudice against their new mother, that the stepmother may over-indulge her new charges in a bid to win their affections, and that the household into which she enters may be disorderly and untidy. However, she also reminds her readers that such an undertaking can be truly rewarding:

> Great as are the difficulties, and strong as are the prejudices the stepmother has to encounter, she may certainly evince the possibility of overcoming these sources of discouragement and anxiety. By steadily pursuing the course of duty in humble reliance on Divine grace; by manifesting a spirit of judicious kindness towards those who may not have the first place in her affections, she may substantiate the claims of woman to those refined and noble attributes, which are the glory of her character. She may be rewarded by the esteem and gratitude of those who realize the advantages her influence confers upon them; to her they will ever look with mingled feelings of reverence and affection, and fondly will they cherish the memory of one who has blessed them with all but a mother's love. But greater still will be her reward in heaven. (p. 290–1)

In this way the new stepmother becomes intrinsically allied to her departed predecessor; her role is one that may win the blessing of heaven and the fact that her memory will be fondly cherished aligns her further with the "angel" who has gone before. Furthermore, although she may face troubles, the stepmother possesses the ability to distance herself from the stigma attached to her breed by displaying the "refined" and "noble" attributes of womanhood, attributes that are necessarily absent in mythical representation of wicked stepmothers.

Stepmothering was also an issue in Bakewell's *The British Mother's Magazine*. Articles on the subject appeared occasionally and spanned the years, suggesting that the topic continued to be emotive. Contributors focused on various aspects of stepmothering: "The Two Step-Mothers" is a discussion between two women in which a successful new mother offers advice to an anxious contemporary (B.B.B. 1858: 203–7); "The Difficulties and Trials of Stepmothers" calls for sympathy from those who can ease the stepmother's task, rather than "watch[ing] all her proceedings, and that with no friendly eye" (A Stepmother 1848: 88–9); "Step-Mothers: Sketches from Life" celebrates a successful stepmother who has "won the hearts" of her surrogate offspring (Author Unknown [2] 1861: n.p.). The poem "To a Step-Child" (Author Unknown [3] 1862: 201) personifies the perfect stepmother as she tends her adopted child and by suggesting that the new and former mother are spiritually connected through the child himself, again fuses images of the stepmother with her heavenly counterpart and lends a semblance of divine blessing to the stepmother's role:

> Thou art not mine; the golden locks that cluster
> > Round thy broad brow –
> Thy blue eyes, with their soft and liquid lustre,
> > And cheek of snow—
> E'en the strange sadness on thy infant features,
> > Blending with love,
> Are hers whose mournful eyes seem sadly bending
> > On her lost love.
>
> Thou art not mine; upon thy sweet lip lingers
> > Thy mother's smile,
> And while I press thy soft and baby fingers
> > In mine the while—
> In thy deep eyes, so trustfully upraising
> > Their light to mine,
> I deem the spirit of thy mother gazing
> > To my soul's shrine.
> They ask me, with their meek and soft beseeching,
> > A mother's care;
> They ask a mother's kind and patient teaching—
> > A mother's prayer.
>
> Not mine—yet dear to me—fair fragrant blossom
> > Of a fair tree,

Crushed to the earth in life's first glorious summer,
    Thou art dear to me.
Child of the lost, the buried and the sainted,
    I call thee mine,
Till, fairer still, with tears and sin untainted,
    Her home be thine.

Sympathetic to the plight of the child and to the departed mother whom she recognizes as "sainted," the surrogate mother of "To a Step-Child" personifies the Victorian ideal of womanhood. Sensitive, devoted and meek, she is portrayed as a worthy caretaker who can adore another woman's child unreservedly, while acknowledging the temporary nature of her own role—but she represents only one image of stepmotherhood.

While Bakewell prioritized a positive portrait of stepmothering, she also acknowledged that there were occasions on which the stepmother might resemble the monster of myth, rather than an angelic caretaker. In *The Mother's Practical Guide* she comments:

> It is but too true that there are women who take upon themselves the important duties of a second mother without any intention faithfully to discharge them; in truth, without considering that the situation involves any. They say by actions, if not in words, "We married the husband, not the children; if we do our duty to him, it is as much as can reasonably be expected." (1843: 269)

Moreover, states Bakewell, it is not always the wife who is at fault. She tells of men "so overpowered by passion, or stimulated by ambition, as to consent to part with their children in order to obtain the woman of their choice" (p. 270). Yet having temporarily laid at least some blame at the door of the male, she swiftly returns to the issue of unkind or injudicious stepmothers, and although she stresses that it is more frequent for a woman to act in this manner "from the pressure of circumstances which she has not foreseen, than from premeditation" (p. 271), she nevertheless admits that unhappy scenarios do exist:

> [The stepmother] probably enters on her new home with a wish to be happy, and to make all around her comfortable, but is received with coldness and suspicion where she expected cordiality and kindness. The children treat her with disrespect, if not with positive insult, and in self-defence she is tempted to retaliate, and in time may become the tyrant of those she was prepared to love. (p. 271)

The potential for the stepmother to become a wicked creature in accordance with myth is thus ever-present and, should circumstances dictate, she may eventually re-emerge. Even for the largely positive Bakewell, the wicked stepmother of fairy tale remains a potential threat to the loving and tranquil environment that typifies the idealized nineteenth-century domestic sphere, although she does not fully discuss the implications of such a notion. Nevertheless, there is evidently a tension between ideology and reality and other Victorian writers chose to focus, although rarely explicitly, not on the saintly stepmother, but on her less desirable and occasionally monstrous counterpart. In doing so, they invited elements of that which had been abjected by writers such as Bakewell to once more take center stage. Moreover, in depicting such individuals and acknowledging their existence, they also simultaneously exposed the domestic ideal as a fragile environment that could easily be shattered by ideologically imperfect surrogate parents from the world outside.

## THE PRECARIOUS NATURE OF HOME SWEET HOME: LUCY LANE CLIFFORD'S "The New Mother" (1882)

The notion of the stepmother as a monstrous creature is foregrounded in Lucy Lane Clifford's extraordinary tale of "The New Mother," although the "interloper" of Clifford's text is not married to the children's father and so is a metaphorical, rather than a literal, representation of stepmotherhood. Heavy with didacticism and highly moralistic, Clifford's story finds its place within a select group of writings by Victorian women that includes works by Christina Rossetti and Anne Thackeray Ritchie. These are often disturbing texts, sometimes possessed of an almost malevolent undercurrent that refuses to grant a comforting closure to the young reader. They are, as Nina Auerbach and U.C. Knoepflmacher suggest, a counterbalance to the "obsessive nostalgia" of Carroll, MacDonald and Barrie, but their subversiveness is disguised by an outward conformity to stereotypically didactic female literary style (1992: 1). Psychologically dense and ultimately nightmarish, "The New Mother" exemplifies the nature of such texts.

Not surprisingly perhaps, there has been sustained and diverse academic interest in the tale; readings have ranged from Alison Lurie's emphasis on its relation to the primitive (1975), to Anna Krugovoy Silver's extensive Bakhtinian analysis (2000). But much remains to be explored, and to focus on the notion of family, specifically mothering and stepmothering, within Clifford's story, is to expose the ambivalences and anxieties of Victorian children who may have perceived the stepmother as a fearful phenomenon. Even today, "The New Mother" is a disconcerting read. Anita Moss has noted that the story offers "a warning which taps deeply into any child's worst terrors—the fear of losing one's mother and the anxiety that terrible transformations will occur, that what is beloved and familiar will, somehow, inexplicably become strange and terrifying" (1988: 57). For a Victorian reader to whom the death of a mother was a much more prevalent threat, its impact must have been even greater.

## An Intriguing Meeting

The story tells how well-behaved sisters, Blue-Eyes and the Turkey,[6] living with their mother and baby sibling in a cottage in the woods,[7] meet a strange girl by the wayside. The children are entranced when the stranger tells them of the little man and woman that live in a box at the side of the peardrum she carries, and further intrigued by the information that both come out and dance when the peardrum plays. During a subsequent meeting, the girl reveals that the little woman, who lifts her petticoat as she dances and sends out a kiss, also tells a secret.

Desperate to see the miniature people, but repeatedly told by the strange girl that they are not sufficiently naughty, the children embark on a regime of deliberate naughtiness. They tell their loving mother nothing about the girl and the peardrum, but their increasingly destructive behavior saddens her and she eventually admits that if Blue-Eyes and the Turkey were to continue to be very naughty, she would have to go away and leave them, and would send home a new mother with glass eyes and a wooden tail (*New Mother*: 23). The children are torn, but continue to be naughty, comforted by the stranger who denies the plausibility of their mother's threat. "'That is what they all say'," she comments (p. 24).

However, the children's mother does leave, as promised. Having warned her daughters that unless their behavior is good on the following day she will have to go away, she witnesses yet more naughtiness and then slowly dresses herself and the baby and leaves the house, telling the children that the new mother will be home presently. The strange girl with the peardrum offers little consolation. When the children meet her, she tells them that the little man and woman are now far away and that she is returning to her own land. Despite the children's belief that their mother will return, the girl asserts that she will never come back (p. 38).

The children continue to hope for their mother's forgiveness and tidy and clean the cottage so that "it [looks] more and more as if the dear mother's hands had been busy about it" (p. 43). They sit and wait, thoroughly repentant, but their mother does not return. Instead, they hear "a sound as of something heavy being dragged along the ground outside, and . . . a loud and terrible knocking at the door" (p. 44). Peeping out of the window, the Turkey sees "a black poke bonnet with a frill round the edge, and a long bony army carrying a black leather bag. From beneath the bonnet there [flashes] a strange bright light," which the Turkey knows is the flashing of two glass eyes (p. 45).

Unable to gain access to the cottage, they hear the visitor say to herself that she must break open the door with her tail and moments later the door is cracked and splintered. The children flee to the forest where they remain, feeding on fruits and sleeping under leaves, but constantly longing for the return of "their own dear mother" so that they can tell her "that they'll be good for evermore—just once again" (p. 46). Sometimes, at night, they creep back to the cottage to watch and listen, but are rewarded only by the sight of a blinding flash that they know is the light from the new mother's glass eyes, or a strange muffled noise that they know is the sound of her wooden tail as she drags it along the floor (p. 47).

In its simplest sense, Clifford's strange tale is patently didactic—the children's naughtiness drives their mother away—but it is simultaneously a psychological study of childhood fears, although it was written in an age that was "still free of psychoanalytic suspicion," as Auerbach and Knoepflmacher point out (1992: 1). To read "The New Mother" as a tale of mother loss and its associated terrors certainly explains the story's enduring effect. Whether the reader is Victorian or twenty-first century, the notion of absolute and final separation from the mother remains distressing. Yet it is not solely the disappearance of the mother figure that is so disturbing. It is also the destruction of what is in many ways an ideologically perfect home, a place of love and harmony, in which happy children and tender mother co-exist.

## A Female World

The beginning of "The New Mother" gives little indication that such trauma will follow. The reader is introduced to the family's perfect home where the bonds between mother and daughters are much in evidence.[8] Theirs is an almost exclusively female Nirvana; father is away at sea throughout the story and the only other male character mentioned, apart from the little man in the pear drum, is the old man, first seen in the village and later depicted following the strange girl toward the city. This female world is one of domestic harmony; the older children go the village to see if there is a letter from father and return to watchful mother, waiting tea, and happily crowing baby. The interior of the cottage is a stereotypically feminine domestic space:

> The cottage room was so cosy; the walls were as white as snow inside as well as out, and against them hung the cake-tin and the baking-dish and the lid of a large saucepan that had been worn out long before the children could remember, and the fish-slice, all polished and shining as bright as silver . . . The baby's high-chair stood in one corner, and in another there was a cupboard hung up high against the wall, in which the mother kept all manner of little surprises. ("The New Mother": 10)

Virginal white both indoors and out, the cottage is metaphorically a pure and unsullied female space in which nurturing and childcare are prioritized. The cake-tin, baking-dish and worn-out saucepan lid are testaments to copious amounts of home cooking, the baby's high-chair, although placed in a corner, is specifically emphasized by the narrator, and the cupboard where "all manner of little surprises are kept" is a magical object of delight for Blue Eyes and the Turkey: "The children often wondered how the things that came out of that cupboard had got into it, for they seldom saw them put there" (p. 10). However,

**Figure 3.1** "Then she kissed them." The unity of the all-female family is emphasised in Dorothy Tennant's opening illustration for the original edition of "The New Mother" in which daughters, mother and baby present a tightly-formed tableau as the girls prepare to leave for the village. © The British Library Board. All Rights Reserved. Shelfmark12810.c.13.

and in contrast to the other domestic items that surround it, the fish-slice is "polished and shining as bright as silver," suggesting that it is unused. The father is apparently away at sea throughout the story, and the pristine implement may signify the absence of the sea-faring member of the family, although its polished condition indicates that it is a cherished item.

The children's mother seemingly epitomizes the Victorian angel in the house. Attentive to her children's physical and moral well-being, she is an equally devoted housekeeper, but her idyllic home is shown to be constantly under threat. The cottage is "lonely" (p. 8) and is located on the edge of a forest; it lies within the domain of fairy tale, bordering both realism and fantasy. Its proximity to the forest is such that "the garden at the back seemed a part of it, and the tall fir-trees were so close that their big black arms stretched over the little thatched roof, and when the moon shone upon them their tangled shadows were all over the white-washed walls" (p. 8). Darkness is an-ever present neighbor and may one day engulf the snow-white building, tainting its virginal purity.

The precariousness of this domestic idyll is further emphasized through the events that befall Blue-Eyes and the Turkey. Having met the strange girl with the peardrum and discovered that their only route to the little man and woman is through bad behavior, both children resolve to be naughty, although at first Blue-Eyes claims that she does not know how to misbehave because no one has taught her, and the Turkey is unsure of her capacity for naughtiness: "'I think I can be naughty if I try,'" she says." 'I'll try tonight'" (p. 19). Ultimately, both prove to be adept at bad behavior, although it takes some time before they are bad enough to drive their mother away. Once again, the perfectly harmonious home on the edge of the forest is exposed as a fragile construct that can easily be shattered by a disruptive element from the world outside, or, indeed, by one that activates dormant dissension from within such an idealized space; the children clearly already possess the potential for bad behavior. Moreover, the mother makes it clear that she can survive only within this ideologically perfect environment; without model children, the angel in the house will vanish. When Blue-Eyes asks her what would happen if she and her sister were "very, very, very naughty and wouldn't be good, what then?" the mother replies:

> "Then" . . . and while she spoke her eyes filled with tears, and a sob almost choked her—"then . . . I should have to go away and leave you and to send home a new mother with glass eyes and wooden tail . . . it would make me very unhappy, and I will never do it unless you are very, very naughty and I am obliged." (p. 23)

Despite their love for their mother, the children yearn for knowledge. If, as Silver (2000) suggests, the sisters are punished for their sinful obsession with the peardrum couple, the little woman's sexual prancing and the secret she has to tell, their rebellion might also be interpreted as a desire for entry into the symbolic order, a yearning for sexual knowledge and a breakaway from the contained and insular world of the maternal *chora*.[9] The domestic world associated with the angelic mother might thus be perceived as an asexual space that cannot be maintained if children seek sexual maturity. But the children are ambivalent about making such a choice; desirous of the world beyond their mother, they simultaneously wish to retain her presence: "[T]hey sobbed bitterly, for they remembered the little man and woman and longed more than ever to see them; but how could they bear to let their own mother go away, and a new one take her place?"("The New Mother": 23). Poised between knowledge and ignorance, they choose the former, and so opt to destroy the idyll that was once their home.

## Death and Destruction

The destruction of the perfect home simultaneously instigates the death of the perfect mother. The sisters try to persuade her to stay, but their attempts are futile. The mother dresses herself and the baby, picks up her bundle and goes slowly out of the door:

> "Come back, dear mother!" cried Blue-Eyes; but still the mother went on across the fields.
> "Come back, come back!" cried the Turkey; but still the mother went on.
> Just by the corner of the field she stopped and turned, and waved her handkerchief, all wet with tears, to the children at the window; she made the baby kiss its hand; and in a moment mother and baby had vanished from their sight. (p. 36)

Despite her seeming devotion to her children, the mother appears to have no choice but to leave them, although she weeps as she departs and takes one final look at her home and family. When the children later meet the peardrum girl, she confirms that their mother will never return; she tells them, "'I saw her by the bridge; she took a boat upon the river; she is sailing to the sea; she will meet your father once again, and they will go sailing on, sailing on to the countries far away'" (p. 38). As Silver confirms (2000:742), the crossing of water is symbolic of dying and the mother's disappearance might thus be interpreted as the death of the angel of the house, a notion that exposes Clifford's work as truly subversive to the Victorian ideological agenda. The mother holds an infant in her arms as she leaves, personifying both the Victorian ideal and the Madonna; unable to exist within a real world of temptation and "sin," she has been "obliged" to go. Moreover, there are also resonances of death in childbirth in this episode which further characterize the mother as martyr. She and the baby vanish together, the mother dressed "in her best gown and her new sun-bonnet" and the baby "in all its Sunday clothes" ("The New Mother": 34).

With the demise of their saintly mother, Blue-Eyes and the Turkey can only anticipate that her replacement will be monstrous. Resistant to the coming of a new mother, as undoubtedly many Victorian children were, they rely entirely on hearsay as they await her steps. Having listened to their mother's description of the newcomer and the peardrum girl's warning that "'she is already on her way; but she walks only slowly, for her tail is rather long, and her spectacles are left behind; but she is coming, she is coming—coming—coming'" (p. 39), they declare their hostility: "'I shall never, never like any other mother. I don't know what we shall do if that dreadful mother comes,'" says Blue-Eyes, while the Turkey states, "'We won't let her in'" (p. 41).

But the new mother does come, or at least the children believe that she does, although the narrator forbears to confirm that she is as monstrous as foretold. Significantly, the children's impressions of the new mother are largely based on how they imagine her to be; while the Turkey peeps out at the figure who knocks on the door, she catches only a glimpse. The "strange bright light" that the Turkey thinks she sees beneath the black poke bonnet is immediately transmuted in her mind into the flashing of glass eyes and it is only the children who hear the voice outside, threatening to break open the door with her tail; there is no corroboration by the narrator. They "almost" hear the visitor lift her tail before the door is "cracked and splintered" (p. 46) and then they flee to the forest where they remain, returning only to gaze on their once-happy home and listen "with beating hearts" (p. 47).

Clifford's depiction of the new mother is highly ambiguous; despite the fact that the children have never truly seen her, she is presented as the stuff of nightmares; she represents stepmotherhood according to popular myth and her diametrical opposition to the idealized angelic mother figure is precisely how children might have characterized a replacement for a much-loved parent.[10] With her phallic wooden tail[11] and lightning eyes, she is an unearthly automaton and a maternal travesty, a hellish interloper that bears no relation to a child's ideal of motherhood. As a result of her arrival, the children are implicitly banished from the family home and find themselves lonely and alone in the forest while the wicked stepmother reigns supreme in the once-idyllic cottage.

"The New Mother" is admittedly complex, but the story clearly explores the loss of a mother and her replacement by an unwelcome outsider. The absence of the father may be literal or figurative but he is largely irrelevant; the domestic sphere is essentially a female space and the Victorian father who remarried often distanced himself from the early interaction between new wife and existing offspring. As "The New Mother" suggests, this was frequently a frightening and traumatic time for children. To have lost a "perfect" mother and to remember her primarily as a saint is, by implication, to deny the possibility of replacement; to accept a counterfeit mother is to demonstrate disloyalty, particularly if the natural mother herself has contributed to the creation of the wicked stepmother myth. Blue-Eyes and the Turkey have no choice but to perceive their new mother as monstrous. Furthermore, until they accept the new mother, they have nowhere to go. Clifford's tale finally and uncompromisingly proposes that having destroyed the fantasy that was once their home and exposed it as an untenable and fragile construct, the children can never regain their domestic idyll.

## A SUBTLY SUBVERSIVE APPROACH: HARRIET CHILDE-PEMBERTON'S *Birdie: A Tale of Child-Life* (1888)

Although Clifford, as author, offered her protagonists little hope of an idyllic domestic future, other children's authors were less dogmatic in condemning their characters to eternal gloom and despair. For Harriet Childe-Pemberton, a happy-ever-after closure appears to have been of prime importance, although Childe-Pemberton, like Clifford, displays a propensity for subversion and her texts invariably require careful analysis.[12]

Childe-Pemberton's *Birdie: A Tale of Child-Life* is the story of the motherless Haviland children whose world is made idyllic once again by their acceptance of stepmother Lady Victoria, a friend of their deceased parent. However, there is turbulence along the way; nine-year-old Birdie resents the arrival of the new stepmother, particularly as it is only a year after her own mother's death, and her loyalty to her dead mama, coupled with a belief that Lady Victoria has deceived her,[13] exacerbates her resistance to the interloper. Birdie encourages her younger brother, Hubs, to join her in her campaign and the two prove disruptive for the newly formed transnormative family.

Childe-Pemberton's portrait of Lady Victoria is intriguing, primarily because although the narrative point of view appears to encourage acceptance of the new mother—"She came among . . . [the children] loving them already" (p. 90)—the narrator persistently over-emphasizes the charms of the new arrival. Most notably, perhaps, it is the narrator's insistence on Lady Victoria's resemblance to a princess that prompts awareness of fairy-tale comparisons and consequently a sense of unreality, and so begins to undermine the apparent authenticity of Lady Victoria. Indeed, the narrator explicitly draws the reader's attention to fairy tale prior to Lady Victoria's first visit to the Haviland home when she arrives merely as a guest. The children learn that Lady Victoria was a friend of their mother's and that the Queen is her godmother and so instantly grant her celebrity status: "And so it happened that, in the imaginations of Mr Haviland's children, Lady Victoria had some of that mysterious importance which belongs to the princess of a fairy tale, and her visit was awaited with impatience and wonder" (p. 31). Furthermore, while Lady Victoria "positively fascinate[s]" Birdie and Hubs, the narrative asserts that she also "seem[ed] to have cast some spell over Grandmama and Aunt Emily too!" (p. 51); the usually strict adults relax in Lady Victoria's presence. She is an accomplished pianist and story teller; she plays the children "dreamy valses (*sic*), and merry swinging airs, and sweet, soothing lullabies" and entrances them with her tales of faraway lands and of "great deeds, strange and noble and terrible . . . that took place hundreds of years ago" (p. 54). For Birdie and Hubs she becomes "their beau-idéal, their good fairy" (p. 64) and when she appears, after her marriage, at the family's ball, Birdie feels that she "loo[ks], for all the world, like the beautiful genius of some enchanted realm!" (p. 169).

But if Lady Haviland is an enchantress, she initially fails to establish her power over Birdie and Hubs; she stands in opposition to the perfection of the children's dead mother and so can never become her equal. However, because her milieu is loss and grief, as Schectman (1993) proposes, it is perhaps only within such an environment that she can become stronger and, significantly, it is in the midst of subsequent mortalities that Childe-Pemberton allows Lady Victoria to finally establish her reign. Hubs, unhappy because his loyalty to Birdie prevents a close relationship with Lady Victoria, is made more wretched by the death of his pet rabbit and when his stepmother offers comfort, repays her affection: "[H]e knelt up on her lap, and put his arms round her neck and kissed her" (*Birdie*: 119). In addition, in response to her questioning, he admits that his earlier behavior to Lady Victoria was prompted by a promise to his sister. Although the relationship between Hubs and his stepmother is consolidated in this episode and it is from this point that Hubs refers to her as "Mamma" (p. 121), the alliance creates a barrier between Hubs and Birdie; the narrative intimates that Lady Victoria has essentially competed with Birdie for Hubs' loyalty and Birdie's jealousy increases her resistance to her stepmother. It requires a further death and some deft emotional manipulation for Lady Victoria to finally win Birdie's complete approval and affection.

Lady Victoria's youngest brother Lionel visits the family, gains popularity with the children and proves himself a chivalrous champion for his sister's cause. When Hubs falls through the ice on the pond, drawn to the scene by Birdie who has deliberately disobeyed her stepmother's orders, Lady Victoria is perceived as negligent by her husband, but chooses not to tell him the truth of the tale. It is Lionel who talks to Birdie and reveals his sister's sacrifice and when Lionel suddenly dies, the child, who has shown immense anxiety for her young brother in the wake of his accident, is united with her stepmother through "a fellowship in sorrow" (p. 186): "[Y]ou and Lion were like Hubs and me, weren't you? Oh! I am so tremendously sorry for you—I am, I am!" proclaims Birdie (p. 185).[14]

Birdie is further comforted by the notion that Lion and her mother will meet each other in heaven, but is also concerned that her behavior will disappoint her mother. Lady Victoria, however, quashes Birdie's anxieties while at the same time asserting her own heaven-blessed position:

> "Ah well, Birdie dear! Up in heaven Mother is happy, and nothing that could make her sad can reach her there."
> "Then do you think, *if* she knew, it would make her sad?"

**Figure 3.2** United through sorrow: Birdie and Lady Victoria are reconciled (p. 186). Illustrator H.W.Rainey. © The British Library Board. All Rights Reserved. Shelfmark 12807.o.4.

"Certainly it would make Mother sad if she knew that any of her children were not trying to be happy and good. And, Birdie, if our dear ones in heaven can see us here, then Mother knows how I have loved her children, and cared for them, and felt for them just as she herself would have done, and how I have longed for them to understand all this, and how I have waited and hoped—oh! hoped so hard that some day they would." (p. 188)

Lady Victoria's speech is her trump card; by aligning herself with Birdie's dead mother, and persuading the child that in accepting a stepmother she is also pleasing her parent in heaven, Lady Victoria's acceptance is assured. While she may not be entirely comparable with the wicked stepmother of fairy tale, she is nevertheless shown to be adept at persuasion; there is a duality to her character that emerges as the text proceeds. Like Clifford, Childe-Pemberton reveals the transnormative family as a phenomenon that is replete with difficulties and, in addition, suggests that in the wake of maternal demise, the domestic ideal can be reasserted only through further tragic circumstances and dubious adult intervention. Superficially, she offers her reader a tale of stepmotherly devotion that is ultimately rewarded, but she also presents a story in which rivalry, unhappiness, death and emotional manipulation play a most significant role.

## DISCORDANT VOICES: FILIAL JEALOUSY AND AUTHORIAL "COMPROMISE" IN CAROLINE BIRLEY'S *We Are Seven* (1880)

While it is the fairy-tale emphases of Childe-Pemberton's novel that alert the reader to its subtextual implications, Caroline Birley's *We Are Seven* is perhaps more subtle in declaring its allegiance to traditional fantasy tales. Yet it bears comparison with those tales that explore rivalry between a stepmother and daughter; the young protagonist might be perceived as exhibiting a female Oedipal complex, while the incoming stepmother achieves her queenship only through the physical and mental disempowerment of her rebellious stepchild. Despite such potentially remarkable characteristics, Birley's text is ultimately a compromise because it insists on a comforting and somewhat awkward closure. Nevertheless, it remains an important publication, not least for its focus on the tension between stepmother and stepdaughter and for its implicit message that in the domestic idyll there can only ever be one queen.

*We Are Seven* features a family of motherless children whose widower father, Colonel Enderby, remarries and whose choice of bride is the woman who was his first love. Despite opposition to the marriage from fourteen-year-old Judy, the eldest daughter, all is resolved in the book's final chapter and the closing paragraphs depict the second Mrs Enderby and her stepdaughter anticipating a harmonious future together as they join in prayer. However, Birley's apparent desire for a reassuring closure to her novel is overwhelming, to the extent that it all but destroys the credibility of what is essentially an otherwise feasible tale. In order to achieve her idyllic and ideologically sound finale, Birley is obliged to silence opposition to the marriage between Colonel Enderby and his second wife and she does so by disempowering the lively, but jealous, Judy. Judy is badly injured in an accident, but conveniently emerges from her sickbed an altogether more compliant creature.[15]

Birley's technique might be perceived as a time-honored tradition in Victorian literature for girls. As Lois Keith comments in *Take Up Thy Bed and Walk: Death, Disability and Cure in Classic Fiction for Girls* (2001),

> At one point in my research . . . it felt like there was hardly a girls' novel since 1850 which didn't have a character who at some crucial stage defied their guardian and fell off a swing or out of a sled, became paralysed through tipping out of a carriage or was suffering from some nameless, crippling illness from which they could, indeed must, be cured. (p. 5)

Judy is injured as a pony cart, containing herself and her small stepsister, Winifred, hurtles uncontrollably toward gravel pits. Remembering a story told by her father, in which a young mother saves the life of her son but sacrifices her own, Judy folds Winnie in "a close embrace, pressing the little face against her bosom" (*We Are Seven*: 131) and hurls herself and the child from the run-away vehicle before it reaches the precipice. Winnie is, of course, unhurt, but Judy suffers "concussion of the brain . . . and probably other injuries" and "hover[s] for days between life and death" (p. 133) as a consequence. However, within the final two pages of the novel she realizes that she has always cared for her stepmother and the two are finally, and somewhat swiftly, united in loving harmony.

## Maternal Instincts

Judy's sudden capitulation is remarkable, as is her apparent readiness to abdicate her role as surrogate mother and wife. Throughout the novel Birley is at pains to emphasize Judy's maternal nature, not least in the final chapter when Judy mimics the heroine of her father's tale in order to save Winifred's life. Introduced as "high-principled, generous [and] determined," Judy has "great power and influence" over her brothers and sisters (p. 9) and is essentially a mother substitute to her sickly younger sibling, Birdie: "Ever since their mother's death, Judith had striven not to let . . . [Birdie] miss the sweet caressing ways to which she had been used," writes Birley (p. 11). When Birdie falls mortally ill, it is Judy who becomes her father's confidante and assumes the maternal role; he tells Judy that they must teach the sick child to "look forward to her heavenly home" (p. 74). Judy rarely leaves her dying sister's side in the last few weeks and she and her father are the only witnesses to Birdie's death.

Moreover, Judy consciously desires to become her father's partner. Her "only consolation" in the aftermath of Birdie's death is her father's company: "Their companionship in Birdie's room and mutual grief, had drawn them very close together, and Judith looked forward to a time when . . . [her father] would treat her as an equal, consult her and depend on her for everything, and teach her how to fill her mother's place" (p. 80). Judy spends "long hours" (p. 81) writing out the contents of an old volume on engineering so that she can be a helpmeet to her father as he prepares a manuscript for publication, and is rewarded when he appoints her his private secretary. In fact, she becomes something of an angel in the house: "It was in [Judy's] nature to devote herself to someone, and she studied to render [her father] every little service that was in her power" (p. 83). Made anxious by the prospect of school in a year's time, Judy hopes to become so necessary to her father that he will be unable to part with her.

Not surprisingly, Judy is intensely jealous when news of a romance between her father and the widowed Mrs Heathcote emerges. For Judy, a girl on the verge of puberty who cannot match her rival's charms:

> her father's second marriage seemed too wild and dreadful an idea even to be thought of, and the marked improvement in his spirits . . . she quietly assigned to her own influence. And yet a vague distrust and jealousy made her hold aloof from Mrs Heathcote, whose . . . manner gained the hearts of all the rest . . . Judith felt always shy and awkward and uncouth beside her, and shrank from the disagreeable sensation of a contrast which produced such envious dissatisfaction with herself. (p. 112)

Judy, displaying the traditional anxieties of an adolescent, feels "shy . . . awkward and uncouth" beside Mrs Heathcote but convinces herself that it is her own ministrations that have improved her father's "spirits," despite the fact that all those around her admire the new arrival. Birley's portrait of Judy as a burgeoning woman, who is nevertheless still a child, is insightful; the "envious dis-satisfaction" that Judy feels when she contrasts herself with Mrs Heathcote succinctly encapsulates the anguish of a young girl confronted with an un-assailable rival, while Judy's belief that her father's remarriage is "too wild and dreadful . . . even to be thought of," betrays the child-like nature of her emotions, as does her response to her father's declaration.

Colonel Enderby intends to marry Mrs Heathcote and confides in Judy after his intended second wife has paid a visit. Judy's reponse is a passionate reproach—"'O father!'" she cries out—but although the Colonel understands that his remarriage "will be a trial to [Judy] at first" (p. 114), he attempts to convince his daughter that all will be well, adding, "I am not going to persuade you that, like many second marriages, this step is taken solely for my children's good . . . but, believe me, my own hopes and happiness would have been sacrificed had I not seen in her one who will as far as possible be like a mother to you all" (p. 115). Colonel Enderby's acknowledgment that "many second marriages" are made "solely" for the good of children is notable; not only does it suggest an authorial point of view, it also exposes the impetus for numerous remarriages and so questions the viability of the transnormative family as a re-creation of the domestic ideal. However, the Colonel's desire to remarry is founded on affection, rather than practicality, although he acknowledges that Mrs Heathcote has the potential to be "like a mother" to his offspring. Despite his explanation, Judy remains resolute in her disapproval: "'I don't much like Mrs Heathcote,'" she comments. "'If it had to be, I wish it had been some one else'" (p. 115).

Judy's reaction to the news of her father's impending marriage derives from her fear that she will lose not only her father, but also her brothers and sisters. Immediately after her father's announcement, she runs to the churchyard to fling herself, weeping, on her mother's grave. As the narrator explains, in a direct reference to the fairy-tale/reality dichotomy peculiar to the figure of the step-mother, Judy is not frightened of "the stepmother of fairy tales who would rule her harshly or perhaps be positively unkind . . . but beyond the natural pang of seeing a stranger in her mother's place, there was the downfall of her hopes and visions of being the future consolation of her father's life" (p. 116). Furthermore, she fears that the new stepmother will win the hearts of her siblings, that Judy herself will be forgotten when she goes to school and that Mrs Heathcote's daughter, Winifred, will become the household's "darling" (p. 117). She yearns for an assurance that her father's love for her has not dimin-ished, but the marriage proceeds and "Poor Queen Judith . . . [feels] as if a usurper were coming to her kingdom and . . . [makes] a valiant effort to keep the hearts of the few subjects who were left within her power" (p. 123). Instead of welcoming her new mother, Judy finds occupation in "methodical resistance" (p. 125); even when her stepmother persuades Colonel Enderby not to send his daughter to school, Judy remains rebellious and insists that she would rather go away.

## Authorial Difficulties

Having created what may well have been a highly realistic scenario for eldest daughters faced with the prospect of a new mother, Birley finds herself at an impasse which results in awkward textual maneuvers. When Colonel Enderby tells his daughter that she has been "unaccustomed" to authority and implies that her resentment is based on fear of discipline (p. 114), his accusation is without foundation; Judy has never been depicted as the "wild girl" (p. 114) that her father proposes. Furthermore, although the narrator's constant emphasis on the stepmother's goodness is excessive, it is sometimes interspersed with details that portray her in a less favorable light. For example, prior to her marriage, Mrs Heathcote unashamedly asks for love from eight-year-old Dulcie

Enderby and presents her with a gold locket—an action that is clearly an act of bribery:

> "You love me a little, don't you dear?" she asked [Dulcie] gently; "and you are very good to Winifred, I know;" to which Dulcie answered with a mute caress.
>
> After a while Mrs Heathcote unfastened from her neck a gold locket with the word "Dulcie" on it in raised letters and put it on the little girl.
>
> "I feel as if your being my little namesake gave us a peculiar right to one another," [she said]. (p. 113)

Such moments are essentially *aporia* that signal a contradiction between rhetoric and thought and expose the conflict between Birley's desire for realism and her obligation to ideology. Having presented Judy's jealousy and resentment of her stepmother as credible and, to some extent, justified, Birley must now renege on her heroine in order to achieve a desirable closure in which the Enderby family can emerge as united and idyllic.

She does so by injuring her central protagonist and rendering her passive, transforming the lively Judy into a sickbed saint. Judy's predicament allows her time for contemplation and her stepmother becomes a favored nurse:

> The shock to [Judy's] nerves had been so great that the least noise or motion brought on actual pain, and all excitement was carefully avoided. There were hours when she lay quite still, thinking of many things, while her stepmother kept her quiet watch beside the fire, and Judy learnt to prize her thoughtful tenderness and gentle voice even more than her beloved Aunt Dolly's visits. (p. 134)

However, whenever Judy is ready to talk, her stepmother absents herself from the room, much to Judy's displeasure. Heavy with "a burden of deferred confession" (p. 134), Judy at last begs Mrs Heathcote, now Mrs Enderby, to stay, proclaiming, "I don't want *anything*, I want *you*" (p. 135). There follows a brief, but emotional, scene in which Judy begs for her stepmother's forgiveness and voices her anxiety for Mrs Enderby's health: "'Now every time you look so tired, and worn and ill with nursing me, I am, oh! much sorrier, and I am so glad to be allowed to try again'" (p.138). Finally, in a moment of supreme repentance, Judy declares, "'It is like a new life given to me to do better with'" and asks Mrs Enderby to help her with it, adding, "'I want it to be unlike the old one in almost everything'" (p. 138). Portrayed throughout much of the book as a most "dutiful daughter" (p. 90), Judy's extreme penitence appears entirely unnecessary.

## Textual Contradictions

It might be tempting to view *We Are Seven* as an archetypal Victorian story in which the protagonist recognizes the error of her ways and is brought to salvation through divine intervention and the ministrations of a positively angelic being. It might also be argued that Birley had no choice but to conform to expectations; Victorian publishers would undoubtedly have questioned a children's text that finally presented a middle-class family as disunited. However, the contradictions inherent in Birley's tale suggest that in order for a children's author to adhere to the tenets of Victorian family ideology, it would sometimes be necessary for her to compromise her integrity. Or, perhaps, to veil any suggestion of subversion by concealing it, consciously or subconsciously, within a superficially conventional and idealistic domestic narrative.

Birley, it would seem, chose the latter method, presenting her audience with a striking paradox that entirely undermines the complacency of the novel's closure and demands that the reader question its assurances. The last chapter of the book deals primarily with Mrs Enderby's attempts to win Judy's affection, and is prefaced with a stanza from Adelaide Proctor's poem, "A New Mother"[16] that reads:

He might perhaps have blamed them, but his wife
Never failed to take the children's part;
   She would stay him with her pleading tone
   Saying she would strive, and strive alone,
Till she gained each little wayward heart. (1903: 110)

Taken in isolation, Proctor's description is highly reminiscent of Mrs Enderby's behavior; in fact Birley may well have modeled her fictional stepmother on Proctor's creation. But, read in its entirety, Proctor's poem asserts that conflict can continue to exist within the household of a transnormative family, despite appearances to the contrary. "A New Mother" is written in the voice of a loyal servant who refuses to acknowledge the stepmother as a replacement for her dead mistress and constantly reminds the children of the mother they have lost. Never "chiding" her charges when they "[shrink] away " from their new mother (p. 244), the servant watches as the children grow closer to their stepmother when their father is called away to war. Prior to his departure, the father tells his family that his dead wife and current wife were once friends, and explains, through metaphor, how both fell in love with him and that Margaret, their stepmother, chose to give up her love for the sake of her friend. While the children appear to accept this tale and their father's reassurance that their mother "is happy now, and . . . knows all" (p. 249), the narrator declares in the closing line that "[she] loved her own dear lady best" (p. 249). Present at her mistress's deathbed, she has already told the reader how the children's natural mother begged that her babies should "still remain [her] own" (p. 241) as she lay dying. The servant will undoubtedly remain loyal, despite changes in the house.

Proctor's poem leaves the reader with a sense of unease; despite the father's palliative tale, there is more than a suggestion that its narrator will continue to cherish her dead mistress and to exhort her in the eyes of the children,[17] and this sense of discomfort is evident in both Birley's tale and Proctor's poem. Although Judy's accident has seemingly silenced her opposition to her new mother and the children of Proctor's poem have apparently been placated by their father's story, there is, overall, a tangible fragility to both situations. The domestic idyll has been established superficially, despite maternal absences, but the ghosts of dead mothers threaten to disrupt what is assuredly a tentative status quo. Judy's saintly new persona, achieved too swiftly, is unrealistic and implicitly untenable. Proctor's servant, having promised her former mistress that "her children's hearts, at any cost, /Should be with the mother they had lost, /When a stranger came to take her place" (p. 240), is unlikely to betray her pledge. By aligning herself with Proctor's "A New Mother," Birley, in spite of her apparently "happy" ending, suggests that while an idyllic transnormative family home may be desirable, it is a environment fraught with conflict. Moreover, for Birley, as for Childe-Pemberton, the accession of the stepmother would seem to invite comparison with the machinations of the wicked step-mother of fairy tale. The incoming queen can apparently only achieve her goal through complete and utter victory over the child, using whatever guiles she may have at her disposal.

## THE FOLLY OF VOLUNTARY SLAVERY: CHARLOTTE M. YONGE'S *The Young Step-mother or A Catalogue of Mistakes* (1861)

However, to allow the child or children of the family to rule in the new step-mother's stead could prove entirely disastrous for the incoming queen, and for Charlotte M. Yonge the indulgence implicit in such a stance was to be abhorred. Writing on the subject of stepmothers in *Mothers in Council*, the publication of the Church of England Union for Mothers which she edited in the 1880s and 1890s, Yonge described stepmothering as "one of the most difficult positions upon which a person can voluntarily embark" and although she admitted that her feature was not written from personal experience—Yonge was never a mother—she explained that she had drawn on "the amount of obser-vations that no one can fail to have made in the course of a lifetime" (n.p.). According to Yonge, it was necessary for the stepmother to "mount her step, and make it clear that she [was] mistress of the house": "[n]othing can go right in a family without just authority and firmness," she wrote. Moreover, for a step-mother to abdicate her responsibilities because she sought to avoid comparison with the wicked creature of fairy tale was highly erroneous: "Some [stepmothers] become almost slaves to their stepchildren in the fear of being supposed to be tyrants," asserted Yonge. "This is a mischief to be deplored" (n.p.).

Yet for the new stepmother to attempt to personify the *converse* of the tyrant of fairy tale is, by implication, for her to seek to emulate the perfection of the deceased mother, a task in which she can never succeed: as Hughes (1991) points out, the myth of perfection is predominant and so it must necessarily preclude replication. Haunted forever by the spectre of the dead maternal ideal, the Victorian stepmother who chooses indulgence in order to secure her reign can only mimic the saintliness of her deceased rival and the result, as Yonge suggests in *The Young Step-mother or A Catalogue of Mistakes*,[18] must inevitably be disastrous.

Unlike the other novels discussed in this chapter, the central protagonist of Yonge's text is not a child, but Albinia Kendal, the stepmother of the title, and although the narrative voice is that of an omnipotent third person, it focuses primarily on Albinia's perspective. Yonge's implicit adolescent readership is admittedly older than that of Childe-Pemberton and Birley, but her text nevertheless addresses similar issues, namely the entry of a new mother into a household of children and the events that ensue. However, while Childe-Pemberton and Birley trace the development of the transnormative family from conflict to resolution and locate their narratives within what is a brief time frame, Yonge's tale tracks the Kendals through a period of years, following the children into adulthood and concluding when two of the original offspring have left the family home and the third has resolved her many psychological crises.

*The Young Step-mother* resists the superficially comforting closure preferred by other writers of transnormative family children's tales. Instead, it proposes that a stepmother who lacks firm resolution and enters her new home bathed in illusions and excessive expectations will endure disappointments. While Albinia begins her married life replete with hope and good intentions, the concluding passage of the novel foregrounds her sense of failure, an emotion that she suffers on many occasions throughout the text. Despite the fact that she has tried to do her utmost for her adopted family, she is clearly unconvinced that she has succeeded. Her clergyman brother Maurice Ferrars, a stalwart friend and helper to Albinia, tells his sister: "[W]hile we are indeed honestly and faithfully doing our best . . . our lapses through infirmity will be compensated, both in the training of our own character and the results upon others." Albinia's answer is assuredly ambiguous—"If we are indeed faithfully doing our best," she replies (*Young Step-mother*. 430)—but it would appear to question that she has performed her duties as she might have wished. Yonge's text suggests that Albinia, as stepmother, will always consider herself a failure.

**An Optimistic Beginning**

Albinia enters her marriage "embrac[ing] joyfully the cares which such a choice must impose on her" (p. 5), although, even in the opening pages of the novel, the reader is forewarned of the difficulties faced by the young bride. Albinia's sister-in-law, Winifred, is frankly opposed to Albinia, "giving her fresh young heart away to a man who has no return to make": "his heart is in his first wife's grave . . . Did you ever see any one so utterly broken down?" (p. 2). Although Winifred's husband, Maurice, points out that Kendal's melancholy is one of his charms in Albinia's eyes, she continues:

> I am sure I pity the poor man heartily; but to see her at three-and-twenty, with her sweet face and high spirits, give herself away to a man who looks but half alive, and cannot, if he would, return that full first love—have the charge of a tribe of children, be spied and commented on by the first wife's relations—Maurice, I cannot bear it. (p. 2)

The difficulties awaiting Albinia are succinctly presented: as the incoming new mother, she will have the charge of three children, the lively Lucy, twelve, the plain and boorish Sophia, eleven, and the sickly thirteen-year-old Edmund, and she will indeed by "spied on and commented on" by her dead predecessor's relatives; Kendal's mother-in-law and her spinster daughter live near to Willow Lawn and have had much influence on the children since their mother's death two years previously. Furthermore, in the wake of spinster aunt Maria's marriage, Mrs Meadows will eventually come to live with Albinia and her husband.

Albinia's husband is also portrayed as something of a barrier to marital harmony. Not only has Kendal lost his first wife to typhus, but his much-loved and promising son Edmund, twin of the sickly Gilbert, also fell victim to the disease. In addition, Kendal has fathered four other children, all of whom died in infancy, and whose deaths are commemorated, along with their mother's, on a mural tablet in the village church (p. 12).[19] Kendal is consequently melancholy and, at first, Albinia's lively character is no match for the sadness that permeates the family home:

> When taken away from the scene of his troubles, [Kendal's] spirits revived; afraid to encounter his own household alone, he had thought Albinia the cure for everything. But at home, habit and association had proved too strong for her presence—the grief, which he had tried to leave behind, had waited ready to meet him on the threshold and the very sense that it was a melancholy welcome added to his depression. The old sorrows haunted the walls of the house and above all, the study, and tarried not in seizing on their unresisting victim. Melancholy was in his nature, his indolence gave it force, and his habits were almost ineffaceable, and they

were habits of quiet selfishness, formed by a resolute, though inert will, and fostered by an adoring wife. (p. 33)

So Albinia must contend not only with the problems inherent to motherless children and cope with the intrusions of her dead predecessor's relatives, but must also bear her husband's intense and continuing grief and the insularity born of his intellectually deficient first marriage. Although the narrator explains that Kendal's first wife had been "no companion," the illusion remains with Kendal: "he had always loved her devotedly, and her loss had shattered all his present rest and comfort; as entirely as the death of his son had taken from him hope and companionship" (p. 33). The dead wife and mother is consequently granted iconic status.

Locked away in his study for much of the time, Kendal is essentially a recluse and claims the space entirely as his own. Inside, the study is "shaded with a mass of laurels that [keep] out the sun and make it look chill and sad," while a portrait of Kendal's first wife hangs over the fireplace and a carved wooden sandal-wood work-box is placed, shrine-like, in a niche in the wall (p. 19). Taken into the study in Kendal's absence by daughter Lucy, a child who is an appalling gossip and who clearly enjoys the drama of the moment, Albinia is alarmed when Lucy announces that her father is coming. Although Lucy is mistaken, Albinia finds herself vexed and dismayed by the experience and "[cannot] help thinking of Bluebeard's closet": "Her inclination was to stay where she was, and take her chance of losing her head, yet she felt as if she could not bear to be found invading a sanctuary of past recollections, and was relieved to find that it was a false alarm" (p. 19).

In this way, and from early in the novel, Yonge portrays Albinia not as a wicked stepmother, but as an individual who strives to identify herself in opposition to mythical representations of stepmotherhood. However, as a consequence, she is also depicted as a victim; like Bluebeard's wife, she is necessarily subject to the vagaries of her husband's behavior. The relationship between Albinia and Kendal does improve; she labors to "raise . . . [his] . . . spirits and rouse his faculties" and she ultimately makes him a more happy and active man, as she vows to do (p. 34). Indeed, he even abandons his study to make space for his first wife's mother when she moves to Willow Lawn, although this is an action based on duty to his first wife. Moreover, there remains a sense of distance between husband and wife and it is Albinia's brother whom she invariably turns to for support and advice; without Maurice, Albinia might easily be drawn into Kendal's melancholia. Albinia's natural family, Yonge's text asserts, is a vital support mechanism that prevents the young stepmother from becoming entirely suffocated by her husband. When the couple's first child is born, Winifred reports that "[Kendal] does not seem to take the slightest pleasure in his baby" and that his gloom has broken down Albinia's "sunny spirits" (p. 67). Albinia is assuredly morose, but her brother understands that "the phantoms of her boy's dead brethren dwel[l] on her imagination" and preclude her from rejoicing (p. 71), while her husband's anxieties have frightened her. "Almost jealous" for her baby son, Albinia is rendered "piteous and incoherent" by her fears for the future and her duties to her family: "I think of Gilbert and the girls—and oh! there is so much to do for them—they want a mother so much" (p. 72), she tells Maurice. The "sunny spirit[ed]" Albinia has become paranoid.

The children may well be in need of a maternal figure, but prove entirely troublesome for their dedicated stepmother. Gilbert is a permanent source of anxiety, whether through his claims to sickness or his association with dubious local characters; Lucy is "intolerable with her airs", as Winifred states (p. 67), while the brusque and depressed Sophia appears to be in a permanent state of despondency, although an undiagnosed spinal illness proves to be the cause of at least some of her behavioral problems. Despite the fact that Albinia is immensely and consistently tolerant with her stepchildren, their transition into adulthood is scarcely gratifying for her and she is forever chiding herself for what she perceives as her failure to produce a more creditable family. In the wake of an accident involving baby Maurice and Kendal's threat to exile Sophia at school, Albinia's sense of self-deprecation is extreme:

> The education of "Edmund's children" had been a cherished vision, and it had resulted so differently from her expectations that her heart sank. With Gilbert there was indeed no lack of love and confidence, but there was a sad lurking sense of his want of force of character, and she had avowedly been insufficient to preserve him from temptation; Lucy whom externally she had the most altered, was not of a nature accordant enough with her own for her to believe the effects deep or permanent; and Sophia—poor Sophia! Had what was kindly called forbearance been really neglect and want of moral courage? Would a gentler, less eager person have won instead of repelling confidence? Had her multiplicity of occupations made her give but divided attention to the more important home duty? (p. 93)

Yonge's text demonstrates that Albinia's expectations of her role as stepmother and her illusions about the way in which her family *should* develop are ultimately at fault. As the novel moves toward its closure, Yonge introduces some "improvements" into Albinia's life; Gilbert distinguishes himself in the 25th Lancers at Balaklava, although he dies shortly afterwards, and the depressed Sophia, thwarted in a romantic relationship, avoids matrimony altogether by embracing a spiritual life. But Yonge also imposes further problems on her protagonist. Lucy, allowed and more than willing to marry the worthless Algernon Dusautoy, is characterized as being "proud . . . of her gilded slavery" (p. 427); she is pale with red eyes and trembling on her wedding day, but Albinia and Kendal marry Lucy "very much as if they had been attending her to the block," although Albinia admits that she has "taken the middle course that she contemned (*sic*)" (p. 316). In addition, Albinia and Kendal's son, Maurice, remains a troublesome, boisterous being. At the closure of the novel the echoes of his former mischievous ways are still in evidence: portrayed in the text as a violent and hyperactive infant who Albinia acknowledges was considered "a plague" by those outside the family (p. 317), school may have mellowed young Maurice, but he has had to be sent away in order to become an acceptable individual. Yonge does offer Albinia a potentially joyful future as a mother through her second child, Winifred, a "chestnut-curled, black-eyed fairy," already capable of chatting fluently in two languages (p. 425), but this ideologically perfect child is also depicted as a precocious infant and she may, or may not, fulfill her mother's dreams. In Yonge's text, nothing is certain.

For Yonge, stepmotherly over-indulgence is clearly a folly, and firmness and determination are preferable to tolerance and patience. But her text also, simultaneously, highlights the difficulties inherent to stepmothering, whatever the nature of the adopted family. Indeed, in her article on stepmothers (1896) she apologizes for what she considers to be "a very unsatisfactory discussion" and concludes:

> The long and short ... [of it] seems to be that, with the fear of God and love of justice and kindness before her eyes, a stepmother is often deeply loved and respected, becoming ... a true mother; but that she will probably have much to undergo, which can only be endured and conquered through love, hope and patience. ("Stepmothers" n.p.)

The role of a stepmother is clearly one that should only be entertained after much thought and without romantic expectations. Even then, devotion and willingness to succeed are no guarantee that the domestic ideal can once more be established—if it has ever truly existed. Kendal's first marriage, to a wife who was "no companion," was evidently not representative of the ideal, but nevertheless engendered sorrow; his second marriage to Albinia is shown to be similarly ideologically deficient, and is marred substantially by his previous relationship. Yonge's narrative emphasizes that while the first Mrs Kendal is not worshipped as a saint, she remains revered by her husband.

All the texts discussed in this chapter propose, to varying degrees, that the nineteenth-century stepmother can never replicate the often-iconic persona of her predecessor. She can achieve a semblance of the domestic ideal through manipulation, as in Childe-Pemberton and Birley's novels, but achievement of such an ideal requires the construction of a relationship that must necessarily be drawn from the ashes of what has gone before if it is, in any way, to resemble the dictates of Victorian ideology. The stepmother is ever the "other" in her new family; standing in opposition to the frequently sanctified perfection of the deceased maternal image, she must always, to some extent, fail to create a second, "perfect" home. If she assumes a tyrannical role, she allies herself with fairy-tale myth and the shades of wicked stepmotherhood; if she employs only persuasion and tolerance, there will be chaos and disillusionment. Moreover and ironically, although she may strive to build a domestic sphere in which her adopted family will flourish, her very presence is a constant reminder of that which has been lost because the stepmother herself, as Schectman (1993) argues, is born of grief and death. The Victorian transnormative family, with stepmother ostensibly at the helm, signifies not the re-creation of the domestic ideal, but a substitute image that is, at best, overlaid with the implications inherent to "making do."

However, the substitution of a stepmother as caretaker was merely one of the ways in which the middle- or upper-class children of nineteenth-century fiction might experience transnormative family life. For many children, parental absence or death necessitated temporary or long-term boarding-out with other relatives while, in the summer, city-dwelling offspring might be sent for a seaside or country holiday with an aunt or grandmother. Even if the child remained at home, a visiting relative or one domiciled with the family might play an extensive part in the child-rearing process. There is a wealth of children's fiction in which the child is absent from the parental home, or away from parental influence, and many such texts attempt to portray the new "home" in accordance with Victorian domestic ideology; they suggest that such surroundings are an extension of the idyllic domestic sphere and that the influence of kindly relatives is beneficial to the child. But, and conversely, such texts also sometimes hint that the domestic space can be severely disrupted by the presence of extended family members, and that the guardianship of an uncle or aunt cannot ensure the creation of an environment that consistently and satisfactorily adheres to the dictates of the domestic ideal.

# Chapter Four
## "Uncles are One Thing . . . [but] Aunts are Always Nasty!"[1] Relational failures and the discourse of gender bias in foster family tales

For Dolores Mohun, the thirteen-year-old protagonist of Charlotte M. Yonge's *The Two Sides of the Shield* (1885), aunts who foster orphans "are ever so much worse than stepmothers" (p. 11).[2] An incorrigible devotee of romantic fiction, Dolores is "well instructed by story books in the hypocrisy of aunts until fathers were at a distance" (p. 26), and consequently anticipates a sorrowful future when her widowed father deposits her at Aunt Lilias' house and departs for Fiji. Aunt Lilias is kind, but Dolores, perceiving herself to be "in the power of one of [those] cruel aunts" (p. 31) about whom she has read, assumes the guise of a romantic heroine, a lonely orphan persecuted by vicious and jealous relatives. In contrast, Dolores has "nothing but pleasant associations" connected with her Uncle Reginald, younger brother to her father, who visits from Ireland, "always made her father's house his headquarters when in London and used to play with her when she was a small child, and . . . take her to the Zoological Gardens" (p. 202).

Dolores' perception of aunts is clearly the product of her penchant for novels and Yonge's text is an often humorous portrait of childish imagination as well as a cautionary tale about the folly of youthful preconceptions. However, the opening chapters of the novel encapsulate a theme that is recurrent in nineteenth-century tales focusing on middle- and upper-class foster children rendered homeless by parental death or absence overseas. While there is often antagonism between foster child and her aunt, an uncle is usually instantly adored. He may be portrayed as playmate, carer or sage, but he is innately empathetic and comprehends the needs of his young kin. He receives their affection easily and reciprocates it unconditionally, albeit that he is willing to chastise, when appropriate. The relationship between a child and her aunt may fail, although there is likely to be reconciliation prior to the closure of the text if the aunt in question is married and a mother, as in *The Two Sides of the Shield*; her innate maternal skills will enable her to win the affections of her troublesome young relative.[3] But it is in the contrast between spinster aunts and uncles that Victorian gender bias fully declares itself. While unmarried aunts are shown to have little or no skill in establishing a domestic idyll, are frequently insensitive to children and may be depicted as manipulative or even harmful, the relationship between a child and her uncle, whether he is a bachelor or husband, is likely to represent an exemplary familial bond.[4] It is a preference that is far more evident within children's literature than mainstream adult fiction[5] and is only occasionally exposed within the same text; the majority of the books discussed in this chapter focus on the relationship between a child and her spinster aunt *or* a child and her uncle. Nevertheless, comparison of such stories reveals a subversive subtext that impacts not only on the reader, but also on the way in which the phenomenon of the transnormative family is ultimately represented.

### Explicit Messages

This "favoring" of uncle over aunt indicates authorial adherence to the tenets of patriarchy and to the concept of male supremacy and Yonge's texts, in particular, demonstrate complicity with such doctrines.[6] *The Two Sides of the Shield* and *Countess Kate* (1862) directly juxtapose aunt and uncle figures and offer an overt comparison that clearly privileges the uncle, but while protagonist Dolores Mohun's comments might well be interpreted as juvenile nonsense, there is a more potent message at play in *Countess Kate*. With its contrasting portraits of the excessively dutiful and embittered Aunt Barbara and the caring, kindly Colonel Umfraville, the text fully embraces the notion of the uncle as the superior individual.

The novel tells how eleven-year-old Kate is suddenly elevated to the peerage and placed under the care of her two spinster aunts, the severe Lady Barbara and the frail Lady Jane Umfraville, who determine to make a lady of Kate, but whose lectures drive the child from London to the former, supposedly "unsuitable" friends with whom she used to live. Kate is forced to return to the city and to her aunts' home, but is ultimately "rescued" by her great-uncle, Giles Umfraville, and his wife Emily. In the final pages of the novel, Aunt Barbara is thoroughly castigated by Giles for her treatment of Kate and denounced for her prejudices:

> "I am willing to confess that I am not capable of dealing with . . . [Kate].
> Only from a sense of duty did I ever undertake it," [said Barbara].
> "Of duty, Barbara?" [Giles] asked.
> "Yes—of duty to the family."

... "I came home, Barbara," continued the Colonel, "resolving that ... if you had found in her a new interest and delight ... I would not say one word to disturb so happy a state of things. I come and find the child a state prisoner ... I find her not complaining of you, but answering me with the saddest account a child can give of herself—she is always naughty. After this ... I can be doing you no injury in asking you to concur with me in arrangements for putting the child under my wife's care as soon as possible."

"To-morrow, if you like," said Lady Barbara. "I took her only from a sense of duty ... I would not keep her for any consideration." (p. 212–13)

Aunt Barbara's response is one that characterizes her as cold and emotionless, and her confession that she is "not capable of dealing with ... [Kate]," and the speed with which she relinquishes her responsibility, further emphasize her lack of "natural" parenting skills. In contrast, Uncle Giles is immediately concerned for Kate's well-being. He instantly comprehends the significance of Kate's statement that "she is always naughty," understands her condition as "a state prisoner" and acts swiftly to resolve the situation and create a happier home for the orphaned child. Recently bereaved by the loss of their own adult children, Uncle Giles and his wife eventually assume responsibility for Kate's upbringing and, as time passes, Kate loses her "childish wildness, and love[s] them more and more" (p. 216).

Yonge's text explicitly denounces the spinster aunts as ineffectual carers, whilst contrasting them with, and promoting, the figure of the uncle. In fact, Giles might be said to display those traits so evidently lacking in Aunt Barbara. In the confrontation between Giles and Barbara, it is Giles who displays the more female tendencies; Aunt Barbara's overall lack of emotion and her severity entirely contravene the prescribed Victorian feminine ideal. Barbara may weep as she confesses, "It was not in me to love that child. It was wrong in me," but she is also unwilling to change: "Now it is too late. Our habits have formed themselves, and I can neither manage the child nor make her happy," she admits (p. 214). Inflexible and opinionated, denied the opportunity for marriage in her youth because she elected to care for her delicate sister, Barbara in many ways epitomizes the spinster aunt of Victorian children's fiction and, indeed, the stereotypical nineteenth-century old maid.

## The Public Face of Spinsterhood

Give youth and hope a parting tear—
Look onward with a placid brow—
Hope promised but to bring us here,
And Reason takes the guidance now.
One backward look—the last—the last!
One silent tear—for youth is past.

Who goes with Hope and Passion back?
Who comes with me and Memory on?
Oh, lonely looks the downward track—
Joy's music hush'd—Hope's roses gone!
To Pleasure and her giddy troop
Farewell, without a sigh or tear!
But heart gives way, and spirits droop,
To think that Love may leave us here!

Have we no charm when youth is flown,
Midway to death left sad and lone?
N.P. Willis: Lines on *Thirty Five.*[7]

If the angel in the house represented the ideal of womanhood for the Victorians, the figure of the spinster was its antithesis. While some contemporary commentators were alarmed by the "plight" of the so-called old maid, others, such as the author of the above lines, perceived her solely as a sad and somewhat pitiful creature. The literature of the day specifically addressed to the middle-aged, unmarried woman emphasized the hopelessness of any dream of marriage and advised the necessity of contentment on the path to old age. Anne Penny's *The Afternoon of Unmarried Life* (1858), a homily to the single woman, couched its verbiage in sympathetic and purportedly empathetic tones, but nevertheless foregrounded the misery of the spinster. In her frontispiece, Mrs Penny presents a scenario rich in metaphor in which she describes the emotional wretchedness that could befall an unmarried woman aged between thirty and fifty:

A lady sits by a table well furnished with books . . . but her forehead is bent down on one hand, and the other has fallen listlessly to her side . . . she rises and goes to the window . . . According to her own notions, she resembles that Anchusa Plant which the gardener has left standing between a glowing Marvel of Peru and a spiked band of red Zinnias; which, having done its regular blossoming, now and then opens a few blue stars on cool mornings, but which is for the most part dull-looking and unsightly, stretching its long prickly shoots on all sides with dim and shapeless luxuriance; leaning on nothing, attaching itself to nothing, with little lovely colour, and no sweet scent. For the person I am describing is no longer young—she is not yet old; she is of middle age, and just now she thinks this age a very dreary one. (pp. 15–19)

No longer capable of blossoming, the middle-aged spinster is depressed, lonely, and bored. "Leaning on" and attached to "nothing," she is a woman without purpose and while she is surrounded on all sides by vibrant, glowing, and younger creatures, she has been "left standing." It is a sobering introduction, and while the remainder of Mrs Penny's text is replete with advice on how to achieve contentment in spinsterhood—through spirituality, cordiality, activity, family ties, and "a well-cultivated mind" (p. 93)—her argument is often unconvincing, primarily because she frequently reminds the reader of that which has been lost. Moreover, with the complacency of one who is married, she concludes: "According to human judgement, it is undoubtedly *happiest* for a woman to be the wife of a good man; but the conditions requisite for this superlative degree of happiness are not easily secured" (p. 313).

For Mrs Penny, as for other contemporary writers, the spinster state was problematic and the married woman was not only to be envied, but congratulated on achieving her "natural" destiny.[8] However, for many women, marriage was a logistical impossibility. At the mid-century, a spinster was unlikely to marry if she was past the age of thirty or thirty-five (Poovey cited in Green and Owens 2002: 2) and the largest imbalance between the sexes was reported in London where the number of unmarried women aged above twenty-five in 1851 outnumbered unmarried men by more than 104,000 (Green and Owens 2002: 2). It was a situation that alarmed some social commentators: "[T]here is an enormous and increasing number of single women in the nation, a number which, positively and relatively, is indicative of an unwholesome social state, and is both productive and prognostic of much wretchedness and wrong," asserted journalist W.R. Greg in 1862 (cited in Vicinus 1988: 3).[9]

Without marriage, the middle- and upper-class woman of mid- to late-Victorian Britain lacked power and prestige; the gradual encroachment of the bourgeoisie with its separate spheres for male and female had effectively placed the spinster in a no-man's land and, as Martha Vicinus comments: "By the mid nineteenth-century, middle-class spinsters appeared to have no larger purpose in life" (p. 3). Certainly the spinster might draw, write, and even publish, but in terms of domestic ideology, she dwelt in a void in which "absolute purity and goodness" (p. 5) were thrust upon her. As Laura L. Doan notes, within the symbolic order, the spinster is defined by absence: "She lacks a primary relationship with a man to fulfil her role as wife and mother . . . [and] . . . [o]ther available kinship roles (aunt, daughter, or sister, for instance) achieves only marginal importance and cannot compensate for the inadequacy of her single status" (1991: 5). Without the opportunity for marriage and procreation, the Victorian spinster was doomed, not only socially, but physically. As early as 1838, Richard Carlile, writing in *Every Woman's Book or What is Love?* warned of the consequences of female celibacy:

It is a fact that can hardly have escaped the notice of anyone, that women who have never had sexual commerce begin to droop when about twenty-five years of age, that they become pale and languid, that general weakness and irritability, a sort of restless, nervous fidgetyness takes possession of them, and an absorbing process goes on, their forms degerate, their features sink, and the peculiar character of the old maid becomes apparent. (Jalland and Hooper 1986: 32)

It was through such imagery that the archetypal Victorian spinster was born—a nervous, agitated creature with no meaningful life of her own, forever destined to perform an extraneous role. Her domicile might well be in the home of a relative, or perhaps she lived in isolation with only a companion or servants for company, visiting her relatives when appropriate, or when invited. Whatever her particular situation, "she took her place in the family as an unsuccessful human being, and, though she might be loved and respected by all the household, a bitter drop of condescension was generally mixed in with the affection," as Janet Dunbar states. "She became the aunt, the nurse, the useful member of the family who had no responsibilities of her own" (1953: 22). She was, in effect, surplus to ideological requirements.

## Children's Literature and the Spinster Aunt

Although her role might well have been perceived as extraneous, the unmarried aunt, daughter or sister was nevertheless a member of the family and her incorporation into the "traditional" domestic sphere is a commonplace feature of nineteenth-century texts for children. If she is youthful, her characteristics are inevitably girlish; the young, unmarried female per se is often depicted as a burgeoning "angel" whose feminine perfection will assuredly secure a successful marriage.[10] The older woman is generally less picturesquely portrayed; beyond marriageable age, she may demonstrate the rigidity of Yonge's Aunt Barbara or the feebleness of Barbara's sister Jane. Often less knowledgeable about worldly matters than her married contemporaries, her experience of childcare is necessarily limited, but she appears to possess little of the maternal instinct and sensibilities "naturally" afforded to her wedded female relatives. Her judgement may be unsound and she may even display jealousy towards those relatives who *have* achieved home and family. Whatever her psychology, the spinster aunt would seem to be incapable of providing, or helping to sustain, an ideologically sound domestic environment. In many ways she is perhaps the most subversive of family members in terms of nineteenth-century domestic ideology; her very existence exposes the domestic ideal as a phenomenon that is both elusive and selective, while her propensity for disruption represents a serious threat to the alleged idyll that is the Victorian home.

## NEGATIVE INFLUENCES AND FAMILIAL DISCORD: MARY LOUISA MOLESWORTH'S *Rosy* (1882)

In Molesworth's *Rosy*, spinster aunt Edith Vincent is depicted as largely responsible for the mayhem that ensues when her young niece is reunited with her mother and father on their return from India. Absent for "some years" (p. 10), Rosy's parents have left the child and her brother, Colin, in England

and while Colin "had the good fortune to be sent to a very nice school, Rosy had stayed altogether with her aunt, who had loved her dearly, but in wishing to make her perfectly happy had made the mistake of letting her have her own way in everything" (p. 10). Rosy is eight when her parents return and they are disappointed to find their daughter wayward, fractious and demanding. Furthermore, her behavior appears irredeemable: "[A]s months passed, and all her mother's care and advice and gentle firmness seemed to have no effect, Rosy's true friends began to ask themselves what should be done. The little girl was growing a misery to herself and a constant trouble to other people" (p. 10). This emphasis on "true" friends is significant; the aunt has been introduced just prior to the statement and so there is an implicit suggestion that she is not among those "true" friends.

Rosy's problematic behavior is exacerbated by the news that Beata, the daughter of a family whom Rosy's parents met in India, is coming to stay because her mother and father are returning to the sub-continent. Due to illness, Beata's grandmother is unable to take care of the child, and so Rosy's parents assume responsibility for her: "It had all seemed so natural and nice. Rosy's mother was so pleased about it, for she thought it would be just what Rosy needed to make her a pleasanter and more reasonable little girl" (p. 18). She is, of course, mistaken. Fearful that Beata will appropriate the love of her little brother Felix (Fixie) and that the family will love the foster child more than her, Rosy embarks on a regime of jealousy and bullying, telling Beata:

> I think I shall like you, if only you don't make a fuss about how good you are, and set them all against me. I settled before you came that I wouldn't mind if you were pretty or very clever. And you're not pretty, and I daresay you're not very clever. So I won't mind, if you don't make everybody praise you up for being so *good* (p. 36)

Rosy's prejudices against Beata eventually subside and in fact Beata is largely responsible for the way in which Rosy improves in both behaviour and self-confidence. However, the manner in which Rosy's spinster aunt has raised the child, and the ineptitude of her child-rearing practices, are portrayed throughout much of the text as the root cause of the child's temperament and Rosy herself is aware of her aunt's failings and appears to have little love for the carer who has caused her so many problems. When Rosy's mother announces that she is writing to Aunt Edith and invites Rosy to send a note, Rosy declines:

> "Then shall I just send your love? . . ." said her mother.
> . . . "I don't want to send my love," said Rosy. "If you say I *must*, I suppose I must, but I don't *want* to send it."
> "Do you think your love is not worth having, my poor little girl?" said her mother, smiling a little sadly, as she drew Rosy to her. "Don't you believe we all love you, Rosy and want you to love us?"

"I don't know," said Rosy gloomily. "I don't think anybody can love me, for Martha's always saying if I do naughty things *you* won't love me and father won't love me and nobody."

"Then why don't you leave off doing naughty things, Rosy?" said her mother.

"Oh, I can't," Rosy replied, coolly. "I suppose I was spoilt at auntie's, and now I'm too old to change. I don't care. It isn't my fault; it's auntie's." (p. 21–2)

Molesworth's sympathies would seem to be firmly with the child at this juncture; Rosy's gloomy supposition that no one can love her renders her pathetic and exposes her desire for parental affection, and her excuse, that she was "spoilt at auntie's" and is "now too old to change," may be humorous, but it is also poignant. Thoroughly insecure and informed by her brother Colin and Martha the nurse that she has been spoilt, Rosy is encouraged to assume a lack of responsibility for her behavior, although her mother tells her: "Your aunt was only too kind to you, and I will never allow you to blame her" (p. 23). Molesworth's stance is ambiguous; while Rosy is not permitted to blame her aunt, the reader is encouraged to do so through a narrative that repeatedly confirms the aunt's culpability. It is an ambiguity suggestive of a social dilemma; Molesworth, as author, may acknowledge that adults can be blameworthy, but simultaneously subscribes to the belief that the child must remain respectful.

As the narrative progresses, it becomes clear that it is not merely Rosy's aunt that has adversely affected her niece's behaviour: Nelson, Aunt Edith's maid, has actively promoted the notion that Rosy's home will be less than idyllic for the child and that life with her aunt was preferable. In conversation with Beata, Rosy comments:

"*I'm* not the favourite, I was at my aunty's though, that I was—but it has all come true what Nelson told me," and she shook her head dolefully.

"Who is Nelson?" asked Beata.

"Aunty's maid. She cried when I came away, and she said it was because she was sorry for me. It wouldn't be the same as *there*, she said. I shouldn't be thought as much of with two brothers, and Nelson knew that my mamma was dreadfully strict. I daresay she'd be still more sorry for me if she knew . . . if she knew *you* had come. (pp. 34–5)

A modern reader might well assume that the absence of Rosy's parents is largely to blame for her insecurities, but Molesworth offers no criticism of Mr and Mrs Vincent; thousands of children were left in England while their parents were stationed abroad, and in *Rosy*, as in many other texts focusing on children of the Empire, the responsibility for those offspring apparently rested squarely on the shoulders of their temporary caretakers.[11] However, if Molesworth, as author, is reluctant to present parents as culpable, she would also seem resistant to the notion that the spinster aunt is ultimately to blame, although her narrative overall suggests otherwise and her opinion certainly vacillates. Having suggested, through the voices of both the narrator and Rosy that Aunt Edith has spoilt the child, the blame is then transferred to Aunt Edith's maid. When Mrs Vincent hears that her sister-in-law is planning a visit, she comments:

> I should not mind Edith herself coming . . . She is *really* good and kind, and I think I could make her understand how cruel it is to spoil Rosy. But it is the maid—that Nelson—I cannot like or trust her, and I believe she did Rosy more harm than all her aunt's over-indulgence. And Edith is so fond of her; I cannot say anything against her. (p. 96)

Aunt Edith, states the narrator, is an invalid and is very dependent on Nelson, which seemingly vindicates her from any responsibility, although as a middle-class mistress of a household, she surely *should* possess sufficient moral judgment to employ suitable staff. However, Aunt Edith's frailty is proffered as an excuse and, as with the earlier fiction of Edgeworth and Sherwood, the lower-class maid is deemed to be most at fault, although both Edgeworth and Sherwood generally apportion blame to those responsible for hiring such individuals.[12] No such blame is explicitly forthcoming in Molesworth's text; in fact there is additional commentary on Nelson's failings:

> Then this very morning too had brought a letter from Rosy's aunt, proposing a visit for the very next week, accompanied, of course, by the maid who had done Rosy so much harm! Poor Mrs Vincent—it was really trying—and she did not even like to tell Rosy's father how much she dreaded his sister's visit. For Aunt Edith had meant and wished to be so truly kind to Rosy that it seemed ungrateful not to be glad to see her. (p. 119)

Paradoxically, however, and within a few pages, the emphasis once again changes, questioning Aunt Edith's judgment as Rosy recalls that her aunt "had not liked the idea of Bee coming" and "that if she fancied the little stranger was the cause of any worry to her darling she would try to get her sent away" (p. 124). Aunt Edith is encouraged by Nelson to be anxious for Rosy's happiness, but her distinct preference for her "pet" (p. 134) renders her foolishly gullible to suggestion and prompts her to question the actions of Rosy's parents. When Nelson complains that Rosy is too subdued and that "it [is] all that Miss Bee's doing," Aunt Edith responds: "We can't take the child away from her own parents. All the same, I'm very glad to have come to see for myself, and if I find out anything not nice about . . . [Beata] . . . I shall stand upon no ceremony, I assure you" (p. 131).

Molesworth, as author, remains ambivalent toward the figure of Aunt Edith as the text moves toward its closure. Beata achieves saintly status when she saves Rosy from serious injury during a fire and consequently becomes unwell and

Rosy is ashamed of her behavior and was "[never] . . . so truly grateful to anyone as she was now . . . to Beata." The narrator comments that "even Aunt Edith's prejudices seemed to have melted away, for she kissed Bee as she said goodnight, and called her a brave, good child" (p. 183), but the words are ambiguous: Aunt Edith has not necessarily lost her prejudices, they only "seemed" to have melted away and despite the fact that her maid is responsible for the events that precipitated the fire, there is no dismissal. Overall, Aunt Edith is certainly blameworthy, although the narrator offers no overt criticism, but by representing the spinster aunt in such a way, Molesworth highlights the flaws of such a creature and suggests that her presence within the "natural" family is problematic. An intrusive outsider, possessed of cloying sentimentality and an impulse to override parental dictate, the spinster aunt, as a relative, must be endured, although she may pose a threat to familial harmony.

## USURPING THE MOTHER: HARRIET CHILDE-PEMBERTON'S "All My Doing; or, Red Riding Hood Over Again" (1882)

The concept of the spinster aunt as intrusive and potentially threatening to family unity is also central to Childe-Pemberton's "All My Doing; or, Red Riding Hood Over Again," but in this multi-faceted tale she is also depicted as manipulative and jealous. In addition, while the story might initially be perceived as validating transnormative family structures, it ultimately questions the wisdom of allowing "outsiders" to assume parental roles. In Childe-Pemberton's tale, neither the "natural" family, nor the transnormative grouping provide an idyllic familial unit for the young protagonist, and although the chaotic "natural" family might be deemed a less precarious place in which to dwell, it nevertheless permits the intrusion of potentially dangerous influences. The domestic ideal would seem to be an entirely elusive phenomenon within Childe-Pemberton's text.

The narrator of the story, Aunt Pussy, adopts what Roderick McGillis refers to as "a mother's language: literal, personal, direct and heartfelt" (1995: 129), to relate a cautionary story to her fifteen-year-old niece, Margery. Margery has dismissed "Red Riding Hood" as "one of the stupidest of all the nursery tales," asserting that "people don't get put to death themselves or cause the deaths of others simply by being heedless and silly" ("All My Doing": 212). Pussy, who likes her niece's "earnestness and sincerity and . . . can pardon her dogmatic tone" (p. 212), tells Margery of her own tragic experience; as a young girl[13] she behaved heedlessly, and her thoughtless actions resulted in the incapacitation of a much-admired grandmother and the crippling of a suitor. While the deaths of grandmamma and Herbert are figurative, the reader learns that Pussy was also "put . . . to death," albeit metaphorically. Her old maid status is, she intimates, the direct result of her thoughtless exploits and she remains embittered by her youthful experiences. "Twenty years have come and gone

. . . and Herbert is still a lame old bachelor and I am a lonely old maid," she declares in the closing paragraphs (p. 247).

Childe-Pemberton's reincarnation of the Red Riding Hood story is ostensibly didactic and its narrator portrays herself as moralistic and self-deprecating throughout, but Pussy is not simply a saintly storyteller; she also seeks to broaden her niece's general education. McGillis asserts that Pussy is a positive influence in that she provides "a corrective to mother–daughter relationships which are in coercion with patriarchy" (1995: 134), yet to perceive Pussy as a wholly beneficient force is inaccurate. Despite Pussy's overt affection for her niece, the subtext of the tale exposes the spinster aunt as a potentially disruptive influence within the family home and suggests that her regard for Margery is essentially the product of frustrated maternal desires. Pussy, it would appear, is a pretender to the maternal throne.

She relishes her intimacy with her niece; in fact she would seem to view it as something of a triumph. As she states:

> To tell the truth, Margery is never dogmatic with me. When I begin to talk and tell her things out of my own experience—as I often do, for it has been a varied one—she always listens in rapt attention, and often answers me quite doubtfully and humbly, which surprises me sometimes, I confess, for *I* have never learnt half the things *she* is being taught, and know very little about mathematics and political economy. ("All My Doing": 212)

Childe-Pemberton's depiction of Pussy identifies her as a character devoted to self-promotion. Pussy's egocentricity is evident throughout her statement; she boasts of a varied experience and of an ability to fascinate her niece and her claim that she is surprised by Margery's "rapt attention" and doubtful and humble answers is indicative of false modesty. Moreover, Pussy's portrait of Margery's parents slyly displays to advantage the aunt's apparent "unconditional" affection for her niece. She tells the reader: "I don't greatly mind at present, as her father does, that her arms and legs are long and awkward and that she is a little careless about brushing her hair and keeping her collars clean, nor am I in a fever of anxiety, like her poor mother, lest she may not know quite as much as other girls of her age" (p. 212). Margery's parents are summarily dismissed; their qualifications are, by implication, inferior to those of Pussy and once Pussy has begun to debate the question of Red Riding Hood with Margery and has fully engaged her interest, she elevates herself to even greater heights, assuming guru status to Margery-the-devotee: "I felt my niece slip off the arm of my chair, and in another minute she was kneeling before me with her elbows on my lap, looking up at me with just the puzzled sort of look I had expected . . . her puzzled gaze having something awestruck in it" (p. 213). Pussy has swiftly and expertly usurped the maternal role and simultaneously claimed ownership of her niece.

Within the terms of the Red Riding Hood scenario, Pussy herself might be deemed somewhat wolfish as she attempts to lure a patently innocent young girl away from the educational path ordained by her parents. As a spinster, Pussy is evidently both envious and critical of her sister-in law; having glanced around the schoolroom and its factual texts, she wonders whether, if she had had children to educate, she would have pursued "precisely the same plan as found favour in the eyes of [her] sister-in-law" and complains, "but I had never had much chance of putting my ideas into practice. They had remained ideas —explained at great length very often to certain of my friends—but not going much further" (p. 212). Childe-Pemberton's phrase "certain of my friends" suggests that Pussy gossips, perhaps among other spinsters, about her sister-in-law's shortcomings as an educator; the selfsame sense of cunning and secrecy that underlies Pussy's musings on education pervades her criticism of Margery's parents. Ambiguous and self-promoting, Pussy appears to be neither an entirely trustworthy mentor, nor, by implication, a reliable narrator, and so the public persona of this "caring" aunt would seem to be something of a sham.

Yet Pussy *is* a gifted storyteller and despite the sense of unreliability that infiltrates the introductory narrative, Margery is swept along by the tale that follows. Located twenty years previously when "the fashions in dress were just the reverse of what they are now" (p. 213), the story is immediately as ambiguous as its narrator; while it displays a sense of historicity which clothes it in the once-upon-a-time agelessness of fairy tale, it also presents itself as a factual, real-time event. The protagonist herself is equally ambiguous. With her favourite red cloak, she departs for her grandmother's house as both Victorian girl and fairy-tale heroine; ignoring maternal and fraternal advice, she dallies en route with a dangerous stranger who subsequently enters and violates grandmamma's home. The parallels between Pussy and Red Riding Hood are explicit and the narrative is fluently delivered. Indeed, Pussy, as a narrator, would seem to be more at ease with the fairy-tale genre than she is with the reality of life at home, perhaps because it is only within such a setting that she can, in her own estimation at least, become something of a heroine.

### To Grandmamma's House

Within her home, Pussy leads an unremarkable life. "Only one" of ten children, she lives in a world of chaos with a father who "never [sits] down from morning till night" and a mother who "[spends] her life in walking up and downstairs" (p. 214). Pussy tells Margery: "Nobody looked after us children very regularly, nobody had the leisure to do it; we had governesses at one time, but we didn't get on with any of them, and they didn't much like our scrambling ways, and so after a while they ceased" (p. 214). Into the midst of this confusion comes a letter from grandmother, asking Pussy to go and live with her. "The reason for the offer was candidly stated," says Pussy. "There was a lot of us, and there might be some advantages for one in having a home elsewhere. My grandmother was a fresh, lively old lady, living in a good house in a nice neighbourhood, and she would much like the society of a young thing about her" (p. 216). After a brief deliberation, Pussy decides to go, attracted by the prospect of less chaos, grandmamma's carriages and horses, and presents of new dresses and hats. The matter is settled in a hurry, "like everything else," she says (p. 217), and although her mother offers her some cautionary advice prior to departure, Pussy is coolly and sardonically critical of her family's behavior:

> [I]f my family did not express so much regret as I should have liked, it was saying a good deal for the interest they took in what was about to befall me, that they all suspended their own occupations to wish me good-bye, and see me off. My father even went so far as to insist on accompanying me to the station. (p. 219)

The parental attention that Pussy lacks at home is equally absent from her grandmother's house. A woman of "indulgent, take-it-easy ways" (p. 225), grandmamma's liking for a placid life contrasts with the behavior of her daughter, the bustling, anxious Aunt Rosa, who in many ways typifies the spinster aunt, but, despite their differences, neither grandmamma nor Aunt Rosa demonstrates an aptitude for assiduous parenting. When their annual holiday to Brighton approaches, they suggest that Pussy remains by herself in the house, and it is this isolation and freedom from parental control that allows the newly independent Pussy to make the disastrous mistake of inviting a stranger—later exposed as a thief—to tour the house just prior to her grandmother's return. The burglary that ensues that night thoroughly debilitates grandmamma and causes former soldier Herbert, shot in the leg by the robbers, to lose his limb and his profession. Having been a suitor to Pussy, he now declares that he "[has] no right to ask any woman to chain her love by a sofa-side" (p. 247). Pussy has, in effect, engendered her own spinsterhood, although the denouement, told in her own words, might also be interpreted as a further attempt to characterize herself as an heroic victim.

Pussy receives little blame for events from those around her, although her constant self-deprecation might be perceived as more than adequate punishment and, in later life, her spinsterhood and childlessness continually remind her of her folly. "And of all sad words, none so sad as the wail, Too late! Of all bitter memories, none so bitter as the thought, It need never have been!" she laments at the conclusion of her tale (p. 248). But her enthusiasm for self-flagellation fails to adequately camouflage the narrator's implicit antagonism toward those who allow such disasters to occur. If blame is to be apportioned anywhere, it would appear to sit squarely on the shoulders of negligent parents.

Parental responsibility is a fundamental issue in Childe-Pemberton's text; Pussy criticizes Margery's parents and subsequently passes blatantly acidic comments on the behavior of her own mother and father. To allow a child to grow without firm parental support and guidance would seem to be a cardinal sin for Childe-Pemberton, but to expect others to assume responsibility for a child whose development has been neglected is to court disaster; indulgent grandmothers and fretful aunts are apparently no substitute for a careful and caring family group and such laxity will inevitably lead to disaster. Grand-mamma and her daughter, in spite of carriages, a nice house, and lavish gifts, are incapable of saving Pussy from error and from a lifetime of regret. Pussy's parents may have the ability to procreate, but lack the time to tutor their offspring in moral rectitude and common sense.

However, Childe-Pemberton offers no solution. Her multi-layered tale leaves the reader wiser in the ways of the world, but forewarned only about the dangers of talking to strangers. She suggests no resolution to the problem of busy families with numerous offspring, but neither does she validate the notion of "outsiders" as parent substitutes. For Childe-Pemberton, there is no domestic ideal. Pussy's family home is chaotic, but her transnormative family experience is both disastrous and dangerous and Pussy herself is, perhaps, the most dangerous individual of all. The supposedly caring, patient spinster aunt who publicly strives to be a helpmeet to her niece is revealed as subversive; the neglected child has become a sterile woman driven by frustration. Her predilection for "good works" is inextricably bound up with condemnation of her sister-in-law and with her own desire for motherhood. Her concern for Margery's well-being would seem to be based not so much on philanthropy, as on a yearning for control. Pussy's story, told *only* in her own voice, is essentially a tribute to herself in which she is finally vindicated and everyone else is to blame. Self-deprecation may permeate the tale, but its very excess renders it questionable. In short, Pussy protests far too much.

Of course it may be that Pussy's tale of her youthful exploits is complete fantasy; there is no corroboration of events by any other character within the story to add credence to Pussy's words, and Pussy's unreliability as a narrator necessarily undermines the validity of her narrative. But there is nevertheless a distinct moral to "All My Doing; or, Red Riding Hood Over Again," although it is hidden deep within the text and is only subtly didactic. It is a caution to the impressionable and, taken in conjunction with Childe-Pemberton's clear indictment of the spinster aunt figure, it might also be interpreted as a warning about "unsuitable" relatives and their moralistic stories. Pussy is discussing past events with her grandmother who is now "strong enough to talk about [them]" (p. 245) and confesses all her misdeeds to the old lady. Her grandmother laughs and chuckles over Pussy's simplicity, pats her cheek and tells her grand-daughter that "it [was] just what she would have done [herself]." Then she adds: "When I was a girl I believed everybody told the truth, and listened to what every one said" (p. 246). Childe-Pemberton's story is indeed a dense and "fascinating narrative," as Jack Zipes comments (1987: 209), but it would primarily seem to assert that maturity comes not through the overt didacticism of would-be instructors, but through learning to differentiate between those who can be trusted and those who are merely self-serving tellers of tales. From Childe-Pemberton's perspective, the spinster aunt would seem to sit squarely within the latter category.

### Trusty and True: Unimpeachable Uncles and the Female Touch

No such suggestion appears to be evident in children's texts focussing on the relationship between an uncle and his nephew or niece. Theirs is an often idyllic pairing in which the uncle is mentor and friend to his younger kin, offering advice and guidance, sensitivity and affection and, sometimes, his skills as play-mate; as an amalgamation of father, brother, and friend, his talents are manifold, and the whole family invariably welcomes his visits. Youth is not necessarily a prerequisite for the "wonderful" uncle; the title character of Molesworth's *Great-Uncle Hoot-Toot*[14] (1889) may be perceived as an "old curmudgeon" by his nephew Geoff Tudor (p. 7), although Geoff has never met him, but he has long been "a sort of autocrat and benefactor in one, to the [fatherless] family. His opinions, his advice, had been asked on all matters of importance" (p. 15). Great-Uncle Hoot-Toot is not a blood relative, merely the dearest friend of the Tudor children's grandfather, but his pedigree and devotion to the family confirm his identity as akin to the traditional avuncular model. He is ever the gentleman. Geoff's elder sister, Elsa, comments that although Great-Uncle Hoot-Toot "looks rather shrivelled and dried up; . . . he's so very neat and refined looking" and draws attention to his small, implicitly well-bred brown hands and very bright eyes (p. 25). Great-Uncle Hoot-Toot, like his contem-poraries, is never subjected to the criticism more commonly levelled at his spinster counterparts. He may be "shrivelled and dried up," but it is possibly his life in India that has damaged his appearance; there is no suggestion that he has become wizened through the lack of "sexual commerce" that, according to Carlile, entirely debilitates the spinster.

This bias toward the figure of the uncle is unsurprising to a degree, given that the Victorian era was notable for its patriarchal structure, and its predominance in the children's literature of the mid-to-late period is clearly designed to inculcate a sense of male supremacy within the young reader. Yet the existence of a male stereotype whose behavior, in particular his tendency to nurture, suggests feminine rather than masculine characteristics, is indicative of a significant evolution that began in the mid-century and that has been the basis of much academic discussion in recent years.[15] In *Boys Will be Girls: The Feminine Ethic and British Children's Fiction, 1857–1917* (1991), Claudia Nelson asserts that manliness for mid-century Victorians encapsulated a "blend of compassion and courage, gentleness and strength, self-control and native purity." The notion of manliness would change in later years to encompass the Empire spirit, but for much of the century, "manliness" suggested androgyny and asexuality and, as shorthand for "humanliness," it sometimes applied to girls as well as to boys (p. 37). Although, as Nelson concurs in her introduction, nineteenth-century male and female were "not so much different sexes as different species" (p. 1), she also points out that evangelical books for children invariably featured androgynous protagonists who were angelic, regardless of sex. Froggy, the central character of Brenda's *Froggy's Little Brother* is one such creature whose duties as housekeeper, cook and nurse to his sibling are entirely comparable with many of the characteristics of the angel of the house, while Sandy, of Stretton's *Lost Gip*, is more of a maternal figure to his younger sister than his mother could ever be.

Within children's literature, the concept of the androgynous, somewhat angelic male extended beyond the child to embrace the adult, and continued to do so late into the century within middle-class domestic narratives. There are certainly un-angelic ruffians and drunks aplenty in tales of street-arab life, but such creatures rarely gain access to the respectable family, let alone claim kinship with them. The male adults encountered within the middle-class domestic sphere are largely fathers and uncles possessed of impeccable manners and keen perception. They understand and adhere to the creed of the gentleman and appear to do so with genuine devotion. However, while the father figure may perform his duties admirably and precisely in accordance with social expectations, it is the uncle, particularly the bachelor uncle, who more often displays traits more commonly associated with the angel in the house, despite his identity as an unmarried man.

## Bachelors and The Question of Marriage

If marriage was the true destiny of woman, she clearly needed a partner, but by the mid-to-late century, the surplus of females of marriagable age was exacerbated by a growing reluctance to marry among men. As John Tosh explains, while men "on the margins of 'respectable' society," or those of the lower middle classes who sought to increase their social status, still perceived domestic life as desirable, "higher up the social ladder the situation was different" (*Manliness*: 106):

> Reluctance to marry was a demographic fact. The age of first marriage rose gradually but steadily in the second half of the nineteenth-century; for professional men it had reached 31.2 years by 1885. Many well-established families, like the Gladstones or the Rhodeses, faced possible termination of the family name because of their sons' preference for bachelorhood. Thousands of young men avoided their marital fate by embarking on careers in the colonies as single men. Much was made by contemporaries of the deterrent effect of the rising cost of marriage, defined as the level of expenditure needed to set up a household in accordance with the bride's expectations. (*Manliness*: 106–7)

Furthermore, as Tosh points out, "rejection of domesticity was also strongly written into the culture of the period" through the "world without petticoats" enthusiastically perpetuated by popular novelists such as H. Rider Haggard, which suggested a deeper alienation from the married state (*Manliness*: 107). Consequently, toward the end of the century, there was both interest in and concern about bachelors, a fascination "that [was] evident, for example, in the novels, stories, poems, and essays about bachelorhood published in mass-circulation periodicals during this period" (Snyder 1999: 3).

This concern is not explicit in the children's literature of the mid-to-late Victorian period. Uncles are inclusive to the family and their single status is not questioned, but if, as Tosh asserts, "home was always an ambivalent marker of masculinity and . . . a man who withdrew from male conviviality and spent his time in the company of women was exposed to the charge of effeminacy" (*Manliness*: 108), then children's authors frequently seem to circumnavigate any potential for such accusations by introducing a potential partner for the unmarried male. For example, Uncle Jasper, the young and sensitive doctor in Ismay Thorn's *Quite Unexpected* (1889), who lives with his elderly spinster aunt and her brother, is reduced to tears by the news that Maggie, a loved sister-in-law, has died and he is immediately willing to foster her four children. He writes to their father, stationed overseas:

> If you will trust them to me as . . . [Maggie] did, I hope that, with God's help, I may bring them up in such a way that you will not regret your confidence in me. Of course . . . I must leave the cottage and set up for myself . . . I have not a bad practice here . . . and [I have as much work as I can manage]. I have hitherto been very much alone, and I hope your children will give me their companionship, and bring a double interest into my life, if you will trust them to me. (p. 11)

As an unmarried but clearly nurturing individual, Jasper is evidently qualified to become a family man, but is denied the opportunity to establish his own domestic space: his aunt and uncle are so reluctant to see him leave that, despite reservations, they agree to accommodate Maidie, Geoff, Jim, and Tot. However, by the closure of *A Flock of Four* (1889), the sequel to *Quite Unexpected*, Uncle Jasper is poised to achieve a family of his own. The children's father has returned and Uncle Jasper is wedded to Roberta, daughter of the local squire, and herself an "angel," about whom Geoff comments: "I never knew anyone like Bobbie. She is *so* sweet" (p. 158). Young uncles in children's novels are frequently dispensed with in this way; not only do they meet a soul mate who is equally thoughtful and sensitive, but their marriage firmly reinforces their identities as "true men," while their new role of husband and potential father eradicates any suggestion of overt effeminacy. Other uncle figures may remain single and live with female relatives, but their masculinity is often emphasized by their occupation as soldier, businessman, or the fact that they are a member of a club "in town." Moreover, bachelor uncles are prolific in children's literature. While they have long featured in fictional narratives generally, the uncle as ally, mentor and friend is characteristic of nineteenth-century children's fiction and in many ways takes as his template the character of Uncle David in *Holiday House: A Book for the Young*, a seminal text that was published at the outset of Victoria's reign, but that continued to be reprinted and read throughout the century and beyond.

## THE ARCHETYPE OF THE "GOOD, KIND UNCLE": CATHERINE SINCLAIR'S *Holiday House: A Book for the Young* (1839)

Sinclair's novel has been acclaimed for its "almost revolutionary attitude towards child-rearing" (Carpenter and Prichard 1984: 256); it celebrates not the idealized child of the late eighteenth, early nineteenth century, but "the species of noisy, frolicsome, mischievous children" that according to the narrator are "now almost extinct" (*Holiday House*: 7). Laura and Harry Graham are clearly members of that species; they are lively, energetic children who are frequently troublesome, but are ultimately always repentant. Older brother Frank is much more a child of Mrs Sherwood; devout, spiritual, and worthy, he dies at the closure of the novel, but despite his presence in *Holiday House*, it is Harry and Laura who are the protagonists of the story.

In many ways Sinclair's novel is an optimistic fantasy that posits the trans-normative family as a more-than-adequate replacement for the "natural" family paradigm. The children's mother dies when they are young and widower Sir Edward, cannot cope:

> Sir Edward felt such extreme grief on the death of Lady Graham, that instead of being able to remain at home with his young family, and to interest his mind as he would wish to have done, by attending to them, he was ordered by Dr. Bell to set off immediately for Paris, Rome, and Naples, where it was hoped he might leave his distresses behind him while he travelled, or, at all events, forget them. (pp. 16–17)

Luckily, as the narrative asserts, the children have "a very good, kind uncle, Major David Graham ... and their grandmother, Lady Harriet Graham" who are happy to take charge of them. Both adults evidently love children and observe "that no house could be cheerful without a few little people being there" (p. 17). Laura and Harry demonstrate no regret that their papa is leaving and, in fact, fail to recognize him when he returns as Frank is dying:

> A tall gentleman of exceedingly striking appearance ... walked rapidly towards the cottage door, and in another minute entered Frank's room ... Harry and Laura shrank close to their uncle when the stranger, now in evident agitation, gazed round the room ... till Major Graham looked

round, and instantly started up with an exclamation of amazement, "Edward! Is it possible!" (p. 315)

Significantly, although Sir Edward has returned, the closing passage of the novel is a comment by Laura to her uncle. Her father has once again vanished entirely from the text, his presence unimportant because it is Uncle David who has always assumed the parental role.

As an optimistic portrait of transnormative family life, *Holiday House* features characters who are credible, if stereotypical. The kind Lady Harriet, "an extremely thin, delicate, old lady with a very pale face and a sweet, gentle voice" (p. 29), the nurse Mrs Crabtree, whose name reflects her "crabby" nature, the gluttonous Peter Grey and "old Andrew," the footman, are familiar representations of their types within children's fiction and are consequently instantly recognizable for a young reader. The "delightful if facetious uncle David" (Townsend 1965: 34) might be deemed an archetype, but his character also displays the qualities that together seemingly comprise the ideal carer. Humorous, tolerant, affectionate and supportive, Uncle David is respected and loved by his surrogate offspring.

Uncle David's bachelor status is never explicit, but the fact that he lives with Lady Harriet and accompanies her on holidays suggests that he has never married. His background is briefly noted in conversation with the children; a soldier, he has traveled extensively, to India and America (*Holiday House*: 122–3), and his baldness and domicile with Lady Harriet, who would seem to be his mother, indicate that he is now retired. He is not, however, entirely devoid of alternative company nor is he gauche with women: he is obviously at ease at the dinner party at Holiday House, the home of Lady Harriet's relations, Lord and Lady Rockville, when a shy Laura appears. Laura approaches her grandmother, but Uncle David, sensing Lady Harriet's confusion, calls out:

> "Come here Laura, I can read what is written in your grandmamma's face at this moment; and it says 'You are a tiresome little puss, that nobody can keep in any order except Uncle David'; therefore sit down beside him, and eat as many almonds and raisins as he bids you."
>
> "You are a nice, funny Uncle David!" whispered Laura, crushing her way in between his chair and Miss Perceval's; "nobody will need a tongue now, if you can read so exactly what we are all thinking."
>
> "But here is Miss Perceval, still more wonderful; for she knows by the bumps on your head all that is contained inside" [said Uncle David]. (pp. 119–20)[16]

Uncle David's priority is the child, rather than the woman, in this brief episode; Laura is permitted to "[crush] her way" between Uncle David's chair and that of the female by his side. Although Uncle David is swift to apportion flattery to the "wonderful" Miss Perceval as compensation, Laura is his prime concern and any further adult conversation is halted by the physical presence of the child. It is undoubtedly a deliberate authorial maneuver that serves to emphasize the child-centered nature of Sinclair's text.

For Uncle David and, by implication, for Sinclair, a happy and contented home life is essential for a child; as Frank departs for life as a mariner, Uncle David comments on the practice of sending brothers to different schools and concludes:

> "Families were intended to be like a little world in themselves—old people to govern the young ones—grown-up brothers and sisters to show their juniors a good example—and children to be playthings and companions to their seniors . . . If people could only know what is the best happiness of this life, it certainly depends on being loved by those we belong to; for nothing can be called peace on earth which does not consist in family affection, built on a strong foundation of religion and morality."
> (pp. 242–3)

There is no differentiation between "natural" and transnormative families in this excerpt; the words appear to validate any loving and supportive family structure as potentially idyllic and so, for Sinclair, it would seem that the family per se is capable of achieving the domestic ideal. Furthermore, Uncle David's transnormative family unit is depicted as idyllic: Frank tells him, "no-one ever had a happier home; and till the east comes to the west, I shall never cease to think of it with gratitude to you and grandmamma" (p. 128). Although Uncle David's speech on families might be perceived as a lecture, he is never pompous or patronizing with the children. In fact, he often connives with them and, in addition, displays a sense of humor that is unsophisticated and thoroughly on a par with their own, and that encourages them to join in. In an early episode, he entertains the children by parodying the severe Mrs Crabtree's preoccupation with rules:

> "In the first place, you are positively not to tear and destroy above three frocks a day; secondly, you and Harry must never get into a passion, unless you are angry; thirdly, when either of you take medicine, you are not to make wry faces, exept when the taste is bad; fourthly, you must never speak ill of Mrs Crabtree herself till she is out of the room; fifthly, you are not to jump out of the windows, as long as you can get out at the door"—
>
> "Yes!" interrupted Laura, laughing, "and sixthly, when Uncle David is joking, we are not to be frightened by anything he says!" (p. 28)

Uncle David's satirical stance suggests that he does not approve of Mrs Crabtree and her doctrine of corporal punishment and he repeatedly allies himself with the children against the "old vixen" (p. 17). Consequently, he is characterized positively, while Mrs Crabtree is negatively portrayed. Early in the text, prior to Sir Edward's departure, Uncle David tells him: "[Mrs Crabtree] ought to have been the drummer of a regiment, she is so fond of beating! I believe there never was such a tyrant since the time when nurserymaids were invented" (p. 17), and when Mrs Crabtree vows to punish Harry, she receives "a sad disappointment"; Uncle David interferes to remove "her tawse" from her, and Harry escapes a beating (p. 61). However, Uncle David is careful not to contradict Mrs Crabtree in front of Harry and Laura and his disapproval is generally delivered via a jest. Indeed, he is ever ready with a joke, even when Harry and Laura misbehave, sometimes with fairly disastrous consequences. On the same evening that Laura cuts her hair off, Harry sets fire to the nursery, and when the drama is over Uncle David comments: "Did any mortal hear of two such little torments!" and is "hardly able to stop laughing" (p. 55).

Uncle David's proclivity for humor is entertaining, but his ability to joke about such incidents is questionable. His regular collusion with the children and his laughter after the fire is indicative not merely of a juvenile sense of humor, but of a child-like disregard for danger and the assumption that all will be well, despite the potential for tragedy. There is a suggestion here of the male who, despite his career as a soldier, has never truly matured, and a subtextual implication that the single man, devoid of true "manliness" as husband and father, remains very much a boy. Yet there is no overt criticism of his behavior; unlike the spinster aunt, whose immaturity is depicted through pettiness and jealousy, Uncle David is portrayed as a trustworthy individual, albeit one who seeks to align himself with the child at every possible opportunity.

For all his humor, however, Uncle David is shown to be seriously committed to his role as carer and the narrator notes:

> As Harry and Laura grew older, they were gradually treated as friends and companions by Lady Harriet and Major Graham, who improved their minds by frequent interesting conversations . . . and thus Major Graham and Lady Harriet succeeded in making that very difficult transition from treating children as toys to becoming their confidential friends and most trusted as well as most respected young associates. (pp. 271–2)

But it is in his dealings with the consumptive Frank that Uncle David emerges as something of an angel, assuming the roles of both caring mother and devoted father as he oversees the sick boy and prepares Frank's siblings for sorrow, although he constantly urges them to be strong for Frank's sake. When the doctor is unable to reply to Frank's question about the possibility of recovery, it is Uncle David's "pale agitated face" (p. 313) that Frank turns to for truth and, despite Uncle David's obvious affection for Frank, the uncle generously welcomes the return of Sir Edward, the children's father. Sir Edward sinks into a chair, overcome with "unspeakable anguish" (p. 315), and, after Frank's funeral, is "too ill to leave his bed," but Uncle David remains with him "in constant conversation" (p. 318). Friend, companion, and guardian to his niece and nephews, stalwart supporter of his adult relatives, just and generous to the poor without "putting on any airs of condescension" (p. 221), Uncle David is, throughout *Holiday House*, and despite his child-like tendencies, an exemplar of the kind, caring, thoughtful, surrogate parent. His "children" emerge as similarly exemplary young adults, although it may be that they will achieve a level of maturity that their uncle will never attain.

## IN SINCLAIR'S FOOTSTEPS: BRENDA'S "Lotty and Georgie" books and the man with the yellow moustache

Uncle William, the yellow-moustachioed, long-whiskered "great favourite" (*Little Cousins*: 53) of cousins Lotty and Georgie in Brenda's *Lotty's Visit to Grandmama* (1877) and its sequel, *Little Cousins or Georgie's Visit to Lotty* (1880), is a direct descendant of Sinclair's Major Graham. In common with Uncle David, Uncle William has an innate rapport with his younger relatives, provides them with moral guidance and frequently shares a joke with the two girls, but his involvement in their lives extends to entertaining them, both at home and on outings, and to chaperoning them around the city. His role is perhaps less obviously masculine than that of Sinclair's character—for example, he takes Lotty and Georgie to a woman's hairdresser in London—but his character overall accords with mid- to late-nineteenth-century ideals of sensitive manliness. Apparently a bachelor, Uncle William lives with Lotty and Georgie's grandmother at Seabeach, "often goes out to dinner" (*Lotty's Visit*: 97), and has lodgings in Jermyn Street in London (*Little Cousins*: 52), where he is a frequent visitor. He is also a soldier, although it is unclear whether or not he has retired: Lotty asks her nurse if Uncle William will give her a ride on his back "as he used to do before he went to battle" (*Lotty's Visit*: 31–2).

Like Major Graham, Uncle William is a member of a transnormative family group; he and Grandmama foster Georgie, whose parents are in India— "[Mama is] in India . . . and father shoots tigers sometimes," Georgie tells Newman, Lotty's nurse (*Little Cousins*: 42)—and Georgie does not appear to regret her parents' posting; she mentions them only on this one occasion. In fact, she seems to be entirely happy at Seabeach, and thus Brenda's texts are clearly not concerned with the problems of transnormative family life. Addressed to young readers, the books are essentially entertaining tales of the experiences of two girls by the sea and in the city, and the narrative largely avoids emphasis on the inner lives of the protagonists.

Yet Brenda's texts provide a rich source of information about the concept of the ideal uncle. Uncle William is a constant in Lotty and Georgie's lives; they anticipate his arrival with glee and are dismayed to find that he will not be joining them for lunch on Georgie's first day in London:

"I never said 'goodbye' to him yesterday!" said Lotty.

"And I didn't, either!" exclaimed Georgie; "how did we come to forget?" . . .

"Well you will be able to beg his pardon this evening," said Uncle Horace, "for he is coming to dinner," at which the little faces brightened up very much. (*Cousins*: 52–3)

It is hardly surprising that the girls enjoy Uncle William's company. When Lottie visits Seabeach, Uncle William takes her to the train in a cab, entertains her on the journey, and promises her a pony to ride. He acts as champion to the children when a "naughty little boy" jumps on and spoils "their beautiful sandheap" (*Lotty's Visit*: 57) and threatens to dip the boy in the sea if he does not apologize, which he swiftly does (*Lotty's Visit*: 58). In addition, Uncle William rebuilds the spoiled sandheap: "tucking up his coat-sleeves, he began in good earnest, laughing and talking all the while, and being so merry, that the children soon became merry too, and forgot all about their disappointment" (*Lotty's Visit*: 59).

Uncle William is ever inventive and enthusiastic in the games that he devises for the girls, amuses them with his often nonsensical but accessible humor, teases them remorselessly, although entirely without malice, and invites them to participate in his jokes. In one particular episode that would have delighted a young reader, and that remains entertaining today, Lotty, Georgie, and Uncle William stage a cat race with Lotty's and Georgie's kittens pitted against Uncle William's cat, and grandmother promises a scent bottle as first prize. Georgie wins, but is sorry that Lottie can't have a similar bottle:

"And you are not sorry for poor me too?" inquired Uncle William, looking very sad.

"No, not a bit," answered Georgie at once, "because you are a grown-up man with a moustache, and you can't want a scent-bottle—men never do have scent-bottles." (*Lotty's Visit*: 85)

While Lotty is consoled by her grandmother's gift of "a beautiful carved needle-book," Uncle William continues to lament his lack of reward:

"And where is *my* present?" asked Uncle William. "Poor me! No one gives *me* a present. Now don't you pity me Lotty?"

"I don't pity you much because you are a tall, grown-up man," said Lotty, "and you can buy what you like in a shop."

"You are very unkind," said Uncle William, "and I shall go out into the garden, and have a good cry!" But the children knew he was only in fun, and that he went into the garden to smoke his cigar. (*Lotty's Visit*: 87)

**Figure 4.1** Uncle William joins in (*Lotty's Visit* 59). Illustration by H.W. Petherick © The British Library Board. All Rights Reserved. Shelfmark 12803.gg.17.

Lotty and Georgie are shown to vacillate in their conception of Uncle William. Sometimes, as in the above episode, they perceive him as a playful adult, but on other occasions he seems to be regarded as a fellow child. When he takes the girls to Madame Tussauds, followed by tea at the confectioner's, Lotty and Georgie are surprised at his choice of food; they obviously anticipate that he will share their tastes. While they feast on "bath buns and cheese cakes and ginger-beer," they "marvel . . . greatly at Uncle William's extraordinary taste in preferring mutton cutlets and a glass of sherry" (*Cousins*: 110). Brenda may characterize the bachelor uncle as child-like, but she also acknowledges the duality of a character who is fundamentally an adult. Despite Uncle William's capacity for playfulness, his tastes at the confectioner's betray his age and this combination of man and boy is evidently perplexing for Lotty and Georgie.

Although Uncle William is portrayed throughout the texts as humorous, he is prepared to chastise Lotty and Georgie when their behavior demands it, although he is never harsh and is inclined to plead for leniency, once again fusing the roles of adult and child. At Seabeach, Georgie is disobedient, is hurt as a consequence, and upsets the port wine, eggs, and soup intended for a poor local woman. When Uncle William learns of the incident, he looks "very grave indeed" and states: "'I'm much shocked. I thought Georgina was a little girl who could be trusted.'" Georgie knows that her uncle is cross with her because "he had called her '*Georgina*' instead of 'Georgie'; and he never did that except when he was much displeased" (*Lotty's Visit*: 73), and she is led off to bed in tears. In the sequel text, when Lotty misbehaves and injures her baby sister, Georgie petitions Uncle William to plead for her cousin and "beg her off" (*Cousins*: 118). Uncle William refuses: "She's nearly been the death of Tottie . . . I don't think I can beg her off—she *ought* to be punished," he replies (*Cousins*: 119). However, he does recant somewhat on both occasions: after Georgie's mishap, encouraged by Lotty, he begs for jam to be sent upstairs to Georgie and, after Lotty's misdemeanor, joins with Grandmama and Lotty's father in begging for Lotty to be forgiven. Lotty's mother does so and Georgie is permitted to take her cousin "a nice little supper of sponge cake and milk" (*Cousins*: 125). Like Sinclair's Uncle David, Uncle William is both firm and fair, but would prefer to conclude a crisis with humor, rather than severe discipline, once the repentance of the perpetrators is assured.

This departure from the trope of the male as strict disciplinarian, a concept evident in the earlier literature of Sherwood, for example, locates Uncles David and William as "new men," but their almost constant desire for fun also characterizes them as boyish, rather than manly, although Brenda's Uncle William is perhaps the more youthful of the two. His enthusiasm for childish pursuits is evident throughout both texts, from the sandcastle building at Seabeach to the trips to Madame Tussauds at the Baker Street Bazaar and the confectioner's, and he is a keen player in the cat race that the girls enjoy. But while Uncle William is an accomplished playmate who appears to devote much of his time to entertaining Lotty and Georgie, there is no real evidence that he enjoys participating in the adult world to the same degree. Admittedly, Brenda's texts are for children and so focus on the lives of the two young protagonists, rather than their adult carers but, nevertheless, Uncle William is depicted almost exclusively as a man who is in many ways a child, and who aligns himself with the childish, rather than the adult, perspective. It is significant that both Uncle William and Uncle David live with Grandmamas; as companions to elderly female relatives who are probably their mothers, their abilities as nurturers are doubly emphasized, although it may be that their residence within a house where they are the youngest adult contributes to their characterization as child-like. Neither has embraced the responsibilities of marriage, home, and family, and in failing to do so, both implicitly lack the maturity of their married counterparts. Indeed, Uncle William is living directly in the shadow of his own boyhood: his home with Grandmama is in the Seabeach cottage where he and his sister were children. Yet such emphases are not presented as problematic in any way by Sinclair and Brenda; their fictional bachelor uncles are portrayed as positive additions to the domestic sphere.

## A "Happy" Transnormative Home

There are clearly differences between Sinclair's and Brenda's texts: Sinclair's is a self-conscious handbook on childcare with a final religious emphasis, and Cousin David transparently embodies Sinclair's expressed belief that children must be allowed to grow and flourish and to be spontaneous, rather than being controlled and force-fed with facts. Brenda's Lotty and Georgie books promote a less political agenda, but the author is nevertheless eager to stress that kindness and concern for the well-being of the child are of paramount importance. Uncle William's overt display of affection for his nieces, coupled with his attention to their enjoyment and his understanding of their desires, characterize him as a friend and companion whom both children adore. Under the guidance of Uncle David and Uncle William, the transnormative home is portrayed as a happy and idyllic space, although in these portraits of the transnormative family the reality of the children's loss of their parents is, overall, minimized. For Frank, Harry and Laura Graham, the death of their mother is mentioned only briefly:

> [They] could scarcely feel sure that they had ever had a mamma, because she died while they were yet very young indeed; but Frank, who was some years older, recollected perfectly well . . . and missed his kind, good mamma so extremely, that he one day asked if he might "go to a shop and buy a new mamma?" Frank often . . . thought of the time also when he kneeled beside her bed to say his prayers, or when he sat upon her knee to hear funny stories. (*Holiday House*: 15)

Harry and Laura may have forgotten their mamma, but Frank evidently missed her and his remarkable devoutness is undoubtedly the result of his adherence to "his mamma's instruction" (p. 16). The disappearance of the father figure, in itself a traumatic experience for a child, is also swiftly disregarded in order to allow the story to proceed, and Sir Edward's reappearance in time for his son's death is presented as a positive and fortunate event with no mention of the fact that he has contacted his children only by letter for many years. Similarly, Georgie's life with her grandmother and uncle may well be portrayed as idyllic, but, as discussed in Chapter One and proposed by Molesworth in *Rosy*, foster children often found it difficult to re-acclimatize, once parents had returned from overseas, if, indeed, they were still children when that moment occurred. Sinclair's *Holiday House* and Brenda's "Lotty and Georgie" books deliberately evade such matters to focus instead on the feasibility of the transnormative family as a site of domestic bliss.

Furthermore, both Sinclair's and Brenda's narratives offer a model of domestic contentment that is achieved, to differing degrees, through the influence of the benevolent single uncle. He may be depicted as immature, but his genuine interest in and devotion to the child or children in his care is portrayed as commendable and while Uncle David and Uncle William are adored by their respective charges, they appear to be equally popular with their adult kin. Yet their overall suitability as carers is questionable; they may provide a cosy environment for their young relatives, but their status as bachelors, coupled with their childishness, suggests that they may lack the experience necessary to prepare children for adulthood. The transnormative home that they offer is not necessarily the idyllic domestic sphere.

However, these uncles are clearly preferable to spinster aunts. Like the bachelor uncle, the unmarried aunt might also be perceived as childish, although she is rarely depicted as charmingly so. Her immaturity is displayed through the favoritism, petulance and jealousies that might be deemed inevitable in an untutored, unsocialized child, but that ill befit a grown woman, although her unmarried status and implicit celibacy might be deemed responsible for flaws in her character, as Carlile asserts (see p. 105). There are clearly gender issues at play regarding celibacy in these children's texts. While spinster aunts are often anxious, fretful, and so implicitly sexually frustrated, bachelor uncles display no such characteristics; in an era where "gentlemen" freely visited prostitutes, there was presumably no need for the male to suffer a similar fate to that which rendered his female equivalent unattractive and, perhaps, impacted adversely on her development. In Yonge's *Countess Kate*, the delicate Aunt Jane is not physically shrivelled, but she is nevertheless a travesty of womanhood whose over-protected life and spinster state have handicapped her potential to mature:

> The one who sat on the sofa had a plump, smooth, pretty, pink and white face, very soft and pleasant to look at, though an older person than Kate would have perceived that the youthful delicacy of the complexion showed that she had been carefully shut up and sheltered from all exposure and exertion, and that the quiet innocent look of the small features was that of a person who had never had to use her goodness more actively than a little baby . . . [her] slow way of speaking was rather wearisome. (p. 25)

Molesworth's Aunt Edith in *Rosy* is childishly gullible and sentimental, while Pussy, the protagonist of Childe-Pemberton's "All My Doing: or Red Riding Hood All Over Again" is revealed as a manipulative schemer who covets the maternal role and remains thoroughly embittered by her lost opportunity for matrimony. Anxious and often insensitive, or perhaps deliberately blind to the overall harmony of the family with whom she is connected, the spinster aunt, unlike the bachelor uncle, is rarely positively portrayed. Metaphorically deprived of her "natural" role in life as wife and mother, she is an inadequate carer who is surplus to requirements and is consequently problematic, and if she was perceived as such by the adult world, as nineteenth-century commentaries would seem to suggest, it was a bias that was reiterated to younger generations through the children's literature of the period. The bachelor uncle appeared to epitomize all that was required from a relative, while the spinster aunt embodied failure, although both had eschewed marriage, whether by choice or circumstance. Boyishness was permissible, but child-like female behavior was undesirable. Furthermore, and ironically, those traditionally female attributes that the spinster was shown to lack—an ability to nurture, to please those around her, and to contribute to the creation and maintenance of the domestic sphere—became not only the property of the bachelor uncle as "new man," but a significant component of his overall success.

The women authors who promoted such gender bias, whether consciously or subconsciously, were clearly reiterating the ideology of the period; as nineteenth-century writers of domestic narratives their focus was primarily on the family and the vicissitudes of family life, and their foundation was implicitly the familial ideal. Their perceptions were often based on first-hand experiences; as middle-class Victorian women they were necessarily part of the world in which they lived and their preoccupations and anxieties were undoubtedly reflected in their writing. Furthermore, their role as author was inextricably fused with their gender identity; their profession was not merely that of writer but that of a writer who was a female and who "naturally" possessed the womanly characteristics demanded of her sex: a caring nature, motherly tendencies, and an ability to resolve family crises or to comfort the sorrowful when problems were insoluble. As an author, a female writer could provide her child readers with entertainment, counsel and comfort them, and encourage both moral and spiritual development. It was in many ways a maternal role and consequently the female author of domestic fiction was essentially a surrogate mother with responsibilities for both educating and edifying future generations. The next and final chapter will focus on the mechanics of children's texts, the way in which narrative voices assume different roles, including that of mother and friend, and the extent to which these voices perpetuate or subvert the nineteenth-century domestic ideal.

# Chapter Five
## Mother, Ally, Friend or Foe?
## The "dependable" female author
## as one of the family

PART ONE: WOMEN'S WORK

> [I]n art and literature . . . woman has something specific to contribute. Under every imaginable social condition, she will necessarily have a class of sensations and emotions—the maternal ones—which must remain unknown to man; and the fact of her comparative physical weakness . . . introduces a distinctly feminine condition into the wondrous chemistry of the affections and sentiments, which inevitably gives rise to distinctive forms and combinations. (Eliot 1854: 37)

In her 1854 essay, "Woman in France: Madame de Sable," George Eliot identifies the maternal tendency as a helpmeet to creativity, an impulse that produces a distinctive and gender-specific artistry. However, and despite the fact that Eliot's statement appears generous, the subtext of her comment underwrites the concept of woman as a motherly, weak creature whose métier is sentiment and emotion. It is a characterization that implicates the female author and that covertly validates the notion that her talents might best be displayed through exploration of the feminine domestic sphere, a notion that was endemic to nineteenth-century gender ideology and that was ratified by the success of numerous works ranging from *North and South* (1854) to *Middlemarch* (1871–2). Moreover, if women generally were eminently suited to writing about the domestic world, then the work of the female children's author, whose texts centered largely on emotions, sentiments, and frequently home, might have been perceived as the perfect employment for a writer who was also a woman "naturally" possessed of maternal instinct.

This emphasis on the "natural" talents of woman was infused, not only with an aura of sanctification, but also of inherent trustworthiness. If woman's ideal sphere was domesticity, maternity, and family, as nineteenth-century ideology asserted, then a female author was obviously entirely qualified to proffer advice on familial matters, particularly to children. Authors for adults, such as Gaskell and Eliot, might well have been perceived as somewhat more contentious, but the female author for children was seemingly a relatively harmless and praiseworthy creature whose perceived femininity guaranteed the appropriateness of her tales. Publishers' descriptions of texts by women writers frequently alluded to the female traits that emphasized their suitability for the young. Brenda's *Lotty's Visit to Grandmama* was "a pretty little story," while her *A Saturday's Bairn* was "a charming tale," wrote the John F. Shaw publicists. They also recommended Ismay Thorn's *Bertie's Wanderings* as "bright . . . [and] sparkling" and her *Over the Wall* as a "thoroughly natural" story.[1]

However, as earlier chapters have shown, in the same way that adult authors such as Eliot and Gaskell employed the domestic narrative to examine the social machinations of their nineteenth-century world, female children's authors often moved beyond their prescribed remit of emotions, sentiment, and the domestic idyll to explore and sometimes expose the flaws of the society in which they lived. Examined superficially, many nineteenth-century children's texts might be viewed as collusive with the ideology of the period and often patently served as moral and behavioral manuals for young readers. Indeed, the female writer for children might well have been considered indispensable. With her "natural" maternal instincts, she was a valuable mother's helper whose moral rectitude could validate and extend the lessons that the child learned at home; as a surrogate mother, with vicarious responsibility for the young, she could seemingly be relied upon to assist with the child's socialization process. Yet those authors who wrote about the vicissitudes of transnormative nineteenth-century family life were subversive simply by dint of their subject matter, consciously challenging the domestic ideal and exposing it as unstable. Furthermore, if they chose to present their work through what might be perceived as a motherly or aunt-like narrative voice, they themselves assumed the role of transnormative family kin and their influence was potentially as duplicitous as that of the surrogate carers whom they often implicitly, or explicitly, criticized.

For, in spite of her supposed dependability, the female author was not one of the family. She was, rather, an outsider offering advice, a stranger whose words and sentiments were freely introduced into the domestic sphere and permitted to permeate the nursery, and her capacity for domestic disruption was equal to that of Childe-Pemberton's manipulative Aunt Pussy in "All My Doing; or Red Riding Hood Over Again," or of the inept Aunt Edith of Molesworth's *Rosy*. In common with female storytellers throughout history, from Sheherazade to Angela Carter, the women authors of nineteenth-century children's tales rarely served merely as passive mouthpieces for the social dogma of the time. Nevertheless, their role as women and as children's authors, coupled with the effusive embellishments of the publishers promoting their work, served overall to characterize them as beyond reproach.

## A Winning Combination

This notion of inherent trustworthiness placed such writers squarely in a position of marketability, and female authors for children utilized their career opportunities to great advantage, providing thousands of texts for the growing children's market. As Maria Andersson notes, "[women] . . . exploited the association between motherhood and education in order to 'excuse' their trespass into the male field of writing" (2005: 1), and this "trespass" was wholly justified by the subject areas on which female writers for children focussed. Domestic tales of home life, such as Brenda's *Little Cousins or Georgie's Visit to Lotty*, dealt with the minutiae of the middle-class child's world; Ismay Thorn's *Quite Unexpected* portrayed an ostensibly idyllic portrait of kindly relatives; Mary Louisa Molesworth's *Rosy* centered on childish jealousy and its pitfalls while proffering a consolatory resolution. The street-arab tales of Stretton drew on the experiences of both adults and children and were philanthropically allied to the middle- and upper-class practice of visiting the poor. In essence then, the most popular areas of women's writing for children were largely based on so-called women's work, the caring and nurturing that had long been associated with the female. In her discussion of nineteenth-century Swedish author Amanda Kerfstedt, Andersson proposes the idea of motherhood as an authorization strategy for Kerfstedt's writing, and suggests that because the nineteenth-century woman writer "had to find a way to negotiate the conflicting demands put on her as a woman and as an author," she sometimes stressed the insignificance of her work, perhaps "through . . . modest subtitles such as 'drafts' or . . . [by pointing] out the flaws of the text in an excusing preface" (p. 2).

Few of the authors discussed here would seem to be truly apologist and their narrative tone is seldom self-effacing. Yet in *Holiday House: A Book for the Young*, there is a hint of justification in Sinclair's writing for the fact that she, a woman, has dared to seize her pen. In the preface to *Holiday House*, Sinclair states:

> In writing for any class of readers, and especially in occupying the leisure moments of such peculiarly fortunate young persons as have leisure moments at all, the author feels conscious of a deep responsibility, for it is at their early age that the seed can best be sown which shall bear fruit unto eternal life; therefore it is hoped this volume may be found to inculcate a pleasing and permanent consciousness, that religion is the best resource in happier hours, and the only refuge in hours of affliction. (1839: 9)

In acknowledging her responsibility as author, Sinclair simultaneously justifies her work as that of a mother figure with "a deep responsibility" for the young.

Her words are a plea for acceptance rather than an assumption that her book will be read and enjoyed and there is, perhaps, a suggestion of that tendency towards self-effacement that Andersson notes. Furthermore, her preface ultimately emphasizes the sentiments and feelings that might be perceived as traditionally womanly traits and so offers a thorough justification for her book. In the final page she amalgamates fiction and fact: "It may add something to the interest, and yet more to the usefulness of those scenes and circumstances relative to the return from abroad and premature death of Frank Graham, to mention that they are not fictitious" she writes (p. 11). She continues:

> [T]he author is mournfully touched by the consciousness that some tears of juvenile sympathy have fallen from eyes that never saw him, for the early fate of a brother deeply loved and deeply lamented. With every endearing and admirable quality of head and heart, few ever held out a brighter promise of excellence than he who, being restored ... for a few weeks to his family, dying, resigned himself without a murmur to the will of God, and has long slumbered in a premature grave. (p. 11)

The preface closes with the words inscribed on the tombstone of her brother Lieutenant James Sinclair, who died at the age of twenty and "was arrested by the hand of death on his way home" (p. 12). Sinclair's reason for authorship is consequently validated in accordance with her identity as a woman. Not only is she concerned for the welfare and well-being of children, as her maternal instincts naturally dictate, but she has also written her text in part as a tribute to a loved brother. She is, in both instances, the personification of the emotional, nurturing nineteenth-century feminine ideal who displays the affections and sentiments appropriate to her gender. She is "angelic," precisely in accordance with ideological expectations.

Even those authors who resisted overt sentimentalism were portrayed as admirable examples of their sex and those who focussed on poor children were often perceived as particularly "angelic." Interestingly, Stretton did nothing to dispel "the sentimental legend [that] grew up about her," as Nancy Cutt points out (1979: 115); it may be that Stretton recognized the benefits of sanctification. Her work in establishing the National Society for the Prevention of Cruelty to Children undoubtedly helped in the growth of such a reputation, but the legend that she was a "truly good and strong and womanly woman ... [who] ... remained ... perfectly natural and sincere"[2] was a complement to her identity as a idealized nineteenth-century female as much as to her skill as a writer. Stretton's numerous texts about the poor were sometimes sentimental, although they were rarely a match for the overt emotionalism of Florence Montgomery's work, for example, but, as author, she spoke with an authority that characterized her as both thoughtful and practical, characteristics that once again identified her as a paradigm of Victorian womanliness who was strong and empathetic. *The Lord's Purse Bearer* (1883), with its focus on beggars and depictions of starving children employed to encourage donations from passers-by, is a harrowing and sympathetic portrait of deprived and destitute childhood. However, Stretton's preface to the reader is replete with pragmatism, rather than pathos. She writes:

> I look upon giving to a beggar as a crime similar to giving strong drink to one already drunken: giving a child who is begging is but tying a millstone about his neck and drowning him in the depths of a sea of crime and misery . . . No one can be a Christian who lets the least of Christ's brethren suffer want. Only let us take care how we give, and what we give. You give money in the streets? Even sinners do the same; and the half-drunken charity of the gin-palace will often exceed yours . . . Every desolate child has a claim upon us; but when he cries to us for food, let us take care than we do not give him a stone, or put a scorpion into his hand. (p. iii)

In a subsequent addition to the preface, composed seventeen years later, Stretton's views remained unchanged, although, as she pointed out, the condition of England's children had greatly improved since her book was first published. She maintained that "to give indiscriminate or inefficient help . . . [was] an injury, not a benefaction" and that "to help a beggar to remain in his beggarhood . . . [was] a blunder very near a crime" (p. vi).

Stretton might be seen in many ways as a woman of action who used her creative skills to encourage improvements in welfare for the poor, but whose agenda for practical aid for the destitute, coupled with forceful and persuasive opinions, identified her as a campaigner, rather than simply as a lady-like philanthropist. Her books for children provided her with the means to express her ideas and, ultimately, to garner support for her work. Her efforts are still tangible; the National Society for the Prevention of Cruelty to Children remains a thriving charity and her words about the pitfalls of donating to beggars foreshadow those of contemporary social workers. However, for all her innovation, Stretton was rewarded with an obituary that categorized her as an archetypal Victorian matriarch with saintly tendencies. *The Sunday at Home* of 1911, writing of Stretton's demise at the age of 79, paid tribute to her "long, happy, useful and noble life" (Demers www.oxforddnb.com).

It was a similarly stereotypified denouement for Brenda. Although Brenda, like Stretton, had campaigned for the poor through her writings, although to a lesser degree, she was revered primarily for her ideologically compliant womanly traits when she died in 1933. *The Times* newspaper of January 3, 1934 carried an effusive eulogy that praised the author's "exquisite pathos" and "gift for . . . sympathy," traits that were evidently laudable for a female children's author. A cutting announcing her death, taken from what would appear to have been a parish magazine, praised her "outstanding gift" as a writer, a gift that enabled her "to enter deep into the heart of the very poor, and so to clothe the appeal from the lonely and the unwanted as to stir the feelings of numbers who would otherwise not have cared." She was, said the article, "characterised by a very real Christian piety."[3] This highly sentimentalized view of Brenda was given even greater intensity by Arthur Gore, the 6th Earl of Arran, who enjoyed a friendship with the author towards the latter part of her life. Having seen Brenda's obituary in *The Times*, Arran was swift to send his condolences to her husband, Castle Smith, and his letter exemplifies the attitude of the Victorian male toward the "worthy" female,[4] although Arran, obviously grief-stricken, might be forgiven for the somewhat excessive nature of his praise. Nonetheless, his choice of words is indicative of a man whose image of perfect womanhood incorporates notions of saintliness. He wrote:

> Your loss will be shared by all the thousands and thousands of readers of "Froggy" . . . Nobody could have written "Froggy's Little Brother" who did not possess the heart of an angel of the Almighty—and I do not think anything in English literature—even that written by Dickens—can equal the pathos of "Benny's" life and death.[5]

Possessed of "the heart of an angel of the Almighty," much concerned for the plight of the poor, and blessed with the "exquisite [sense of] pathos" and "gift for sympathy" so cherished by ideology, Brenda's identity as a writer and mother-of-five appears to have been of less importance than her categorization as an exemplar of the feminine ideal.

## A Female Enclave

If women writers for children, whether authors of middle-class domestic tales or street-arab stories, were perceived as personifying the ideal of womanhood, it at least allowed them admission to the world of publishing. For children's writers, as for women authors of adult fiction, the domestic narrative was essentially a means to a voice and, in some cases, to much-needed earnings. Although they undoubtedly conformed to a degree with the expectations of their public and the criteria ordained by publishing houses, it would appear that many resisted complete obeisance. The voices that emerge may sometimes be emotional and sentimental, but having gained an audience, albeit through adoption of a "traditional" and sanctioned role, numbers of these writers ultimately subverted their given function, whether consciously or subconsciously, and guided their readers to question, rather than collude with, prescribed doctrines, although they may have done so under the guise of a narrative voice that appeared familial and was therefore implicitly reliable. Moreover, they were together creating a niche for female authors. A contemporary reader might envisage their position as authors as in some way a compromise; in order to achieve a public voice, it might be argued, such women colluded with social expectations and limited their authorial exploits to a field deemed appropriate to their gender. Yet while that may be true, there is an alternative perspective that locates such writers as confederates. There were, of course, male writers for children in the nineteenth century; authors such as Kingsley, Carroll, and MacDonald were pre-eminent in children's publishing, both then and now, while Silas Hocking was renowned during the Victorian period for his Evangelical texts. But it was female writers who dominated domestic fiction in the second part of the century and whose opinions were transmitted throughout the country.

The notion that women writers have long comprised a confederacy has been enthusiastically explored, most notably by Elaine Showalter in her seminal text, *A Literature of Their Own* (1977), in which Showalter proposes that although women have been regarded as "social chameleons" who assume "the class, lifestyle and culture of their male relatives," it might also be that they have "constituted a subculture within the framework of a larger society and have been unified by values, conventions, experiences and behaviours impinging on each individual" (p. 11). Although Showalter's text centers on female writers of adult fiction, her words would seem to be equally applicable to those who wrote children's texts; indeed, to suggest otherwise is to marginalize the children's author, to diminish the potency of her voice, and to disregard the immense influence of her books on both child and adult readers. Subsequent critics of children's literature, including Lissa Paul (1987) and Shirley Foster and Judy Simons (1995) have extended Showalter's work into the field of juvenile fiction to identify "the coded messages" (Foster and Simon 1995: 23) contained within nineteenth-century texts written by women. Their emphases are feminist and their subject area is girls' stories, but their recognition of female authors as a political force exposes such writers' potential for subversion within *all* areas of society, particularly in those that were a part of the supposedly female domain. It is difficult—and perhaps unnecessary—to try to separate the issue of gender from broader social criticism in the texts discussed in this book; gender identity is clearly an inherent component of women's writing and, as such, necessarily informs their work. But it is the power of women authors collectively that is particularly pertinent here because, as Foster and Simons suggest, the supposed "innocence" of female authors for children is ultimately empowering:

> [D]espite the fact that female children's writers may not appear to be directly political in the sense of engaging with what Chris Weedon has called the universal women's "struggle to transform patriarchy," the issues and themes with which their works deal may well be iconoclastic in challenging existing gender hierarchies or behavioural patterns. The apparently "innocent" and non-central arena within which they operate also empowers them to speak in disguise, as it were. (p. 25)

As writers of domestic fiction, female authors were, as a group, not only privy to the vicissitudes of family life, but permitted to publicly portray their observations. While the children's author may have been discouraged from explicitly proclaiming her political or social opinions—unless, as with street-arab stories, they served a useful purpose—the very act of authorship granted her the freedom to do so, if she wished, although she may have done so covertly or "in disguise." It is, perhaps, not surprising that challenges to the notion of the family ideal are relatively commonplace in the texts discussed here, given that women in general were familiar with the intricacies of the domestic sphere. What is more significant, however, is that there is substantial agreement between authors that the domestic ideal is largely untenable, although this is admittedly subtextual rather than overt. It would appear that such authors did indeed comprise a subculture and that it was not necessarily a subordinate grouping. As Showalter explains:

> It is important to understand the female subculture not only as what Cynthia Ozick calls 'custodial'—a set of opinions, prejudices, tastes and values prescribed for a subordinate group to perpetuate its sub-ordination—but also as a thriving and positive entity . . . Women writers were united by their roles as daughters, wives and mothers; by the internal-ized doctrines of evangelicalism . . . Sometimes they were united in a more immediate way, around a political cause. . . . From the beginning, however, women novelists' awareness of each other and of their female audience showed a kind of covert solidarity that sometimes amounted to a genteel conspiracy. (1977: 13–14)

The writers of children's literature were not directly addressing an exclusively female readership, but those responsible for children's education would usually have been female and children's authors frequently demonstrate their aware-ness of a dual child–adult audience. While this audience will be discussed in detail later in the chapter, the existence of such a readership suggests at least the possibility of "a covert solidarity" consisting of children's authors and the women who read their texts. Furthermore, while Showalter comments that "the training of Victorian girls in repression, concealment and self-censorship was deeply inhibiting, especially for those who wanted to write," she also cites the words of a female novelist, writing in 1860, who pointed out that "women . . . [were] greater dissemblers than men when they wish[ed] to conceal their own emotions" (p. 25). The female writer who, consciously or subconsciously, gave vent to her opinions, albeit in genteel fashion, might consequently *appear* to subscribe to prescribed ideological tenets, whilst allow-ing more subversive notions to emerge subtextually. Alternatively, it may have been a deliberate authorial decision. As Lisa Sternlieb contends in *The Female Narrator in the British Novel: Hidden Agendas* (2002), "narratives that have been noted for their artlessness, naturalness and directness *work* because of their artfulness, artifice and self-protectiveness"; her book, she says, celebrates "the capacity of a woman narrator to design, construct and baffle while appear-ing to ingratiate with artless candour" (p. 1). If narrators of children's texts written by women did indeed "design, construct and baffle," while appearing to ingratiate, Sternlieb's assertion might well serve to explain the ambiguity of many children's texts as authors apparently strive, but ultimately fail, to perpetuate the feasibility of the domestic ideal. It is through the authorial and narrative voices that such ambiguities often become apparent, and, consequently, it is on the author and narrator, and the readers to whom they speak, that the subsequent section will focus.

## PART TWO: A MULTIPLICITY OF VOICES

> Children's fiction belongs firmly within the domain of cultural practices which exist for the purpose of socialising their target audience. Childhood is seen as the crucial formative period in the life of a human being . . . [and] the use of story as an agent of socialisation is a conscious and deliberate process. (Stephens 1992: 8–9)

Stephens' discussion in *Language and Ideology in Children's Fiction* (1992) is centered largely on contemporary texts, but his comments are also appropriate to a study of nineteenth-century literature for children; Victorian authors and audiences were perhaps more conscious of the didactic power of children's literature than those of today. In an era renowned for its elevated public moral stance, the correct acculturation of the child was a prime concern and one that could be approached most effectively through parental guidance. Both the family and literature, as Louis Althusser was later to claim in his identification of Ideological State Apparatuses, were perfect media through which ideologies could be internalized, and thus they assisted in the production of offspring who acted in accordance with the dominant culture. But it was not just the child reader who was the intended recipient of authorial endeavors. In *Alice to the Lighthouse* (1987), Juliet Dusinberre points out that "even before the Evangelical book gained its hold on children's reading, writers of books for children evinced an uneasy awareness of a double readership, the child with the adult peering over his shoulder, purse and principles equally to hand" (p. 45). Thus the Victorian parent, anxious to protect a child from bad influences, was a similar presence for authors to acknowledge, and publishers clearly recognized the necessity of appealing to both the child and the adult who might be persuaded to purchase the book.

For nineteenth-century mothers, faced with the task of educating their offspring, the choice of reading matter for the child was of vital importance and the quest for "suitable books for children" prompted numerous articles in the journals of the day. In "Literature for the Little Ones" (1888), Edward Salmon asked:

> If to determine what works shall be placed in the hands of a boy or a girl of fifteen gives the mother and father anxiety, what shall we say of the

difficulty they must feel in choosing a book for the babe? The teens are an impressionable period, but the period which a child has lived before it reaches its teens, is not only impressionable but charged with the gravest potentialities. It is almost a truism to urge that the child, whose future is to be moulded definitely between the ages of thirteen and twenty, will be capable of higher or lower motives in proportion as his finest appreciable contact with the world has tended to the noble or base . . . At the outset it may be admitted that mothers,—who are the responsible parties in this matter—have much to be grateful for in the books published for their children. (p. 46)

So books, or at least the right kind of books, could save a child from the "gravest potentialities" and ultimately avoid any risk that he would develop base motives.

In this somewhat fearful climate, publishers were swift to allay parental anxieties by promoting the moral solidity of their texts. Those publishing houses whose religious inclinations were emblazoned in their business names—The Society for the Promotion of Christian Knowledge or The Religious Tract Society for example—were implicitly trustworthy, but even *they* strove to impress their reliability on the book-buying parent. Among the pages of advertisements at the rear of Stretton's *Alone in London*, published by the RTS, is one extolling the virtues of *Jessica's First Prayer* from *The Sword and Trowel* magazine, the highly religious publication of Baptist preacher Charles Haddon Spurgeon: "One of the most tender, touching and withal gracious stories that we ever remember to have read. A dear little book for our children," enthuses the reviewer. Those publishing houses without an overt religious emphasis were equally eager to publicize their texts as edifying for young readers. "This book will teach children the lesson of true courage," proclaimed an advertisement for Ismay Thorn's *Courage* in the author's *A Flock of Four*, and a review of Brenda's *Lotty's Visit to Grandmama* by *Literary World*, reprinted in the rear pages of the author's *Victoria-Bess*, was similarly enticing. "An admirable book for little people . . . We most cordially recommend parents and others on the look-out for the replenishment of the children's book-shelf to get this," it read.[6]

An author's awareness of an adult "peering over [a child's] shoulder, purse and principles to hand," would certainly explain what Barbara Wall refers to as "the double" address inherent in nineteenth-century children's fiction, which she defines as an adult narrative voice, "which exhibited strong consciousness of the presence of adult readers and its replacement by a voice concerned more genuinely and specifically with child readers" (1991: 9). Wall's text, a seminal study of narrative in children's literature, offers a highly effective categorization of the female voice: Yonge is a governess and Sunday School teacher, *Little Women* is discussed under the title "Adolescent Chatter," while Turner's writing is expressed as "The Voice of Equality." Yet Wall's stance might also be perceived as highly subjective and while I have drawn, to a degree, on her methodology, my own perception of Molesworth and Yonge extends Wall's work with additional, and sometimes alternative, analyses.

However, I would agree wholeheartedly with Wall that "the double address" is evident in much Victorian fiction for children written by women. While numbers of authors consciously incorporated elements that would amuse both the adult and the child, they did so in a voice that was seemingly intimate and so carried with it the dependability of a mother's friend and family ally. Others, including Molesworth and Brenda, appeared, to varying degrees, to write specifically for the child, although their texts suggest that they too were fully aware of the presence of the adult and indeed sometimes saw the adult reader as a priority. It was an ambiguous stance and, occasionally, its very existence exposed the machinations of authorship as writers attempted to perpetuate the construct of the domestic ideal through a voice that *seemed* both friendly and reliable, a narrative position that could ultimately prove potentially problematic for the reader, whether adult or child, as Wayne C. Booth notes:

> What are the grounds of trust and affection? Everyone in the classical tradition begins with the obvious point that we feel friendly toward anyone who seems to offer us any sort of benefit or gift . . . Though the offer of disinterested friendship is by its nature a claim to the highest kind, and the offer of utility a claim to superiority over "mere pleasure," we never know until after long acquaintance whether or not an implied author can really distinguish true friendship from false. He or she may prove to be a wolf in sheep's clothing or . . . a snake in the grass. (1988: 173, 177)

Many of the authors of nineteenth-century children's fiction attempted to infuse their work with the sentiments of friendship, whether their implied reader was child or adult. But, and particularly for a child reader, it may have been difficult to differentiate between "true friendship" and the professed sentiments of a writer who was endeavoring to please all of her readers all of the time, and whose main focus may not even have been the child. As Aidan Chambers comments, "It does not follow . . . that a writer who places a child at the narrative centre of his tale necessarily or even intentionally forges an alliance with children" (1980: 260).

## Mrs Molesworth: A Friend to All

The "double-voice[d]" Molesworth, one of the most prolific of nineteenth-century children's authors, who penned some one hundred texts, commented that children's stories "should be like the pure bracing air of some mountain height—unconsciously strengthening towards all good, while assimilated with no realised effect" (Carpenter and Prichard 1984: 355). Her tales are often highly didactic and are infused with the moralistic sentiments of a mid- to late-Victorian with her roots in an Evangelical past; her child characters who behave inappropriately are invariably reformed by the conclusion of the text, although the narrator may well sympathize with the plight that drove them to such actions. According to Molesworth, writing for children called for "a peculiar gift" which was difficult to define. In "On the Art of Writing Fiction for Children" she stated:

> It is more than the love of children . . . It is to some extent the power of clothing your own personality with theirs, of seeing as they see, feeling as they feel, realizing [sic] the intensity of their hopes and fears, their unutterably pathetic sorrows, their sometimes even *more* pathetic joys, and yet—*not* becoming one of them; remaining yourself, in full possession of your matured judgement, your wider and deeper views. Never for one instant forgetting the exquisite delicacy of the instruments you are playing upon, the marvellous impressionableness of the little hearts and minds; never, in commonplace words, losing sight of what is in the best sense *good* for them. (1893: 341)

Although Molesworth's many books continue to both delight and repulse literary critics, her concern for the child reader is rarely disputed. However, it is evident that the child reader was not always her prime focus, and although only one of her stories, *Rosy*, is under detailed discussion here, its narrative voice, tone, and awareness of a dual audience is representative of a number of Molesworth's other tales.

Wall asserts that in developing her "nursery" voice, Molesworth constantly exploited the gap between her adult self and her inexperienced child readers, that "she did not try to evolve a way of sharing a story with a child without superiority or condescension" and that she ultimately "exposed both the children addressed—the narratees—and the child characters to the amusement of adults" (1991: 83). The opening pages of *Rosy* would certainly seem to confirm Wall's allegation. The text begins:

> Rosy stood at the window. She drummed on the panes with her little fat fingers in a fidgety cross way; she pouted out her nice little mouth till it looked quite unlike itself; she frowned down with her eyebrows over her two bright eyes, making them seem like two small windows in a house with very overhanging roofs; and last of all, she stamped on the floor with first her right foot and then with her left. But it was all to no purpose, and this made Rosy still more vexed. (*Rosy*: 1)

A child reader might well have been interested in the author's depiction of the troubled and troublesome Rosy, but Molesworth's descriptive phrases are far more likely to appeal to sentimental parents than to their offspring. "Little fat fingers," "nice little mouth" and "two bright eyes," encapsulate a cuteness that suggests adult adoration of a child, while the narrator's comments on Rosy's facial distortions are precisely those that a mother might make to an ill-behaved juvenile in order to tease her into a more compliant state of mind. Molesworth's subsequent passage actively invites the adult reader both to smile at Rosy's childish behavior and to acknowledge the subordinate nature of childhood: "'Mamma,' [Rosy] . . . said at last, for really it was too bad—wasn't it?—when she had given herself such a lot of trouble to show how vexed she was, that no one should take any notice. 'Mamma,' she repeated" (p. 1). In this small excerpt, the narrative voice is firmly in collusion with the adult; the child's bluff has been exposed and called and she is revealed as entirely dependent on adult acknowledgment if her irritation is to be validated. Even in absentia, the mother is a more powerful figure than her daughter, and the text has only just begun.

Direct address is a commonplace technique for Molesworth, but here again it often serves to validate the superiority of the adult at the expense of the child. Once more in a rage because her brother identifies her jealousy, Rosy throws herself onto the floor, crying. The narrator comments:

Her fits of temper tired her out, though she was a very strong little girl. There is *nothing* more tiring than bad temper, and it is such a stupid kind of tiredness; nothing but a waste of time and strength. Not like the rather *nice* tiredness one feels when one has been working hard . . . But to fall half asleep on the floor or on your bed, with wearied, swollen eyes, and panting breath and aching head, feeling or fancying that no one loves you . . . all these *miserable* feelings that are the natural and the right punishment of yielding to evil tempers, forgetting selfishly all the pain and trouble you cause—what *can* be more wretched? (pp. 11–12)[7]

Highly didactic throughout, this passage displays Molesworth's narrative voice at its most insistent; a parent intent on reasoning with a child in the throes of a violent tantrum might have echoed every word. It is a voice that could, arguably, have been addressed to the child reader, but its loyalty to the adult is pronounced. Moreover, the authorial signature for which Molesworth is possibly best remembered, and frequently criticized, is her preoccupation with pseudo-baby voices that once again invites objectification of the child. In *Rosy*, the protagonist herself occasionally slips into this purportedly juvenile language, although it is Rosy's younger brother Fixie whose linguistic ineptitude provides a constant source of humour:

"Poor Losy," he said softly. "Fixie are so solly for you. Poor Losy—why can't her be good? Why doesn't God make Losy good all in a minute. Fixie always akses God to make her good."

"Don't wake, poor Losy," he said. "Go on sleeping, Losy, if you are so tired, and Fix will watch aside you and take care of you." (*Rosy*: 13)

**Figure 5.1** "But she wanted to quarrel with somebody" (2) Rosy considers arguing with cat Manchon (n.p.). Illustration by Walter Crane. © The British Library Board. All Rights Reserved. Shelfmark 12810.b.23.

Such scenarios may well have entertained an adult or an older child whose linguistic skills were markedly superior to that of the fictional girl or boy, but while they invite sentimentalism, they also encourage mockery.

Molesworth is seemingly tireless in her efforts to perpetuate picturesque images of family life in excerpts such as the above. Her tales for younger children are often couched in emotional indulgence; she closes *Rosy* with a direct speech from the author to her young readers:

> And again, dear children,—little friends, whom I love so much, though I may never have seen your faces and though you only know me as somebody who is *very* happy, when her little stories please you—again, my darlings, I wish you the merriest of merry Christmases for 1882, and every blessing in the new year that will soon be coming! (p. 204)

Affectionate, effusive, and evidently determined to establish a powerful emotional bond between herself and her readers, Molesworth's authorial voice is thus ever paradoxical. She may be perceptive in her portraits of childish behavior but, in *Rosy*, she clearly asserts that the child is infinitely inferior to the adult; she not only betrays her own declaration that she "wrote *for* children" (Salway 1976: 342), but her consistent objectification of her fictional juveniles creates a relentlessly hierarchical domestic space whilst simultaneously professing loyalty to the child. Hers is a caricature of domestic unity that is at best a fantasy, at worst duplicitous; the domestic idyll in *Rosy* is neither "natural" nor easily sustained as the central character ricochets back and forth from displays of loving generosity to outright rudeness. *Rosy* may question the usefulness of the spinster aunt as transnormative family parent, as discussed in the previous chapter, and so demonstrate the danger of outside influences and the frailty of the domestic ideal, but for Molesworth all should be perfectly restored prior to closure. The child must be persuaded to the adult will and the author is an accomplice who can assist in orchestrating such a metamorphosis. Ironically, Molesworth's insistence on the potential for domestic bliss was never realized in her own life and this may explain her determination to adhere with such conviction to the notion that the family ideal was both desirable and attainable. As Mary Sebag-Montefiore notes: "[Mrs Molesworth] was separated from her husband, but presented herself falsely as a widow in order to prevent scandal harming herself or her [five] children . . . She was proud of her exemplary, middle-class ancestry, though she knew there was a mystery about her father. She did not know, however, that he was illegitimate" (2002: 378). Intrusive as a narrator, Molesworth is an outsider who nevertheless assumes the role of "mother's friend" to comply with and consolidate parental power, whilst donning the guise of ally to the child reader. Her apparent desire to become a friend to all significantly marrs her work. But her authorial confusion encapsulates the inherent duality of her role as a real woman who had experienced the actualities of life, but was nevertheless—in accordance with her role as writer for children—striving to promote the myth of domestic bliss.

## An All-embracing Motherhood: Brenda and the Parenting of the Poor

Brenda, unlike Molesworth, largely resisted the impulse to patronize the child, although her books for younger children occasionally incline toward the mawkish. As author and individual, she seems to have subscribed whole-heartedly to the feasibility of a happy family life; *The Pilot's House or The Five Little Partridges* (1885), an amusing, if idyllic portrait of a family holiday by the sea, was based on her first-hand experiences with her own offspring and her "Lotty and Georgie" books propose an enviable childhood of fun and treats within a secure environment. However, while Brenda portrayed middle-class family life largely in keeping with the Victorian concept of the domestic ideal, her portraits of destitute Londoners depicted an altogether contrasting scenario. The representations of maternity that appear in *Nothing to Nobody* and *Froggy's Little Brother* are depictions of failure; children starve and die because they lack adult support, and implicit in such texts is the supposition that, without shelter and care, more will perish.

As the author of *Froggy's Little Brother*, Brenda assumed the role of surrogate parent to her fictional children, offering a transferable maternal sympathy for the trials of orphans Froggy and Benny that recognized their frailty and humanity. It was assistance that was essentially metaphorical; by exposing the boys' wretchedness to the public, real children in similar predicaments might be helped by those who possessed the power to make a difference. In addition, it was a maternal sympathy that extended beyond London to embrace poor children nationwide and that further characterized the female author of street-arab literature as akin to an angel. If woman's "grand function" was maternity, as G.H. Lewes suggested (cited in Showalter 1977: 68), her ability to embrace children everywhere ratified her extraordinary capacity as a mother. As Queen Victoria supposedly extended her arms to the family of Empire and guarded its welfare, so the female author could be depended upon to nurture those children who were patently "other," but who belonged, nonetheless, to the home country.

Moreover, the seeming realism of Brenda's text suggested personal know-ledge of the deprivations of children less fortunate than those to whom the story was addressed, and so simultaneously intensified the credibility of her narrative voice and further validated her identity as transnormative family parent. The narrator's portrait of Froggy, his family and the Punch and Judy show is convincingly authentic:

> While the father was showing off Punch inside the green curtain, and making those funny nasal noises which all London children know so well, the mother used to stand by with Benny asleep in her arms, watching that no inquisitive ones should come too close, and peep into the mysteries behind the green curtain. Then Froggy, the elder boy, who was not much

more than a baby either in size, but was very wise beyond his years, used to stand by the drum, keeping shrewd watch on all the windows from which people could see . . . so that . . . [when] the time came for collecting the money, he could tell mother exactly where to go. (*Froggy*: 7–8)

Precise and fulsome in its detail, this introduction to the family that appears early in the text would assuredly have verified them as realistic representations, particularly for those middle-class parents and children who themselves had witnessed such a show.[8] Consequently, when the narrator proceeds to describe the squalid home in which the family live, it too carries a semblance of credibility:

*Home* did they call it? Ah well! Home is home whatever it is like, isn't it? But theirs was a peculiarly wretched one;—only a very bare garret, at the top of a dark, dingy house, the upper part of which was scorched and blackened from the effects of a fire . . . [The] windows afforded a considerable amount of ventilation . . . [and] the careful mother had pasted sheets of brown paper over some of these broken panes, and stopped up small holes in others with such rags as she could spare;—even *rags*, my little readers, are precious things in some homes! (p. 10)

The comment that opens this paragraph was probably striking to the middle-class child who was domiciled in cosy contentment, but it might have been even more shocking for the adult reader. For the narrator to describe the garret as "home," and for her to suggest that, "home is home whatever it is like, isn't it?" is a question that begs a negative response and entirely ridicules the concept of the ideal domestic sphere.[9] A "home" in which a mother dies and children perish for want of basic sustenance is a travesty; the middle-class adult reader would quite possibly have been horrified by the narrator's emphases. With its dual address to both child and adult, Brenda's paragraph is a masterly device that offers opportunities for both superficial and more considered reading. The address to the child reader is clearly indicated—"even *rags*, my little readers, are precious things in some homes!"—but it is the exposé of the domestic idyll as a concept that is class-specific, and consequently unavailable to all, that subverts the Victorian notion of home and that would surely have provoked both compassion and consideration in a perceptive and thoughtful adult mind.

There are further poignant moments within the text that would seem to appeal directly to a maternal instinct or that were, perhaps, intended to breed and foster such emotions within a female child reader. Brenda's text was read by both sexes, but her emphasis on maternal sentiments may well have been a device to harness and promote the "natural" compassion of her female readers who were en route to womanhood and might eventually become mothers themselves. The episode when the hungry and tired Froggy returns from a day out with Mac, having discovered that the boy is a thief, is one of particularly potent emotional resonance:

> By-and-by a strange sensation crept over Froggy—an overpowering feeling of faintness . . . He made his way to a doorstep, where he sat down to recover himself . . . [and] he fell fast asleep and dreamed that he was a little boy again . . . taken care of by his mother and father . . . He dreamed he was in his little night-shirt sitting on his mother's knee, and she was rocking him to sleep with her arms round him, and singing to him a soft lullaby, as she used often to do. Froggy woke with a little sob, because he knew it was all a dream. (p. 103)

The narrator's appeal to the mother-as-reader or, indeed, to the reader who will one day be mother, is unmistakable. Her portrait of a child, desperate for a mother's love, who can only dream of the embraces that should be his by right, once again disrupts middle-class societal norms and posits a defamiliarized world in which the child is no longer entitled to the most natural of affections.

It is an episode that reaches to the core of the maternal impulse and that is, perhaps, more ultimately effective than the strident plea for support with which Brenda closes her text: "Parents and little children, you especially who are rich, remember it is the Froggy's and Benny's of London for whom your clergyman is pleading, when he asks you to send money and relief to the poor East End!" (p. 222). Throughout the novel there are many more direct addresses to the adult female. As Benny lies dying, the narrator asks: "We all know what it is, do not we? To be sitting by the bedside of some beloved one after a night or day of feverish tossing, and to be watching and praying for the blessed repose of sleep to come" (p. 197). It is a question that is scarcely appropriate for the young child reader, but it asserts a bond, based on shared experience, and inherently initiates a dialogue between narrator and adult female reader.

As author, Brenda clearly sought, or anticipated, some level of commonality with the adult readers of her text, whether through gender or experiences, or both. By empathizing with the narrative voice and comprehending its sentiments, the child and her female parent—for that is implicitly who the adult reader would have been—were invited to view the destitute child through the narrator's eyes, to share in the maternal lamentations that were so evident in the narrative voice, and, ultimately, to join with the narrator in assuming responsibility for the rescue of such children, although perhaps at a distance. Furthermore, it was not only the children of the poor for whom such writers and readers might have adopted the mantle of the surrogate mother. Whether or not they were the authors or readers of campaigning texts, the middle-class female involvement in philanthropy and charitable works characterized woman as a metaphorical parent to the destitute classes who were clearly incapable of fending for themselves. Indeed, such women and their "charges" might be perceived as comprising transnormative family units in which the female, as carer and nurturer, "adopted" those who were impoverished and attempted to instill the ideologies of the middle classes into her wayward, often dissolute "kin."

**Figure 5.2** Asleep on a doorstep, Froggy dreams of being rocked to sleep in his mother's arms (n.p.).
Illustration by Castle Smith, husband of Brenda.

## Firm but Fair: Charlotte M. Yonge as Maiden Aunt

It is unlikely that Yonge, as author, would have ever actively sought to encourage her adult reader to immerse herself in the sentimentalism so avidly displayed by Brenda, whatever the purpose of her text. As Carpenter and Prichard point out, "the moral development of children . . . was . . . a principal theme [of Yonge's children's books], [and] was presented in realistic and credible terms" (1984: 584). In accordance with Yonge's reputation for realism and credibility, the narrative voice of *Countess Kate* is not indulgent or overtly severe, but neither is it identifiable as the maternal tone of the Victorian feminine ideal; like Ismay Thorn in *Quite Unexpected*, Yonge clearly preferred a less intimate style of narration. What Yonge offers instead is the voice of the maiden aunt who resists direct addresses to the reader and displays a no-nonsense approach to morality that, somewhat ironically, contains echoes of the voice of the brittle and inflexible spinster, Aunt Barbara, herself a character in Yonge's text. It is a narrative style that is distinctly different from many of the children's texts by women writers of the period and appears remarkably objective by contrast, but nevertheless, Yonge's tale was, and remains, successful.[10] *Countess Kate* gained a place among the twenty-two texts selected as Children's Books of the Year in the *North American Review* of 1866, the only British story to do so, and the editorial covering the event was fully enamored with the tale:

> Superior in literary execution is the only imported story of the higher order which the year can offer. "Countess Kate" is a tale of girlish life in England, carefully and thoroughly written, full of childish character, and with an admirable moral. It aims to show the superior efficacy of love over sternness in dealing with a spirited child; and is thoroughly wholesome and truthful, although the "Countess" part must afford some bewilderment to those small readers as yet happily unacquainted with the British peerage. (merrycoz.org)

"Wholesome" and "truthful" it may have appeared, but for Wall, Yonge's narrator is preoccupied with instruction and the result is "a disconcerting and narrative stiffness, resulting from the distance between narrrator and character" (1991: 80–1). Admittedly, there is a discernible distance between the narrator of the text and the protagonist, and what might also be viewed as a certain lack of narratorial warmth, but the absence of indulgence in the text's central character and the tale's "narrative stiffness," as Wall terms it, effectively emphasize Kate's isolation. Moreover, Yonge's story is subtly presented through the eyes of both child and adult; Kate's feelings and those of the adults around her are explored as the narrative point of view moves from Kate's perspective to that of her carers, and her sometimes irritating liveliness may well have resonated with an adult reader. Kate is "spirited," but in the rare and genteel atmosphere of her aunts' city dwelling she is an intruder whose behavior is frequently seen as reprehensible by both Kate's aunts and the narrator. When the aunts are seeking a governess, Aunt Barbara temporarily fills the post and proves to be a strict and demanding teacher, but Kate is shown to take advantage of her aunt's absences:

> Lady Barbara could not always be with her, and when once out of sight there was a change. If she were doing a lesson with one of her masters, she fell into a careless attitude in an instant, and would often chatter so that there was no calling her to order, except by showing great determination to tell her aunt. It made her feel both sly and guilty to behave so differently out of sight, and yet now that she had once begun she seemed unable to help going on; and she was sure, foolish child, that Aunt Barbara's strictness made her naughty! (*Kate*: 133)

Kate is not positioned as an inherently bad child; she is obstinate, sometimes wayward and often involved in misadventures, but she is understandably resistant to the move from an adoptive home, with a family she loves, to her new and titled position as her aunt's ward. In true didactic style, the narrator enumerates Kate's sins as she commits them, but finally, through the character of Uncle Giles, offers an explanation for Kate's unhappiness that demonstrates a profound understanding of the child. Giles tells Kate's aunts: "I find her . . . answering me with the saddest account a child can give of herself—she is always naughty" (p. 212).

Firm but fair, Yonge's narrator strikes a balance between the voices of reason and compassion. Although she is swift to castigate Kate for her faults, she is also sympathetic to a degree, and occasionally describes Kate's convincingly child-like behavior in a tolerant and humorous manner that avoids condescension. For example, the description of Kate's arrival in London and her first introduction to the aunts displays a thorough comprehension of the child's feelings:

> "Sit down, my dear," said one of the ladies, making a place for her on the sofa. But Kate only laid hold of a chair, pulled it as close to Mr Wardour as possible, and sat down on the extreme corner of it, feeling for a rail on which to set her feet, and failing to find one, twining her ankles round the leg of the chair. She knew very well that this was not pretty; but she never could recollect what was pretty behaviour when she was shy . . . And when one of the aunts asked her if she were tired, all she could do was to give a foolish sort of smile, and say, "N-no." (p. 25)

The narrator's depiction of Kate's awkwardness is perceptive, and although no obvious endearments are offered and there is chastisement in her words, her explanation that Kate is unable to "recollect what was pretty behaviour when she was shy" is a viable excuse for the child's behavior. Similarly, when Kate is released from the room to meet her new governess, the narrator presents her reader with a portrait of childish action in a voice that is tolerant and witty:

> Kate had been silent so long, that her tongue was ready for exertion; and she began to chatter forth all the events of the journey, without heeding much whether she was listened to or not, till having come to the end of her breath, she saw that Mrs Lacy was leaning back in her chair, her eyes fixed as if her attention had gone away. (p. 30)

The episode is notable both for its authentic description of childish enthusiasm and for the sense of breathlessness with which it is written, but it is also sympathetic toward the child. Kate, just removed from the family with whom she has spent her childhood and thrust into a strange world populated by virtual strangers, is confronted with a governess who is more immersed in her own anxieties than in tending the child. Mrs Lacy, saddened at having to leave her family, is too preoccupied to offer warmth to her new charge. As a mother figure, her maternal tendencies are clearly not transferable and the narrator's implicit criticism of excessive female emotion is echoed later in the text through her portrait of Kate's Aunt Jane. Although Mrs Umfraville, who finally adopts Kate, might be viewed as the personification of the tender, maternal creature of gender ideology, Kate's Aunt Jane also offers her niece affection, but affection without substance. A sickly, delicate creature, Jane is the antithesis of her sister Barbara, and her occasional efforts to introduce what might be described as maternal tenderness into Kate's life are largely ineffectual because of her inherent feebleness. Rendered "pale and trembling" by Kate's tantrum, she later visits the child's bedroom:

> "Poor little dear!" again said Lady Jane; "it is very sad to see a child who has cried herself to sleep. I do wish we could manage her better. Do you think the child is happy?" she ended by asking in a wistful voice.
>
> "She has very high spirits," was . . . [Mrs Lacy's] answer.
>
> "Ah, yes! Her impetuosity; it is her misfortune, poor child! Barbara is so calm and resolute, that—that—" Was Lady Jane really going to regret anything in her sister? She did not say it, however; but Kate heard her sigh, and add, "Ah well! If I were stronger, perhaps we could make her happier; but I am so nervous. I must try not to look distressed when her spirits do break out, for perhaps it is only natural."
>
> . . . Lady Jane bent over the child, and Kate reared herself up on a sudden, threw her arms round her neck, and whispered . . . "I am so sorry."
>
> "There, there; have I waked you? Don't my dear; your aunt will hear. Go to sleep again. Yes, do."
>
> But Aunt Jane was kissing and fondling all the time. (pp. 87–8)

Such effusive mothering ultimately does Kate little good, although the narrator insists that "Kate went to sleep with more softness, love and repentance in her heart, than there had been since coming to Bruton Street" (p. 89). In fact, the episode serves largely to emphasize Kate's overall lack of love and her craving for affection. Furthermore, the narrator's comment that Aunt Jane was "kissing and fondling" Kate, despite entreating her to sleep in case Aunt Barbara overheard, suggests that Yonge deplored sentimentality without commitment and that, for her, the maternal instinct was laudable only when it was accompanied by practical aid, as with her portrait of the dependable Mrs Umfraville.

As author, Yonge does not offer her reader a traditionally maternal voice, nor does she insist that the domestic sphere is invariably an ideologically perfect space. Moreover, she acknowledges the problems inherent to the transnormative family: Kate's first adoptive family home is loving, but ultimately inappropriate, her second is a disaster, her third a substantial improvement. Yonge, ever the realist, may shy away from the concept of the domestic ideal, preferring to present a relatively detached narrator who is also an instructor, who achieves realism without excessive emotion, and is consequently credible. Her narrative voice is assuredly "unmotherly" in comparison with those created by other female authors for children, but it is rational, informative, and perceptive. *Countess Kate* may not reduce its readers to tears or prompt a child or her parent to sentimentalism, but it ultimately permits the possibility of a happy transnormative home, while recognizing that domestic bliss is frequently and fundamentally elusive.

## Lucy Lane Clifford: The Voice of Mother Goose

While Yonge's *Countess Kate* neither subverts nor perpetuates the concept of the domestic ideal, Clifford's "The New Mother" denounces it as nothing more than a fragile construct and simultaneously deconstructs and invalidates the trope of the iconic and dependable mother. In addition, the tale's use of a narrative voice more common to fairy tale than nineteenth-century fiction for children poses a challenge to both the realism and verisimilitude of the tale's apparent message.[11] Clifford's narrator is neither a maternal figure nor a comforting children's friend; in contrast to her contemporaries, hers is an alien role. "The New Mother" is ostensibly a didactic story in which the young protagonists are punished for their bad behavior, but its narrative voice disrupts expectations and offers not a happy-ever-after finale, but a never-ending solitude and despair for the central characters. Its defamiliarization of accepted fairy-tale norms is both disturbing and refreshing; the narrator disrupts expectations traditionally associated with such tales, but simultaneously encourages the young reader to acknowledge the existence of alternative endings through the device of a linear, rather than a circular plot, a most unusual impulse for a nineteenth-century children's author. As Maria Nikolajeva comments:

The basic pattern in children's literature is the circular journey, that is, the plot development home–departure from home–adventure–return home. This pattern, which has its origin in the European Romantic philosophy, can be traced in practically any children's text, and not necessarily only to what is traditionally labelled as adventure genre . . . But the return home is a matter of security; whatever hardships and trials are endured, safe home is the final goal . . . The linear code . . . presupposes the author's total confidence in the reader. It demands a good deal of courage for a child to accept the absence of security that brings the protagonist back home . . . Children's books with ready solutions bind the child's imagination and free thought . . . [t]he open ending . . . [which should be seen as a modification of the linear code] is a way to stimulate questions. (1995: 46–7)

Clifford's story is certainly stimulating in that it denies the reader a comforting closure and its suggestion of a substitute mother-figure with a wooden tail and flashing eyes effectively serves to distort more commonplace images of the Victorian feminine ideal. More disturbing, however, is that the tale, with its monstrous mother figure and abandoned children, is recounted by a narrator whose tone, in many ways, resembles the archetypal teller of fairy tales:

The children were always called Blue-eyes and the Turkey, and they came by the names in this manner. The elder was like her dear father who was far away at sea, and when the mother looked up she would often say, "Child, you have taken the pattern of your father's eyes"; for the father had the bluest of blue eyes, and so gradually his little girl came to be called after them. The younger one had once, whilst she was still almost a baby, cried bitterly because a turkey that lived near to the cottage . . . suddenly vanished in the middle of the winter; and to console her she had been called by its name. (*New Mother*: 8)

This is the voice of woman-as-storyteller, self-consciously reminiscent of the oral narrator who supposedly related folk stories or old wives' tales around the fireside, the "archetypal crone by the hearth" who "emerge[d] as a mouthpiece of homespun wisdom" (Warner 1994: xx) and who was otherwise Mother Goose—a character believed to have developed from the stock figure of the old peasant woman, spinning stories to villagers and watching over the village geese (Carpenter and Prichard 1984: 362). It was perhaps her narratives that evolved into many of the children's fairy tales of today; it is thought that she had her counterparts in Germany and it is possible that it was from such sources that the Grimm's tales developed. Yet although traditional fairy tales may be violent and bloody, the central protagonists are inevitably saved, elevated, or in some way rewarded, largely because fairy tales inevitably juxtapose the good and the bad, and decree that those of essentially sound morality emerge victorious. The children in Clifford's story misbehave, but are not forgiven; instead, they face consequences more usually experienced by the evildoers of the fairy tale. In a traditional fairy tale, there are rarely, if ever, children who are eternally punished, unless they are truly wicked, but in Clifford's text the children reap the rewards of their misdemeanors without hope of salvation.

From the outset, Clifford's narrator is deceptive. She lulls the reader into a false sense of security with her depictions of home and recounts various episodes that accentuate the affectionate nature of the mother figure:

> "Dear children," the mother said one afternoon late in the autumn, "it is very chilly for you to go to the village, but you must walk quickly, and ... you may bring back a letter saying that dear father is already on his way to England."
>
> ... "Don't be long," the mother said, as she always did before they started.
>
> ... "No, mother," they answered; and then she kissed them and called them dear good children, and they joyfully started on their way. (*New Mother*: 10)

The mother's affection for her offspring is thoroughly emphasized—she twice refers to them as "dear children" and kisses them before they depart—and this narrative insistence on her maternal sentiments is repeated frequently throughout the tale that follows; the mother rushes to meet the children when they return, "quarrelling and crying" from their initial encounter with the peardrum girl (p. 19), is sympathetic because she believes them to be tired and hungry, and swiftly prepares their tea: "Then she went to the little cupboard ... and took out some bread and put it on the table, and said in a loving voice, 'Dear little children, come and have your tea; it is all quite ready for you'" (p. 20). Even when the children admit their desire to be naughty she is comforting and consoling, while gently reminding them that unkindness and wickedness have no power over love (p. 22). However, when the children provoke her to extremes, she leaves them as she has threatened to do, taking the baby with her and so vacating her place for the new mother, although, as she does so, she weeps, kisses the children goodbye, and waves to them as she turns the corner of the field—gestures that are all indicative of maternal affection (p. 35).

Throughout the story the narrative voice remains calm and controled, offering little comment on the children's actions or on the mother's disappearance and this is, perhaps, one of the most disturbing elements of Clifford's tale. No consolatory explanation is suggested to offset the drama of the story or to hint that all may be well in the future; there are merely the gentle tones of the narrator, and even as the tale moves toward its closure, the narrative voice remains relatively unperturbed:

> [The children] wander about among the tall dark firs or beneath the great trees beyond. Sometimes they stay to rest beside the little pool near the copse . . . and they long and long, with a longing that is greater than words can say, to see their own dear mother again, just once again, to tell her that they'll be good for evermore—just once again. And still the new mother stays in the little cottage, but the windows are closed and the doors are shut and no one knows what the inside looks like. (pp. 46–7)

Indeed, perhaps it is these gentle tones that are the most horrifying element of all. It is not simply that they offer no resolution, but that they remain tranquil in the midst of chaos and heartbreak. For an adult narrator, which surely this is, to tell a tale to a child that offers only hopelessness is controversial; for that narrator to offer such a story in a tranquil manner, and deliver the conclusion in a present tense that implies the continuation of such a scenario, completely contravenes the Victorian predilection for comforting and appropriate narratives for the young.

Whether Clifford's text was actually read by children is impossible to verify although the fact that it was included in *Anyhow Stories—Moral and Otherwise* (1882), a storybook apparently aimed specifically at the young, suggests that this was likely. There is no overt narratee, but the story's relative simplicity of language and its descriptive style—"the tall fir trees were so close that their big black arms stretched over the little thatched roof" (p. 8), for example—would appear to prioritize a child reader. The story adheres neither to the rules of traditional fairy tale nor to those subject areas that were pre-scribed and approved for children's literature written by Victorian women. It proposes the fallibility of the maternal figure and the damnation of the child. But, and finally, it also claims no association with realism; its fairy-story overtones confirm that it is essentially a fiction and so Clifford's passive narrator is ultimately, and fundamentally, simply a teller of tales.

## Alternative Agendas

If there is such a thing as a dependable narrative voice in fiction, then it might be expected to exist within the ostensibly transparent and didactic narratives of nineteenth-century fiction for children. However, as Molesworth's narrative voice demonstrates and Clifford's text suggests, no such comforting assumption can be made. While much Victorian literature for children is superficially simplistic, texts such as Clifford's invite re-evaluation of the field as a whole, because they question the role of the narrator, the narrative voice, and, finally, the author. Moreover, as analyses of *Rosy*, *Froggy's Little Brother*, *Countess Kate*, and "The New Mother" show, the female writer for children, in common with many writers of adult fiction, was seldom simply a tool for the perpetua-tion of ideologies. She may have been perceived as a helpmeet to the family, but she was primarily an individual with her own preoccupations and agendas.

Having won her public voice, the female author of children's fiction appears to have taken full advantage of the opportunities that allowed her to speak about the domestic sphere, the environment in which she was commonly believed to be most "naturally" at home. She sometimes did so unconventionally, as Clifford illustrates, and at other times appeared to adopt a naïve narrative stance that ostensibly allied itself with ideological dogma. She presented authorial personas who were motherly or aunt-like characters and whose moral judgments were seemingly faultless in terms of their adherence to societal norms, and her sentiments were often delivered with apparent conviction. Her tales encompassed a breadth of voices, from the intimate tones of Molesworth to the apparent realism of Brenda; they demonstrated the ideal woman in all her glory, from affectionate but instructive aunt to savior of the poor. But if the female author's mission was to replicate the dictates of domestic ideology, she did so only partly successfully; although Victorian girls may have learned early in life to repress, conceal and self-censure (Showalter 1977: 25), the female children's author, although undoubtedly well-versed in such skills, was not always effective in disguising the paradoxes of domestic life. The reputation of woman as a potentially angelic, nurturing creature was generally upheld, but it was the domestic sphere that was often exposed as unstable. Moreover, despite the valiant efforts of fictional stepmothers, aunts, uncles, welfare organizations and the female author herself, the family, in particular the transnormative family, could never truly resemble the domestic ideal.

The ambiguities that clearly exist within nineteenth-century texts for children—sometimes overt, sometimes implicit, but invariably present—may have been attempts to tell the truth about domestic life in a world that celebrated idealism in all its aspects. As acknowledged throughout this book, these revelations may have been conscious or subconscious. Many of the authors discussed do indeed strive to maintain a semblance of conformity with ideology, despite the evident difficulties that a fusion of ideological dogma and realism must inevitably present. As Victorian women who were also writers for children, most depicted a world which was familiar to the child reader, offered a positive resolution, and educated him in the ways of the society in which he would grow to adulthood, but their texts were also available to other women and many appear to have invited a dialogue between the author and her adult female readers. There is the very real possibility that under the guise of writing "charming" and "natural" tales for the little ones, such writers were also reaching out to other women who were socially obliged to adhere to the myth of the domestic ideal whilst simultaneously acknowledging, albeit perhaps only to themselves, that it was nothing more than a fantasy.

# Conclusion
## Into the Future: The Enduring Potency of the Nineteenth-Century Domestic Ideal

The children's literature of the nineteenth century depicted a myriad of family types, from the destitute of London's East End to the wealthy of the city's Eaton Square. Incorporating images of exemplary and incompetent parenting, fostering and adoption, it nurtured and perpetuated the myth of the domestic ideal in all its aspects, largely vaunting the "natural" family as the superior form, although such emphases were variable and essentially class-related. For the street-arab child, a transnormative family environment with middle-class mores was generally portrayed as preferable to a squalid home inhabited by a destitute, often dissolute, natural parent, but for the children of the middle classes, the domestic ideal of mother, father, and offspring continued to represent the desirable norm, although authors strove to emphasize the viability of recreating the domestic idyll within transnormative family units.

However, and despite their apparent collusion with ideological dictate, those Victorian female authors who wrote about transnormative family groups as potentially idyllic phenomena served primarily to question the validity of the domestic ideal as a concept by undermining its very feasibility. The mere *existence* of transnormative groupings implicitly challenged the notion that the "perfect" home and family were freely available, while the tensions between reality and ideology that emerged in transnormative family narratives exposed the domestic ideal as a fragile illusion that could rarely, if ever, be sustained.

Nevertheless, the concept of the domestic ideal remained the template by which all was gauged and it has proved resistant to change, regardless of the new paradigms of family life that are now intrinsic to the Western world. I suggested at the outset of this book that we remain late Victorians, nostalgic for a mythical golden age of supported, united families, and that we have internalized diverse elements of nineteenth-century ideology. Do we still yearn for what we perceive to have been an ideal, despite the realities of contemporary, trans-normative family life? And, are we, as late Victorians, imbued with the ideologies of our predecessors, continuing to transmit nineteenth-century sentiments to children through contemporary literature?

The transnormative family is now a highly visible presence in Western society; in 2004 in Britain alone there were 1.8 million one-parent families. While one in fourteen dependent children lived with a lone parent in 1972, by 2004 one in four were resident only with their mother or father (Economic and Social Research Council www.esrc .ac.uk). However, in the twenty-first century, images of the nineteenth-century domestic ideal are still endemic to the child's world and perhaps nowhere more overtly so than in the toy market. In his essay, "A Semiotic Analysis of the Representation of 'The Family' in Children's Commercials" (2001), Justin Watson explores the signs, codes and social myths in commercials for children's toys. The adverts he viewed were shown between 3.30 pm and 5.00 pm on children's ITV in Wales and were clearly aimed at the child. Although Watson discusses a number of toys, he focusses much of his analysis on "The Family Love Doll House," a plastic house complete with a family of man, woman, young girl, smaller boy, baby and dog. As Watson explains:

> The significance of the toy family is the central theme of this advert and is reflected in its name. These pieces of plastic forming representations of humans have deeper meanings, especially when placed together . . . The model of the woman is not just a woman because we are led to believe this is a family . . . We know that this group of plastic 'figures' is a family, because society tells us that man + woman equals a couple, and if there are children present, they are the couple's children and therefore a family . . . The family is complete even down to the dog, and this completeness leads to connotations of fulfilment and happiness . . . [and] the toy suggests another level of completeness. This new level is 'love.' (n.p.)

The song that accompanies the advert, says Watson, links linguistically with the iconic representations of the family to compound the message that the family is love. It states: "Would you like to see what we do each day, / When my little brother and I play./ This is where we live in the house that's filled with love" (n.p.). Watson suggests that removal of the linguistic signs, or role changes within the toy family, could significantly alter the appearance of the advert: "If the family had only one parent, the 'completeness would be fractured' . . . If the couple were a gay couple, would the advert still work?" (n.p.). He asserts that because the advert is based on Western, capitalist, consumerist and Christian readings of completeness and fulfilment, such changes would not be acceptable to those specific groups and concludes, "Mass media is still not capable of giving the audience an alternative view of modern day society" (n.p.).

Watson's comments on "The Family Love Doll House" would seem to be equally applicable to numerous other contemporary toys.[1] The card game, Happy Families, first published in the 1860s, is still easily available and continues to feature mother, father, and two children, or their equivalents, depending on the theme of the pack. The Playmobil range of toys offers a family play set of mother, father, boy, baby and dog and the description accompanying the online advert states, "the happy family walks the dog." Moreover, a nineteenth-century theme is implicit to many ranges. Playmobil's Victorian family unit lacks the dog, but the characters are remarkably similar to their modern-day counterparts, other than their costumes, and so are presumably also a "happy family." The hedgehog "Sylvanian" family of father, mother, brother, and sister, again replicates the domestic ideal and can be housed in Victorian splendor, thanks to the Victorian Living Room Set. It is evident that the connection between the ideal family and Victorian ideology has survived and flourished, and that it continues to be enthusiastically consolidated via children's toys.[2]

**Books for Children**

The domestic ideology of the nineteenth century also survives within fiction for children, although, unlike the toys outlined in the previous section, adherence to its tenets is often implicit, rather than overt. The Western world is not exclusively inhabited by happy men and women living contentedly with their 2.4 offspring, but there is a sense, as Ann Alston suggests (2004: 55), that contemporary authors privilege such images of the family and this, in turn, suggests a shying away from positive promotion of what might be perceived as the less idyllic realities of twenty-first-century domestic life. Even those authors who ostensibly focus on the children of transnormative families frequently incorporate a longing for the familial ideal which is both nostalgic and poignant, a maneuver that reinscribes the desirability of the idyllic domestic sphere and introduces a sense of loss into the narrative. However, this tendency might also be perceived as entirely truthful and in accordance with what Roni Natov (2003) sees as a vital element of the "best" texts for children. Natov writes:

> In the best recent literature for children, the darker sides of childhood experience are conveyed with a depth of emotional expression. However, the vision at the heart of each story is not exclusive of hope, even in the portrayal of the darkest, often imaginable pain that is, horrifyingly enough, the truth of some children's lives. Even in writing about incest, poverty, bigotry, and other trauma, the thrust is toward achieving balance. The experience must be recounted with the unflinching honesty that serves to witness and acknowledge the child's experience . . . The story should also include a kind of chronicle of how one survives—and further, an indication of what one retrieves from such a painful experience. (p. 220)

For Natov, authorial honesty lies at the center of the "best" literature. Although children's authors of past eras have evidently "protected" their young audience from over-exposure to the harsher aspects of life, today's authors for children are seemingly more outspoken than their nineteenth-century predecessors. Consequently, the transnormative family in all its guises and with all its failings may be fully and frankly displayed but, and at the same time, any positive aspects are often undermined by the ghost of the familial ideal.

Award-winning author David Almond's third novel *Heaven Eyes* (2000) is replete with images of family and might be described as an archetypal post-modern text in that it forbears to offer absolutes, invites the reader to create her own meaning and exposes the duplicitous nature of the literary text. However, and despite the fact that the novel is skillfully crafted and ultimately appears to celebrate life, an overwhelming sadness resonates throughout, created, in part, by the three central protagonists' desire for parental affection. Erin, January and Mouse, described by narrator Erin as "damaged children" (p. 3) and resident in children's home, Whitegates, have only memories of their "natural," although transnormative, families to sustain them. Erin herself yearns for her dead mother and invokes her smell, voice, and touch through memory; Mouse, whose mother died "soon after he was born" (p. 8) and who was abandoned by his father, nevertheless believes that his father loved him, despite the fact that he tattooed "Please Look After Me" on his young son's arm prior to departure. January recounts his story as a melodramatic fantasy that excuses his mother's actions by casting her in the role of martyr:

> [H]e told the story of a frantic woman in a stormy winter night. She was very young and very beautiful and very desperate. She carried a tiny baby wrapped in blankets in an orange box. She loved the baby very much but knew that she couldn't care for him. She kept in the shadows as she approached the hospital. She waited for deepest night, trembling with cold, with pain, with love. Then she hurried through the storm and laid him on the wide doorstep before rushing back into the night. (p. 6)

Heaven Eyes, the strange, surreal child that Erin, January, and Mouse discover living with her grandfather in the Black Middens, has lost her family at sea and only newspaper clippings and notes remain to inform her of her ancestry. For each of the children, other than Heaven Eyes, who is only just beginning to be told about her past as the story ends, "natural" families are of paramount importance. In order to claim identity, there must be roots, and for the children of Almond's story, even the memory of an inadequate family will suffice. Although January's mother returns to claim her son, her abandonment of January and his consequent years of yearning for her, blight what might otherwise be a fairy-tale closure. The frequently less-than-idyllic nature of the children's former parental care serves vicariously to highlight that which they have lost, or have never had. To reflect on children forced to reside in a children's home is to acknowledge their lack of a "natural" family sphere and to re-inscribe, if only subconsciously, the desirability of the domestic ideal.

The children's home, Whitegates, might initially be perceived as replicating the familial sphere; headed by Maureen, who "smile[s] and strok[es] . . . [the children's] shoulders" (p. 4), it is reminiscent of the familial environment into which Brenda's Froggy of *Froggy's Little Brother* is finally introduced. Indeed, Erin, January and Mouse might be likened to the disadvantaged street-arab children of nineteenth-century literature, whose natural parents cannot provide for their offspring. However, Almond's portrait of Whitegates does not equate with the transnormative family environment of the children's home as depicted by Brenda; Maureen may display affection, but she is clearly not constructed as the maternal ideal. While the rumors that circulate through the children's home suggest that Maureen is unable to have children, bore a child that died, or lost her offspring when their father took them away, Erin claims that Maureen's eyes "so often were cold, cold, cold," adding: "Those eyes wanted to love us and trust us, but so often they saw us as simply damaged, and beyond repair" (p. 5). In contrast, Brenda's admittedly brief characterization of Mrs Holt, the "kind, motherly" matron of *Froggy's Little Brother* (*Froggy*: 217), emphasizes her maternal traits. The traditionally comforting resolutions of many Victorian children's texts implicitly seek to reassure the child reader, rather than disturb her, but Almond's novel offers no such conclusion. Whitegates provides little consolation for children bereft of their natural parent and although Erin, January, Mouse and Heaven Eyes might comprise a transnormative family group, with Erin and January as carers and Mouse and Heaven Eyes as dependants, Erin's natural family remains predominant in her memory.

### Transnormative Family Emphases

Almond's books for children are not generally preoccupied with transnormative families, although a number of such groupings appear in his novels. However, other authors *do* focus substantially on the transnormative family, and Jacqueline Wilson might be perceived as the writer who most frequently engages with the subject. Wilson is prolific as an author and her many publications for the children's market cover a multitude of transnormative family scenarios, from *The Story of Tracy Beaker* (1991), who lives in children's and foster homes, to April, the foster-child protagonist of *Dustbin Baby* (2001). Such scenarios are clearly popular subjects among book buyers; Wilson has received numerous accolades, including the Smarties Prize and the Whitbread Children's Book Award, and twenty million of her books have been sold in Britain alone. Her stories transparently address the problems facing thousands of children, and are largely unflinching in their efforts to express the emotions of children within transnormative family groupings, but an emphasis on that which is missing reverberates throughout a number of her tales and is often explicit. Tracy Beaker longs for a "real" family and in *Clean Break* (2005), Emily and her younger step-siblings Vita and Maxie are desperate for their father Frankie's return,[3] although his predilection for partners other than the children's mum, Julie, questions his reliability throughout the story. Nevertheless, the children desire only that their family is reunited. Injured when she is running to catch her father after spotting him in the street, Emily is taken to hospital:

> "I'm staying," Dad said firmly.
> "Let me phone Julie on your mobile. Em needs her mum, not you," said Gran.
> Dad handed it over and Gran started phoning. The second she told Mum, she said she was on her way. I was so relieved, but I still had to hang onto Dad.
> "I need Mum *and* Dad," I said.
> "So do I!" said Vita.
> "So do I!" said Maxie. (p. 285)

The tale ends on Christmas Eve. Emily, who has realized and acknowledged her father's unreliability, is now unsure whether or not he will return as he has promised. In fact, she is beginning to doubt many of his claims. But while Wilson does not explicitly produce a fairy-tale finale for her story, there is, in its closing lines, a strong suggestion that all will be resolved:

> Then we heard a noise downstairs. A tapping at the door. Then the letter box banging.
> "Who's that?" Mum called, her voice high-pitched.
> "Ho ho ho!" someone called.
> We all four sat up, and then we jumped up and started running downstairs. It looked like there was a Father Christmas after all. Maybe it was going to be the best Christmas ever. (p. 302)

The implication is that Frankie has returned, at least for the present, and it is in that sense of temporality that the strength of Wilson's novel lies. *Clean Break* suggests that within such a transnormative family group there is the potential for both happiness and unhappiness, as there is within a "natural" family unit; that while the domestic idyll can be achieved, it is, in reality, fragile and ever-tenuous, an assertion that is implicit to many of the nineteenth-century texts discussed in this book but one that is only rarely explicitly confronted by Victorian children's authors.[4] For Wilson, as author of *Clean Break*, little is assured, but there is joy to be found within the transnormative family, although it may be transient rather than everlasting.

Wilson's *Clean Break* is patently a story of familial disruption, but it offers a model of domesticity that captures, in part, the idyllic sphere prescribed by Victorian ideology whilst acknowledging the potential problems of transnormative family life. It rarely moves away from its central theme, that of a breakdown in family relationships and the experiences of the child, but despite its loyalty to its core subject, it consistently avoids overt didacticism. This is achieved largely through Wilson's choice of Emily as narrator; her first-person voice places the reader squarely within the tale as Emily becomes ever more aware of reality, but simultaneously, and increasingly desperately, clings to hopes and wishes. There is little judgment; only the voice of Gran rebukes children, mother, and wayward father, although Gran's own domestic unhappiness has contributed to her critical nature and the children and their mother largely disregard her comments. But, and significantly, there is ultimately no resolution to Wilson's tale, other than Emily's hope. Hers may be hope for a traditional family model, but there is no assumption that all will finally be well.

This proclaimed resistance to a happy-ever-after closure in portraits of transnormative family life is perhaps the most distinctive feature of many contemporary texts and one that differentiates them from their nineteenth-century equivalents. It is an impulse that accords with Natov's requirements for children's literature in that it appears to offer "unflinching honesty," but recognizes the child's predicament, incorporates a sense of hope, and, perhaps, some guidance for survival. Elizabeth O'Loughlin's *Mum and Dad Split Up* (2005) from the "It Happened to Me" series produced by Pangolin Books, a UK-based publishing house with a number of concept books on its lists, is a sensitively written picture book that acknowledges the emotional distress of a child whose family life is disrupted, but it avoids palliatives. Again written in the first-person voice of the child, the text promises only the possibility of a happier future, although parental reunion is not implicit:

> Gran says we may never all live together again. She thinks I believe her, but secretly I don't. I think that if I am very good, Mum and Dad will want to live together with me again./ I have two friends who are sad like me. They live sometimes with their mum and sometimes with their dad, but never altogether . . ./I still often get frightened, and sometimes I feel angry. Then I want to break things. I hope everyone understands how I feel. I think Gran does. /Gran says that one day I will not be so frightened. I hope she is right. She says she is sure, and she will be sure for me until I can be sure for myself. (n.p.)

*Mum and Dad Split Up* boldly addresses the issue of fractured families and the resultant transnormative groupings, but its effectiveness lies in its admission that the future cannot be predicted, although Gran offers at least a semblance of optimism. While it is clearly a concept book, it displays a realism and appreciation for the difficulties of transnormative family life that is only superficially addressed in such prescriptive texts as the (in)famous *Jenny Lives with Eric and Martin* (1983) and the less contentious *Heather Has Two Mommies* (1989), both of which deal with contemporary transnormative family units.[5]

## Drumming the Message Home

*Jenny Lives with Eric and Martin*, written by Susanne Bosche and illustrated with photographs by Andreas, is a picture book with black and white photographs, and traces a weekend in the lives of Jenny, her father Martin, and his partner Eric. It features a birthday party and a visit from Jenny's mother, addresses the issue of homophobia and presents the transnormative grouping as a happy family unit. The book initiated something of a moral panic in the UK when it was found in a school library; as a result, in 1988, Margaret Thatcher's government introduced the legislative Clause 28 which effectively banned the promotion of homosexuality by local authorities. The clause was repealed in 2003, but the book itself, no longer easily available, has become a collector's item.[6] Today, it seems somewhat quaint; indeed, a contemporary reader might view *Jenny Lives with Eric and Martin* as a reasonably inoffensive text, although the wisdom of using a photograph depicting Jenny in bed with her two fathers, one of whom *may* be naked, remains questionable. However, and images aside, it is a publication that is dated and, overall, ineffectual. The message, that there are different sorts of loving families, is undoubtedly genuine, but its extraordinary lack of subtlety reduces the book to mere propaganda.

Equally propagandist in tone is Lesléa Newman's *Heather Has Two Mommies* which focuses on lesbian relationships and employs relatively strident emphases. Newman's text, like Bosche's, is illustrated in black and white, although Diana Souza's drawings, some accompanied by juvenile representations of individuals, are perhaps more traditionally child-friendly than Andreas' photographic prints. The story centers on Heather who is cared for by Mama Kate and Mama Jane and who is disturbed by a playgroup conversation about fathers' occupations: "I don't have a daddy," Heather says. She'd never thought about it before. Did everyone except Heather have a daddy? Heather's forehead crinkles up and she begins to cry" (n.p.). However, Molly, the playgroup leader, steps in to offer consolation: "Molly picks up Heather and gives her a hug. 'Not everyone has a daddy,' Molly says. 'You have two mommies. That's pretty special. Miriam doesn't have a daddy either. She has a mommy and a baby sister. That's pretty special too'" (n.p.). There follows a catalogue of family types as each child describes their domestic arrangements and the discussion concludes with the children drawing representations of their own family group.

*Heather has Two Mommies* is a brave attempt to normalize a transnormative family headed by two women, but it offers an excessively simple solution to Heather's dilemma:

> Molly hangs up all the pictures and everyone looks at them. "It doesn't matter how many mommies or how many daddies your family has," Molly says to the children. "It doesn't matter if your family has sisters or brothers or cousins or grandmothers or grandfathers or uncles or aunts. Each family is special. The most important thing about a family is that all the people in it love each other." (n.p.)

The book's simplicity may well be explained by its target audience; the young age of the central protagonist and the straightforward illustrations and story-line suggest that it is for a pre-schooler. Overall, it presents a world in which all family types are available, acceptable, and "normal" and so could be perceived as challenging the numerous "natural" family models that might also surround the child reader, although it does so in a strictly non-confrontational manner.

## A New Understanding of Family?

The transnormative family models that appear in contemporary children's literature are evidently spearheading a movement that seeks to align reality and the family, and although some texts are more successful than others, writers such as Wilson appear to confront the complexities of twenty-first-century family life. Yet the fact that the domestic ideal lurks in the hinterland of such texts suggests that any depiction of transnormative family groups, however effectively they are portrayed, will inevitably incorporate shadowy images of the idealized norm, and will thus implicitly remain affected by nineteenth-century social dogma.

However, this adherence to nineteenth-century idealism may prove increasingly problematic. In "Families of Choice: Children's literature's response to the changing nature of the family" (2005) Kimberley Reynolds explores Francesca Lia Block's *Weetzie Bat* (1989) and Meg Rossof's *How I Live Now* (2004) and concludes that both novels intimate that alterations are necessary "if we are to change our troubled cultural and political dynamics," stating: "[I]f Rossoff and Block are right . . . we may need to start by exploring sympathetically and making provision for new kinds of 'family' groups, bound together by choice rather than blood" (n.p). What Reynolds terms "families of choice" are also evident, she points out, in popular television serials such as *Friends* and *Buffy the Vampire Slayer*, although, as she says, "groups of children functioning as families in children's literature is not new" (n.p.). She comments:

> It is a commonplace of children's literature criticism that adventure fiction tends to begin by getting rid of any parents/responsible adults, and when this happens in early twentieth-century texts, for instance, the books of Arthur Ransome and Enid Blyton—or even in Barrie's *Peter Pan*—the older children generally take on the traditional, gendered, roles of parents: providing food, establishing routines, taking responsibility for situations . . . They do this consciously and often eagerly, in the knowledge that the circumstances are temporary; their relatively unsupervised interludes act as rehearsals for adult life. (n.p.)

They also frequently return to the traditional domestic sphere when their adventure is over. However, as Reynolds relates, the seemingly revolutionary theories of commentators like R.D. Laing in the 1960s saw "a spate of cultural attacks on the family" and the resulting "anti-traditional-family climate" was one in which many of today's children's authors were reared (n.p.). She adds:

> So perforce, and by choice, the supremacy of the biological family and the ideologies circulating around it have been eroded. The image of the ideal nuclear family gave way to the image of the repressive family which was superseded by the fallible, preoccupied and atomised family—the kind of family that is in danger of being made redundant. We're left with a curiously paradoxical situation where the period of youth is in some ways being prolonged, with increasing numbers of the young remaining economically dependent—often living in parental homes after completing their education—while at the same time, their social and emotional allegiances and support systems have shifted to their peers. (n.p.)

Contemporary children's literature is recording the changes that are taking place, but whether such changes will ultimately engender an entirely new model of "family" living is debatable. The ideology of the family may well have been challenged, but it is nevertheless largely intact and continues to be perpetuated. Despite books such as Wilson's, that privilege transnormative family models and assert that alternatives to the "natural" family are a possibility, today's children's literature market displays a loyalty to nineteenth-century family ideology that reflects a broader social desire for so-called Victorian family values. And it is an impulse that is particularly evident among the mainstream popular novels that are currently the blockbusters of the children's literature field and that have the ability to influence the perceptions of thousands of young readers in the UK alone.

Anthony Horowitz's Alex Rider series is one such example. Teenager Alex, orphaned when young and parented by his emotionally detached uncle who dies in an accident at the outset of the first of the six novels, *Stormbreaker* (2000), is conscripted by MI6 and has been likened to a junior James Bond, although Alex is often resistant to the life that has been forced on him. The Rider books are popular; some nine million copies have already been sold worldwide and publishers anticipated increased sales with the release of the film of *Stormbreaker*. Alex, as something of a "Boy's Own hero," is an unlikely candidate for pity, although he is exposed as a lonely child, despite the excitement of his life:

> Alex thought of the man who had been his only relation for as long as he could remember. He had never known his own parents. They had died in . . . a plane crash, a few weeks after he had been born. He had been brought up by his father's brother [never "uncle"—Ian Rider had hated that word] and had spent most of his fourteen years in the same terraced house in Chelsea, London, between the King's Road and the river. But it was only now Alex realised just how little he knew about the man. (*Stormbreaker*. 9)

At this stage Alex has yet to embark on his career in espionage, but he is categorized as a child without family as the series begins. He does not achieve a family of his own; only through the kindness of Edward and Liz Pleasure, parents of his friend Sabina, does Alex experience the apparent normality of "natural" family life. Staying with the family in Cornwall, Alex reflects on his own, parentless situation:

> [H]e thought about Sabina Pleasure and her parents; her father a slightly bookish man with long grey hair and spectacles, her mother round and cheerful, more like Sabina herself. There were only the three of them. Maybe that was what made them so close . . . From the moment he had arrived, they'd treated him as if they'd known him all his life. Every family has its own routine and Alex had been surprised how quickly he had fallen in with theirs, joining them on long walks along the cliffs, helping with the shopping and the cooking, or simply sharing the silence—reading and watching the sea. Why couldn't he have had a family like this? Alex felt an old, familiar sadness creep up on him . . . Sometimes he felt as isolated as the plane he had seen from the veranda, making its long journey across the night sky, unnoticed and alone. (*Skeleton Key* 69–70)

As a child bereft of family, Alex longs for what he perceives as the familial ideal and, in this episode, evidently believes himself capable of becoming assimilated into what is a seemingly idyllic domestic space. Outside the Pleasure family, Alex's closest familial relationship is with his uncle's former housekeeper, 28-year-old Jack Starbright, who becomes Alex's guardian and is the only individual who consistently cares for and worries about Alex. She is ostensibly a mother substitute, but her youthful approach and frequent absences render her more friend than carer; Alex, in common with other youthful fictional heroes, is very much alone and obliged to find his own way in the adult world.

Horowitz's series is essentially a rite-of-passage saga; Alex must confront and vanquish those who would oppress him as he makes his way toward manhood. In doing so, he must separate himself from "home." As John Kornfeld and Laurie Prothro explain in "Comedy, Conflict and Community; Home and Family in *Harry Potter*'" (2003):

> This transformational journey—which all young people must take to discover who they are and where they fit in the world, to create their own version of home out of the strangeness they encounter when they are "away"—forms the basis of young adult, coming-of-age literature. And unless they leave, they cannot know what it is they seek. (p. 187)

For Alex Rider, the transnormative home that he shares with his uncle scarcely resembles the ideal, but his journey takes him away from that which is familiar and safe and thus his "home" represents the base from which the adolescent begins his travels. For J.K. Rowling's Harry Potter, "home" is a similarly unconventional environment. Orphaned and subsequently fostered by his aunt and uncle, Vernon and Petunia Dursley, parents of the bullying Dudley, Harry is an abused child who is treated as a slave and confined to the cupboard under the stairs, although he "escapes" to the Hogwart's School of Witchcraft and Wizardry when he becomes eleven. Kornfeld and Prothro point out that Rowling devotes "considerable attention in each book to family dynamics in the non-Hogwart's world" (p. 189) and it is true that Rowling's emphasis on the appalling antics of the Dursleys and the contrasting beneficence of the wizarding Weasley family is extensive. However, Kornfeld and Prothro also assert that:

> The scenes at both Harry's and Ron's homes read like theater of the absurd, reducing family life to slapstick comedy. Unfortunately, by relying on stereotypical family roles and relationships to give us a few laughs, Rowling risks reifying family roles and relationships in the mind of her young readers, creating a troubling vision of home and family. (p. 189)

Theirs is a somewhat harsh criticism. There is certainly an element of slapstick in Rowling's depictions of the two families, particularly the Dursleys, but the Weasley family also epitomize the nineteenth-century familial ideal; loving and supportive to each other, welcoming and comforting to Harry and his friends, although, as Kornfeld and Prothro point out, the Weasley home runs entirely on stereotypical lines with Mr Weasley as the wage-earner and his wife as home-maker. Nevertheless, their home, The Burrow, a name that exemplifies the Weasley's cosy nest, provides a hospitable environment for Harry who fully appreciates the laissez-faire disorder of The Burrow after the obsessive and repressive atmosphere of the Dursley home. It is, perhaps, the very traditional nature of The Burrow that is so enticing to Harry; family life centers around the kitchen where Mrs Weasley cooks up copious amounts of food for her family and their friends. The Burrow is a self-contained world of unconditional affection in which the family is inclusive and all-important:

> [Mrs Weasley] turned to look at a large clock that was perched awkwardly on top of a pile of sheets in the washing basket at the end of the table. Harry recognised it at once; it had nine hands, each inscribed with the name of a family member, and usually hung on the Weasley's sitting-room wall, though its current position suggested that Mrs Weasley had taken to carrying it around the house with her. (*Harry Potter and the Half-Blood Prince*: 85)

The nine-handed clock that indicates the location of every member of the family at all times symbolizes the unity of the Weasleys as effectively as their red hair. Inextricably bound together, ever watchful for each other's welfare—although son Percy distances himself from the family—they may offer warmth to Harry, but he is always the outsider. With his own parents dead, killed by the evil wizard, Voldemort, his godfather Sirius murdered and his transnormative family a parody of the familial ideal, Harry has only the The Burrow or Hogwarts as a substitute home. Hogwart's headmaster, Dumbledore, may represent a surrogate father, but he too dies in Rowling's sixth book, and Harry must forge his way alone, without the support of a mother and father. However, his yearning for a "traditional" family remains evident in his affection for the Weasley home—"Harry's spirits soared: the thought of Christmas at The Burrow was truly wonderful" (*Harry Potter and the Order of the Phoenix*: 399)—and this desire for family echoes the longing that he experiences during his first year at Hogwarts, as he gazes into the Mirror of Erised and sees the faces of his past:

> "Mum?" he whispered. "Dad?"
>
> They just looked at him, smiling. And slowly, Harry saw other pairs of green eyes like his, other noses like his, even a little old man who looked as though he had Harry's knobbly knees—Harry was looking at his family, for the first time in his life.
>
> The Potters smiled and waved at Harry and he stared hungrily back at them, his hands pressed flat against the glass as though he was hoping to fall right through it and reach them. He had a powerful kind of ache inside him, half joy, half terrible sadness. (*Harry Potter and the Philosopher's Stone*: 153)

Harry's "natural" family ultimately emerges as more powerful and reliable than any transnormative grouping could ever be. Harry's mother, Lily, the epitome of the iconic Victorian mother who sacrifices herself in an attempt to save her son, protects him from Voldemort as she dies, gives Harry life for a second time, and so bequeaths him the protection of "an ancient magic," as Dumbledore explains:

> "I am speaking of course of the fact that your mother died to save you. She gave you a lingering protection . . . a protection that flows in your veins to this day . . . I put my trust, therefore, in your mother's blood. I delivered you to her sister, her only remaining relative . . . she may have taken you grudgingly, furiously, unwillingly, bitterly, yet still she took you, and in doing so, she sealed the charm I placed upon you. Your mother's sacrifice made the bond of blood the strongest shield I could give you . . . While you can still call home the place where your mother's blood dwells, there you cannot be touched or harmed by Voldemort." (*Harry Potter and the Order of the Phoenix*: 736–7)

Thus maternal love and the "natural" family is shown as the ultimate power and although Harry finally determines to sever connections with his transnormative family and break Dumbledore's magical protective bond, it is to the "natural" family and his parental home at Godric's Hollow that he intends to return:

> "I'm going back to the Dursleys' once more . . . But it'll be a short visit and then I'll be gone for good . . . I thought I might go back to Godric's Hollow . . . For me, it started there, all of it. I've just got a feeling I need to go there. And I can visit my parents' graves, I'd like that." (*Harry Potter and the Half-Blood Prince*: 606)

It is from that family base that Harry, an adolescent embarking on the final stage of his journey toward manhood and independence, will take his initial steps.

For Harry Potter, as for numerous young protagonists of children's fiction today, the family, specifically the ideal family, remains a tantalizing vision, as indeed it was for the children of nineteenth-century fiction. While Harry aches for a family of his own, Froggy and Benny, Jessica, Sandy and Gip, Judy, Birdie and Countess Kate all yearn, whether explicitly or implicitly, for a Ruskinian domestic idyll, a "place of Peace; [a] . . . shelter, not only from all injury, but from all terror, doubt and division" (Ruskin 1965: 59). The transnormative families of both contemporary and nineteenth-century children's fiction may suffice as substitutes, yet they never truly equate with the paradigm of domestic bliss so vehemently propagated by Victorian ideology. The value of the transnormative family seemingly no longer fluctuates; the class prejudice that was evident in nineteenth-century texts is largely absent from today's children's literature. But overall, and regardless of the social background of the child protagonist, the contemporary transnormative family is generally positioned as inferior to the supposedly "natural" grouping of mother, father and children because it is often shown to be unstable, unreliable or deficient in the unconditional love that is seemingly available within the "natural" and ideal family unit.

The nineteenth-century family ideal is at best untenable, at worst a myth, but it nevertheless survives as a potent force within children's literature, as it does within the common consciousness that cherishes and celebrates all things Victorian. Today's children's authors are attempting, sometimes successfully, sometimes poorly, to address the multitude of transnormative family types that exist within the Western world, and that may, one day, be represented fully and without compromise in children's literature. However, it would appear that despite their efforts, the domestic ideal, a concept harnessed by the Victorians and effectively and relentlessly perpetuated throughout the nineteenth century, is currently unassailable. And it may be that it will remain the fantasy by which transnormative groups are forever measured—and that they will, consequently, always be found wanting.

# Appendix

### Note to Appendix

Although a number of female authors have been featured throughout this book, the appendix focusses largely on those whose works have been explored in some depth or about whom little has been published.

### Caroline Birley

Few details are currently known about Birley, author of *We Are Seven* (Gardner Darton and Co: 1880), although she produced a number of books for children and adults during 1880–90, published through the Society for the Promotion of Christian Knowledge, Walter Smith and Co., and Hodder and Stoughton. My own research among museum archives and census returns suggest that Birley was born in Manchester and may have also been a geologist, and that she later moved to London.

Information from Liz Thiel, unpublished research (2006).

### "Brenda" (1845–1934)

Georgina Castle Smith, née Meyrick, was born and raised in London and was the fourth of eight children of solicitor, William Meyrick, and his wife Eliza. Her writing career began in 1873 at the age of twenty-eight with the publication of her first book for children, *Nothing to Nobody*, which was followed two years later by *Froggy's Little Brother*. Married to solicitor Castle Smith in 1875, and subsequently the mother of five children, Castle Smith produced a total of twenty-three books during her 59-year-long writing career, many of which were for children or young adults. She often focussed on social issues, particularly the plight of the inner city poor, but her oeuvre extended beyond the street-arab genre and her "Lotty and Georgie" books (1877, 1880) and the largely auto-biographical *The Pilot's House or The Five Little Partridges* (1885) are particularly noteworthy for their portraits of Victorian family life. During the beginning of the twentieth century, Castle Smith and her husband left London and lived for some time on the Isle of Wight before taking up residence in The Corner Cottage at Lyme Regis with their daughter Eva. Castle Smith predeceased her husband and is buried in Lyme Regis cemetery.

Information from Liz Thiel (2002).

### Harriet Childe-Pemberton (1852–unknown)

Born in St Leonards On Sea, Sussex, Childe-Pemberton was the daughter of magistrate and landowner Charles O.C. Pemberton of Millichope Park, Munslow, Shropshire. Following the death of her father and the sale of the family estate, she moved to Marylebone, London where she lived with her mother, elder sister and six servants. The precise details of Childe-Pemberton's life remain unknown, although she produced many books, plays and poems for children in the late nineteenth century, including publications for the Christian Knowledge Society. *The Fairy Tales of Every Day* (Society for Promoting Christian Knowledge: 1882), with its rewritings of "Cinderella," "Jack and the Bean-Stalk," and "Red Riding Hood" is perhaps of most general critical interest, and Childe-Pemberton's "All My Doing; or Red Riding Hood Over Again" is an intriguing tale that covertly exposes the elusiveness of the family ideal.

Information from Liz Thiel, unpublished research (2006).

### (Sophia) Lucy Jane Clifford (1846–1929)

Although Clifford, née Lane, is commonly believed to have been born in Barbados, Marysa Demoor, the author of Clifford's biography in the *Oxford Dictionary of National Biography* (2004) asserts that Clifford was, in fact, born in London. Married to the mathematician and philosopher William Kingdon Clifford in 1975, Clifford was widowed in 1879 and was left with little money and two young daughters. However, as Demoor points out, she "decided to take matters into her own hands" and became a successful novelist and the hostess of a literary salon in London. Among her first books for children were *Children Busy, Children Glad, Children Naughty, Children Sad* (Wells Gardner, Darton and Co: 1881), a collection of short stories and poetry, and *Under Mother's Wing* (Wells Gardner, Darton and Co: 1885). The latter was dedicated to her children, nicknamed Blue Eyes and the Turkey, the protagonists of Clifford's most famous children's text, "The New Mother," which appeared in *Anyhow Stories—Moral and Otherwise* (Macmillan: 1882), and has been described by Alison Lurie as "one of the oddest and psychologically most disturbing [stories] in Victorian juvenile fiction."

Information from: Marysa Demoor, "Clifford, (Sophia) Lucy Jane (1846–1929)." *Oxford Dictionary of National Biography*, Oxford University Press, Sept. 2004. Online edn, May 2006. (www.oxforddnb.com/view/article/57699). June 8, 2006; Alison Lurie, "A Tail of Terror." *New York Review of Books.* 22.20. (1975). (www.nybooks.co./articles/8993). June 25, 2003.

**Agnes Giberne (1845–1939)**

Giberne was born in Belguam, India, one of four daughters of Major Charles Giberne of the Indian Army and Lydia Mary Wilson. The youngest child died in infancy. When Giberne's father retired, the family returned to England but traveled to Switzerland and Belgium and the girls were educated by their mother during their trips overseas. Giberne's older and younger sisters died when she was sixteen and her mother became her companion. Always an avid "scribbler," Giberne published her first story anonymously at the age of seventeen but later advised young writers to delay publication, because "it was better to give more time to preparation, especially to the study of language and of human nature" (Robson 1900: 83). She was an active author for some seventy years, producing over one hundred texts for children and adults, many published through the Religious Tract Society, and contributing to magazines including *Sunday at Home, The SPCK Magazine* and *The Treasury*, but she was probably best known for her books for beginners on astronomy and other aspects of science, including *Sun, Moon and Stars* (1879). Giberne died in a nursing home in Eastbourne, Sussex.

Information from: Robson, Isabel Suart, *Story Weavers: or Writers for the Young.* London: Robert Culley, 1900. "Agnes Giberne: A Pioneer of Popular Science." *The Times.* August 22, 1939 (n.p.).

**Hesba Stretton (1832–1911)**

Sarah Smith, known by the pseudonym Hesba Stretton (the initials of her five siblings and part of the name of the Shropshire village All Stretton), was born in Shropshire. She began her career as a journalist at the age of twenty-six, contributed regularly to Dickens' *Household Words* and *All the Year Round* and became a highly successful author; Patricia Demers, her biographer in the *Oxford Dictionary of National Biography* reports that Stretton's dealings with publishers from 1859–71/2, detailed in her log books, show her to be "tart and censorious, prickly in negotiations about payment, fully aware of her own worth, impatient with servants, and driven by the detection of 'bugs' from one lodging-house to another." Between 1866 and 1906 Stretton produced fifty books, published mainly through the Religious Tract Society, which included *Jessica's First Prayer* (1867). Stretton's many books for children are often overtly moralistic, but there is no doubt that she was genuinely appalled at the plight of the poor; many of her texts feature authorial comments about the destitute and social reform and she helped to found what was later to become the NSPCC. Throughout her life, Stretton had traveled and lived with her sister, Elizabeth, and her final home was in Ham, Richmond, where she died after a long illness.

Information from: "Hesba Stretton. Profile." *Literary Heritage West Midlands.* (www3.shropshire-cc.gov.uk/stretches.htm). January 3, 2006; Patricia Demers,

"Sarah Smith (1832–1911)." *Oxford Dictionary of National Biography*. Oxford: Oxford University Press, 2004. (www.oxforddnb.com/view/article/36158). June 8, 2006.

### Mary Louisa Molesworth (1839–1921)

Established during her lifetime as a leading writer for children, Mrs Molesworth was born in Rotterdam, one of six children of Charles Augustus Stewart and his wife Agnes. Stewart, born illegitimately, returned to England with his family and became a merchant and shipping agent in Manchester and Mary Louisa spent her childhood in the Manchester area. In 1861 she married Richard Molesworth of the Royal Dragoons, but the marriage ended in 1879, leaving Mrs Molesworth to care for her three daughters and two sons. She wrote prolifically, producing over one hundred books, and her texts for children attempted, sometimes more successfully than others, to engage with the feelings of the child reader. *Carrots—Just a Little Boy* (1876) and *The Cuckoo Clock* (1878) were, and remain, particularly popular, although their charm today lies rather more in their quaintness than in their narrative excellence. In addition, as Gillian Avery comments, "they are difficult to revive for the young of another generation because of their preoccupation with social status."

Information from: Jane Cooper, *Mrs Molesworth: A Biography*. Crowborough: Pratts Folly Press 2002; Gillian Avery, "Molesworth, Mary Louisa (1839–1921)." *Oxford Dictionary of National Biography*. Oxford: Oxford University Press, 2004. (www.oxforddnb.com/view/article/37776). June 8, 2006.

### Florence Montgomery (1843–1923)

Montgomery was born in London, one of seven children of Admiral Sir Alexander Leslie Montgomery and his wife Eliza. Her first cousin, Sibyl Montgomery, mother of Lord Alfred Douglas, illustrated a first story that was originally printed for sale at a charitable bazaar and later published as *A Very Simple Story; Being the Chronicle of the Thoughts and Feelings of a Child* (Sleaford: 1867). As Charlotte Mitchell comments, Montgomery's "breakthrough" was with *Misunderstood* (1869), "a notorious tear-jerker" in which a son's true character is revealed to his father just prior to the boy's death. Sentimentality features highly in many of Montgomery's books, as in *Wild Mike and his Victim* (1875), although *Wild Mike* and *Misunderstood* were, according to Montgomery, not for children, despite the fact that they were evidently popular with younger readers. Montgomery is largely under-researched and current criticism tends to focus on her flaws as an overtly didactic, moralistic, and emotional author, but her work survived into the twentieth century and *Misunderstood* might be considered a classic text of its period.

Information from Charlotte Mitchell, "Montgomery, Florence Sophia (1843–1923)." *Oxford Dictionary of National Biography*, Oxford: Oxford University Press, 2004. (www.oxforddnb.com/view/article/55637). June 8, 2006.

## Catherine Sinclair (1800–64)

The daughter of Scottish philanthropist Sir John Sinclair and one of thirteen offspring, Sinclair was born in Edinburgh and was secretary to her father from the age of fourteen. Also a writer of tracts, adult novels, and travel books, Sinclair's most famous and enduring tale is *Holiday House: A Book for the Young* (1839) which, as Carpenter and Prichard suggest, flouted the conventions of the moral tale and "is one of the first books that accepts children as they really are" (p. 485). Sinclair's contribution to children's literature is distinguished but limited; her other children's novel, *Charlie Seymour; Or the Good Aunt and the Bad Aunt* (1832), the tale of a boy who has to choose a guardian, lacks the originality of her most notable text. However, Sinclair's interest in children re-emerged toward the end of her life when she produced a series of picture letters (1861–4), bringing together words and hieroglyphics. These were highly successful, and reportedly sold up to 100,000 copies of each. Sinclair died at the Kensington home of her brother John.

Information from Humphrey Carpenter and Mari Prichard, 1984. "Catherine Sinclair." *The Oxford Companion to Children's Literature.* Oxford: Oxford University Press, 1995. Charlotte Mitchell, "Sinclair, Catherine (1800–1864). *Oxford Dictionary of National Biography,* Oxford: Oxford University Press, 2004. (www.oxforddnb.com/view/article/25612). June 16, 2006.

## Ismay Thorn (1853–1919)

Ismay Thorn, otherwise Edith Caroline Pollock, was born in London and was one of twelve children of baronet and barrister Sir Frederick Pollock and his second wife Sarah Anne Amowah. There were a further eleven siblings from her father's first marriage. Much of her childhood was spent at Hatton, the Pollock country house near Feltham in Middlesex where visitors included Forster and Thackeray; although she went away to school, she was "constantly petitioning to go home and . . . usually got [her] . . . own way" (Robson 150). She began writing as a child, but published her first children's book, *Pinafore Days*, in 1878 with John F. Shaw, who published many of her subsequent texts; she wrote some thirty in all. The "Harringtons" series, which includes *Quite Unexpected* and *A Flock of Four* proved to be among her most memorable work, but despite the sense of realism in the Harrington texts, Pollock stressed that her characters were not drawn from real life. Pollock's last known home was in Putney with her sisters Emily and Ada.

Information from: Isabel S. Robson, *Story Weavers: or Writers for the Young.* London: Robert Culley, 1900; "The Pollock Family." (www.tudorean.pwp. blueyonder.co.uk.placesnpeople/pollock.htm). November 9, 2003.

## Charlotte Mary Yonge (1823–1901)

The seventh child of a Devonshire clergyman and his wife, Charlotte Yonge was born near Winchester and educated at home. A best-selling author in her time, Yonge's *The Daisy Chain* and *Countess Kate* remain in print and clearly display the interest in family structures and tribulations which inform much of her work. During her career as an author, Yonge produced more than two hundred works of fiction and non-fiction as well as contributing articles for magazines including her own, *The Monthly Packet*, a Church of England publication for girls, which she edited for fifty years. Carpenter and Prichard comment that Yonge may seem the archetypal religious Victorian spinster to modern eyes, but that her books show great insight into children's characters: "A reader may feel that inside the careful Church of England Sunday school teacher there was a novelist of real distinction trying to get out" (p. 584). Today, she is frequently the subject of academic study.

Information from: "The Charlotte Mary Yonge Fellowship." (www.cmyf.org. uk). 3 October 2005. Humphrey Carpenter and Mari Prichard, 1984. "Charlotte M(ary) Yonge." *The Oxford Companion to Children's Literature*. Oxford: Oxford University Press, 1995.

# Notes

## Introduction

1. The "we" that Gilmour refers to here would seem to apply primarily to the British middle class, although I would argue that "Victorian values" remain an intrinsic element of today's upper- and working-class communities.
2. Although the term "nuclear" is conventionally used to depict such family types, it sits awkwardly in a discussion of the nineteenth century and is consequently avoided.
3. James' concept of the family ideal remains highly relevant to some twenty-first-century readers. Last published in 1997 by the US-based Christian Soli Deo Gloria Ministries, *A Help to Domestic Happiness* can be bought through Amazon.com. "Pass it on to those you love," suggests an enthusiastic reviewer on the Amazon site Amazon.com/gp/product, while Still Waters Revival Books of Canada recommend: "This is James' book on how to rightly order the family" (n.p.).
4. The book ran to at least five editions, the last published in 1905, and was commended in a foreword by the Rev. C. Pritchard, then Savilian Professor of Astronomy at the University of Oxford. In her section on Giberne in *Story Weavers or Writers for the Young* (1900), Isabel Suart Robson comments that *Sun, Moon and Stars* was "reaching its twenty-fourth thousand, a remarkable success for a work of this kind" (p. 87).
5. This term should not be confused with our contemporary understanding of "science fiction." It would appear that Giberne was describing herself as an author of both fiction and science.
6. Trans—prefix. 1. Across; beyond; on or to the other side of. 2. Through; into another state or place; transcending (Pearsall 1999: 1521). Normative—relating to or deriving from a standard or norm (p. 971).
7. The term "reality" relates to ostensibly factual data and information, although I freely acknowledge the potential for a lack of objectivity in historical records.
8. Greg's attitudes are further discussed in Chapter 4.

9. Although Brenda is occasionally referenced in literary directories, I located only one article about her: Lennox-Boyd, Charlotte. "Brenda and Her Works." *Signal*. 1990. 62:114–130.

## Chapter 1

1. Ross reviewed George K. Behlmer's *Friends of the Family: The English Home and Its Guardians, 1850–1940*, Leonore Davidoff et al.'s *The Family Story: Blood, Contract and Intimacy, 1830–1960*, and John Tosh's *A Man's Place: Masculinity and the Middle-Class Home in Victorian England*.

2. A "boarder" lived with the family and ate meals with them while a "lodger" occupied a separate space within the house. In *A Clearer Sense of the Census* (1996), Edward Higgs comments that "an attempt was made to make a distinction between a boarder who shared a common table with the household of which he or she was a member, and the lodger or group of lodgers who ate separately and constituted their own household. But the attachment to the Victorian ideal of the family was strong enough to ensure that the latter remained 'lodgers' in relationship to the head of the 'family' until at least 1891." Information from Mary H. Rootsweb Discussion List.

3. Waters explains that "hegemony" was used by Antonio Gramsci to "describe the 'moment' of collective political consciousness when a class brings about an 'intellectual and moral unity' in which the dominant group disappear into the 'common sense' of everyday life" (1997: 209).

4. See Chapter Three for a more detailed discussion of Childe-Pemberton's text and of the implications of Lady Victoria's statement.

5. As Peters points out, "orphan" could also describe a child with only a father or mother (2000: 1).

6. Paul Newland offers a clear definition of the *unheimlich*. "In his 1919 essay 'The Uncanny' (*Das Unheimlich*), Freud suggests that the uncanny 'is undoubtedly related to what is frightening—to what arouses dread and horror.' The phenomenon of the uncanny can be understood as 'that class of the frightening which leads back to what is known of old and long familiar.' At first, Freud followed Schelling's definition [of] 'everything that ought to have remained secret and hidden but has come to light.' But Freud suggested that the *heimlich* and *unheimlich* should not be seen within a purely oppositional, binary paradigm . . . *unheimlich* is in some way or other a sub-species of *heimlich* . . . in other words . . . the uncanny imbricates the familiar and the unfamiliar." Newland, Paul (n.d.). Derrida's main tool in deconstructing Plato's "Phaedrus" is *pharmakon*, a Greek word that translates as "medicine" but that also means both "cure" and "poison." It also embodies many other roles including scapegoat, imitation and magic, and it is these qualities that Derrida employs in relation to the literary presence of ambivalence, playfulness, transience, paradox, etc. Information from Mohan, J. (n.d.).

7. See Chapter Four for a full discussion of Childe-Pemberton's text.

8. Mrs Harrington's inability to "look after herself" suggests that she is either naïve or too busy tending her children. In either case she conforms to Victorian gender expectations of women as innocent and/or preoccupied with maternal tendencies and, overall, epitomizes the self-sacrificial Empire mother.

9. "The surgeon deposited [the baby] in her arms. She imprinted her cold white lips passionately on its forehead; passed her hands over her face; gazed wildly round . . . fell back—and died" (Dickens 1838: 46).

10. Although of course there are notable stepfathers in nineteenth-century fiction—Mr Murdstone in Dickens' *David Copperfield*, for example.

11. Hollingshead's *Ragged London in 1861* (1861) provided a first-hand view of London poverty without the sensationalism of Henry Mayhew's more famous and similar work.

12. Although the schools provided meals, children rarely lived "in the house" but were often placed in paid-for lodgings if they had no other shelter.

## Chapter 2

1. In *Street Arabs and Guttersnipes* (1884), Geo. Needham refers to the "low, infamous" streets of cities as "the very seed-plot of our future criminals" (464). Although Needham's work was published in the U.S. and focusses to some extent on the street arabs of American cities, he also details life in England.

2. The emigration of so-called "orphan" pauper children was endemic in the nineteenth century, and estimates suggest that between 1870 and 1914 some 80,000 children were sent to Canada alone, although the Ragged School Movement and the earlier Children's Friend Society sent dozens of children to Australia in the first half of the century. There were numerous other Victorian emigrant organizations including those of Maria Rye, who was based in Peckham, and Dr Thomas Barnardo, who sent children out to Canada in the 1870s with Annie MacPherson. Child emigration was sometimes a contentious issue; there were reports of children being abused overseas and the legalities of the process were often questionable. Until 1889, the law could not intervene in cases of parental child abuse, and so Barnardo adopted what he termed "philanthropic abduction"—and consequently frequently appeared in court. Bean and Melville (1989) point out that there were also pragmatic motives for child emigration; while it would cost £12 a year for a child housed in an English institution, sending one overseas required a one-off £15 payment (p. 5). Information on child emigration from the National Museums Liverpool Maritime Archives and Library, Information sheet 10; notes on Barnardo from Philip Bean and Joy Melville (1989).

3. The term "street arab" appears to have been introduced by Lord

Shaftesbury. Geo. Needham describes the nomadic Arab as "uncertain, vindictive, and selfish . . . the source of apprehension to every traveller . . . living in clans or hordes, for self-protection" and then states: "It was therefore with acute discernment, that, more than thirty years ago, Lord Shaftesbury discovered the resemblance. To this noble Earl . . . we are indebted for the epithet, so unique and suggestive, of STREET ARAB" (1884: 22).

4. Many second-hand copies of popular street-arab tales were rewards; for example, my copy of Brenda's *Nothing to Nobody* (n.d.) is inscribed, "All Saints Sunday School. First prize. Alice Keefe Jan. 1887."

5. The population of London at the 1861 census was 3,188,485. Information from Kings College London Humanities and Applied Computing website (http://www.kcl.ac.uk./humanities/year1/numerical/problems/london/london-pop-table.html 14 June 2005).

6. Despite the strength of his expressed sentiments, Greenwood was not merely a scaremonger: he offered solutions to the various "curses" of London, although as Jeffery Richards, writing in the introduction to Greenwood's text, comments, they were "almost always reiterations of long-canvassed views" (1869: viii).

7. Montgomery stated that her tale is "not intended for children," as was the case with *Misunderstood*, but, as Jacqueline Bratton points out (1981: 200), *Misunderstood* was given to children to read. It is likely that *Wild Mike* was treated similarly.

8. The implication is that children raised in such a manner will replicate their parents' behavior and there are resonances of Herbert Spencer's evolutionary theories in this passage. Spencer (1820–1903) is remembered primarily in relation to Social Darwinism which, at its most radical, subscribed to the belief that retrograde classes proliferate, but weaken racial stock.

9. The absent parent is also occasionally represented in street-arab tales as in Hesba Stretton's *Alone in London* (1869) where Susan, the mother of Dolly and the estranged daughter of Oliver, abandons her child in order to follow her soldier husband. Dolly is deposited at Oliver's house and Susan returns some years later to find that Dolly has died. However, my research has shown that few street-arab tales follow this formula; sickly, dead or negligent parents are far more commonplace and indeed Tony, the street child who joins Oliver's household, tells how his mother died when he was small and states that he "never had any father" (p. 23).

10. The minister is a positive paragon of virtue; not only is he holy, but he is a single parent who has nurtured his children alone since their mother's death.

11. Entirely in keeping with the Romantic image of the child as inherently good and innocent, Jessica's interest in the chapel appears to be instinctive: she cries as she listens to "the sweet music" (*JFP*, 35).

12. Although Sandy does appear to show genuine affection for his mother towards the end of the text.

13. Again there is the implication that the degenerate poor breed "like rabbits."

14. The pastoral setting is frequently depicted as beneficial in street-arab tales, a sentiment that is echoed in the work of charities such as The Children's Country Holiday Fund, which sought to provide days in the country for poor children.

15. Although there is a certain ambiguity in Brenda's characterization. The cobbler, Michael, who lives in the same building as Daddy confirms: "She's real honest, that I does know. She'd never go picking and stealing and that like . . . Oh yes, she's honest, that I *will* say for her" (*NtN*: 47). This over-emphasis on Daddy's honesty is puzzling, but may suggest that, in Michael's estimation, all street children are dishonest.

16. A conversation between Michael and Miss Barbara reiterates the potential dangers of Daddy's lifestyle. "[S]he's out a'most days all day long," said he. "She only comes in when she gets too hungry to stop out, I suspects. It's a bad lookout for a young'un like her to be roaming about the streets o' London like that, b'aint it, miss?" "Yes, that it is," said Barbara gravely (p. 46).

17. Daddy's rudeness to a beneficent outsider is unusual in such texts; street-arab protagonists invariably welcome those who offer kindness. But Brenda was aware that charity ladies could be problematic for the poor and that their presence was sometimes an annoyance. In *A Saturday's Bairn* (1877), the narrator comments: "[The] nerves [of the poor] are often strung at a painful tension . . . without intention, it is easy to ruffle them . . . I have seen people . . . go into the homes of the poor and pick their way about . . . as if they were treading on hot bricks . . . and then I have heard them wonder . . . why the poor are always such a grumpy, unget-at-able set" (p. 251).

18. Although the term "brothers and sisters" draws on religious terminology that suggests equality, the addition of the word "poor" identifies the destitute as "other."

19. Froggy does attend night school, but the premises are closed when "a great railway company, wanting more land to build warehouses upon, had begun clearing away whole streets" (p. 33).

20. Although, of course, the fate of crippled John undermines the Shaftos' characterization as successful parents.

## Chapter 3

1. Schectman's work echoes that of Bruno Bettelheim in *The Uses of Enchantment: the Meaning and Importance of Fairy Tales* (1976): Bettelheim presents the figure of the wicked stepmother as a psychological device through which the child can comprehend and accommodate both good

and bad elements of a parent. Sandra Gilbert and Susan Gubar also focus on the wicked stepmother as monstrous alter-ego in their 1979 text, *The Madwoman in the Attic: The Woman Writer and the Nineteenth-Century Literary Imagination*.

2. Hughes draws on the feminist theories of Simone de Beauvoir in this excerpt.

3. The term is used here in its Kristevan sense to imply that the abjected remains a threat despite its expulsion to the borders of consciousness.

4. *The British Mother's Journal* was launched in January 1845, published under the sanction of the London Central Maternal Association, and changed its name circa 1860. It appears to have survived into the 1860s, although very few records of the publication remain and the British Library has no issues beyond those of 1864. Although the first editions of *The Mother's Practical Guide* appeared in 1843, it ran to several editions in later years both in the UK and America and continued to be read. My own edition is inscribed: "To Mrs L. H. Keble from her affectionate Husband. 1st January 1864."

5. This may have been absent from early editions. Its inclusion in the preface notes to the third edition of the book suggests that it is a recent addition.

6. These were the nicknames of Clifford's daughters.

7. The children's father is absent; he is, says the narrator, "far away at sea" (*New Mother.* 8).

8. Although the baby is referred to simply as "the baby" much of the time, she is clearly female. "And see, there is the baby waking up from her sleep," says the mother (*New Mother.* 20).

9. There is a noteworthy comparison here between Clifford's tale and Christina Rossetti's poem "Goblin Market," first published in 1862. While Blue-Eyes and the Turkey might be perceived as desirous of adult sexual knowledge, Rossetti's Laura chooses to eat the forbidden goblin fruit and so metaphorically breaks away from the maternal *chora* to embrace adult sexuality.

10. She is certainly a fabrication of some sort, perhaps in both senses of the word. The peardrum girl claims that a mother with glass eyes and a wooden tail "would be much too expensive to make" (p. 25), implying that the new mother is a manufactured creation.

11. The tail, as phallus, introduces a distinctly masculine element into the female space and further emphasizes that the new mother is entirely remote from the maternal ideal.

12. Childe-Pemberton's work is further explored in Chapter 4.

13. The notion of deception arises from a conversation between Birdie and Lady Victoria in which the child confides: "'I should never, *never* like Papa to marry another wife—because Mother couldn't be pleased at *that*, could she?'" (p. 61). Birdie is subsequently horrified to learn that Lady Victoria is to marry her father.

14. There are further suggestions of fairy tale in Lionel's characterization. Known as Lion, he is his sister's arch-defender and it is largely through his death that the family becomes united.
15. *We Are Seven* predates Ethel Turner's *Seven Little Australians* by fourteen years, but there are striking similarities between the texts which suggest that Birley's novel may have influenced Turner's work. The fathers of both families are military men, both teenage "Judys" are described as clever and freckled with wayward hair and a tendency to general disorder, and both girls are injured saving a step-sibling, although Turner's Judy dies as a result.
16. "A New Mother" was first published in Charles Dickens' *Household Words, Or All the Year Round*, but Proctor's complete writings were republished as *Legends and Lyrics* by George Bell and Sons in 1881. References to the poem are taken from the 1903 edition of Bell's publication.
17. The subject matter of Proctor's poems in *Legends and Lyrics* is sometimes controversial, which supports the notion that "A New Mother" (p. 239) takes an unconventional stance. For example, "Homeless" (p. 382) attacks British complacency toward poor children, while "A Legend of Provence" (p. 204) deals sympathetically with a "fallen" woman.
18. Although the novel originally carried a subtitle, this appears to have been removed from later editions. My own 1889 edition is simply entitled *The Young Stepmother*.
19. Interestingly, it is mainly the English-born children of the family who have died. Lucy, Sophia, Gilbert and Edmund were all born in India where Kendal lived for the early part of his first marriage. Yonge's attitude to the climate of India is unusual; for writers such as Ismay Thorn and Hodgson Burnett, England is clearly a healthier country in which to live. However, Willow Lawn is depicted as a particularly blighted spot: when Albinia first looks out of the window she sees "the gray outline of trees and shrubs, obscured by the heavy mist; and on the lawn below, a thick cloud that seemed to hang over a dark space which she suspected to be a large pond" (p. 9). The whole area is damp and Albinia later orders the pond to be filled in.

## Chapter 4

1. The words of Dolores Mohun in *The Two Sides of the Shield* (Yonge 1885: 10–11).
2. Interestingly, Dolores differentiates between "proper aunts" and those who have orphans left to them; it is only the latter that appear to have a propensity for cruelty (p. 6).
3. There are, of course, exceptions. For example, in Mary Louisa Molesworth's *Hermy: The Story of a Little Girl* (1880), Hermy's foster mother, Lady Katherine, despite the fact that she has young children of her own, is

impatient with her niece and describes her as "rather slow and stupid" (p. 14). Lady Katherine and Hermy are never truly reconciled.

4. There is a profligate "uncle" in Yonge's *The Two Sides of the Shield* who leads Dolores astray, but, as Colonel Mohun points out, Alfred is not a true uncle, merely "the only son of Dolores' mother's stepmother by her first marriage" (p. 202). Thus the "true" family remains honorable.

5. In fact, attitudes to spinster aunts vary in much adult fiction of the same period; Dickens' Betsy Trotwood and Miss Murdstone (*David Copperfield*) are respectively delightful and dreadful. In contrast, bachelor uncles are sometimes depicted as entirely unpleasant characters, as with Sheridan Le Fanu's Uncle Silas and Dickens' Ralph Nickleby.

6. Other texts featuring a bachelor aunt and uncle may be less overtly biased, although they may still display sexist emphases. In Ismay Thorn's *Quite Unexpected*, for example, although spinster great aunt Bethia is unwelcoming and relatively disinterested when her nieces and nephews arrive at her home, she learns to love them through the encouragement of sensitive and caring bachelor uncle Jasper.

7. Nathanial Parker Willis' stanzas appear as an introduction to Chapter 1 of Anne Judith Penny's *The Afternoon of Unmarried Life* (1858). Little is known of Penny's life, but she also wrote *Morning Clouds (consisting of advice to the sorrowful etc.)* (1857) and *Spring and Autumn* (1865).

8. Numerous commentators declared the unmarried state to be unnatural, but even with the rise of the New Woman, or perhaps *because* of her existence, this notion persisted. Eliza Lynn Linton, writing in 1891 in *The Nineteenth Century*, declared: "The continuance of the race in healthy reproduction, together with the fit nourishment and care of the young after birth, is the ultimate end of woman as such and whatever tells against these functions, and reduces either her power or her perfectness, is an offence against nature and a wrong done to society." E. Linton, (1891) "The Wild Women as Politicians." *The Nineteenth Century* (cited in Jalland and Hooper 1986: 25).

9. Greg's solution to the problem of surplus women was that the bulk should emigrate to Canada, Australia and the United States where men were in the majority. He also suggested that those who remained in England should learn to be so agreeable to men, that bachelors would prefer marriage to mistresses and clubs (Vicinus 4).

10. For example, Charlotte Constable, surrogate aunt to the Partridge children in Brenda's *The Pilot's House or The Five Little Partridges* (1885), is a clergyman's daughter who is "devoted to little children . . . [and] a very merry young lady . . . [with] beautiful dark hair and eyes, and rosy lips, and even white teeth, and cheeks with the bloom of a white peach on them" (p. 107). When the children meet her, she is wearing "a very delicate white dress . . . all lace and little gauffred frills" (p. 108). By the end of the text, she is engaged to the children's Uncle Bob.

11. For a more detailed discussion of the children of the Empire, see Chapter One.

12. See Edgeworth's "The Birthday Present" in *Rosamond—A Series of Tales* (1796) and "Fatal Effects of Disobedience to Parents" in Sherwood's *The History of the Fairchild Family* (1818), for example.

13. Pussy's age as a young girl is unspecified, but she describes herself as having "just grown up" (p. 213) and talks of parties, which would suggest that she is "out" in society and at least sixteen or seventeen.

14. The nickname Hoot-Toot derives from Great Uncle's habit of saying "Hoot-toot, hoot-toot!" if ever he is "perplexed or disapproving" (Molesworth 1889: 16).

15. See for example M. Roper and J. Tosh, eds, *Manful Assertions: Masculinities in Britain since 1800*, London: Routledge, 1991; J. Tosh, *Manliness and Masculinities in Nineteenth-Century Britain: Essays on gender, family and empire.* Harlow: Pearson Longman, 2005; A. Bradstock et al., eds, *Masculinity and Spirituality in Victorian Culture.* Basingstoke: Macmillan, 2000; K. Snyder, *Bachelors, Manhood and the Novel, 1850–1925.* Cambridge: Cambridge University Press, 1999.

16. A reference to the science of phrenology, developed from the theories of Viennese physician Franz Joseph Gall (1758–1928).

## Chapter 5

1. All references are taken from the rear pages of Brenda's *Nothing to Nobody* and *Victoria Bess: The Ups and Downs of a Doll's Life* as detailed in the list of Works Cited.

2. The words of a reporter who spoke to Stretton in 1892. He also described her as having "a grave sweet face, large grey eyes and silvering curls" (cited in Cutt 1979: 115). However, Cutt points out that Stretton was "as good an example of Victorian stubbornness, inconsistency and idealism as the old Queen herself" (p. 117).

3. There is no further identity to this article. It was found by Brenda's great-granddaughter and myself among Brenda's memorabilia (Thiel 2002: 17).

4. Although this letter was written in 1933, Arran was born in 1868 and consequently can be classified as a Victorian.

5. Gore, A. Letter to Castle Smith dated January 3, 1934 from Georgina Castle Smith's memorabilia. (Thiel 2002: 22).

6. All references are taken from editions in the list of Works Cited.

7. Molesworth's penchant for italicizing is displayed in many of her works. Interestingly, she continues to use such emphases when addressing an older audience. For example, writing for the readers of *Atalanta* in "On the Art of Writing Fiction for Children," she recommends: "Good English, terse and clear, with perhaps a little more repetition, a little more *making sure you are understood* . . . [D]o not be too slavishly afraid of using a long

word—a word even which, *but for the context*, your young readers would fail to take in the meaning of" (1893: 343). This lack of differentiation would suggest that she employed one style of narrative voice, regardless of audience, although such a technique does not preclude a double address.

8. Brenda certainly experienced Punch shows as an adult, according to her daughter's notes (Thiel 2002: 28). Eva writes of Punch performances in the Castle Smiths' London home and a depiction of Punch and Judy performers appears in *Little Cousins or Georgie's Visit to Lotty*.

9. These words may well echo the sentiments of the song, "Home, Sweet Home," that was written in 1823 and that became popular in England some years later.

10. *Countess Kate* is still in publication and is easily available.

11. See Chapter Three for a detailed discussion of Clifford's text.

## Conclusion

1. As Watson also acknowledges, many of the "family group" toys are implicitly aimed at the female market. This suggests that, as with the Victorians, the domestic space is still perceived as a primarily female domain. More significantly perhaps, it is evident that girls are encouraged to internalize domestic doctrines through the production of such toys.

2. Mattel's Barbie doll has yet to produce a family of her own, whether contemporary or Victorian, but the Midge doll, known as Barbie's friend, was manufactured as a pregnant model. Sold in the USA as part of a "Happy Family" set with husband Alan and three-year-old son Ryan, she wore a pink skirt, a tiny wedding ring and a detachable stomach with a curled-up baby inside. However, following customer complaints, giant retailers Wal-Mart removed the set from their outlets ("Barbie's Pregnant Friend Gets the Push" 2002: n.p.).

3. The family in *Clean Break* are doubly transnormative. Emily is the daughter of Julie's first partner while Vita and Maxie are Frankie's and Julie's offspring. Significantly, Emily's first home with her natural parents was violent and unstable, and although Emily occasionally feels separate from the new family, there is a sense of unity that is ultimately sufficient for her and that in many ways echoes notions of the domestic ideal.

4. Lucy Lane Clifford's "The New Mother" (see Chapters 3 and 5), is the only text discussed here that explicitly depicts the domestic idyll as tenuous and vulnerable to destruction.

5. Although both books were written outside the UK, *Jenny Lives with Eric and Martin* was published in Britain (London: Gay Men's Press) and *Heather Has Two Mommies* (Los Angeles: Alyson) is easily available in the UK.

6. At the time of writing, the cheapest copy available in the UK was second-hand and cost £50.

# Works Cited

## Primary Sources

Almond, David. *Heaven Eyes*. London: Hodder Children's Books, 2000.

Birley, Caroline. 1880. *We Are Seven*. London: Wells Gardner, Darton and Co., n.d.

Bosche, Susanne. *Jenny Lives With Eric and Martin*. London: Gay Men's Press, 1983.

Brenda. 1873. *Nothing to Nobody*. London: John F. Shaw, n.d.

—— 1875. *Froggy's Little Brother*. London: John F. Shaw, n.d.

—— 1877. *A Saturday's Bairn*. London: John F. Shaw, n.d.

—— 1877. *Lotty's Visit to Grandmama: A Story for the Little Ones*. London: John F. Shaw, n.d.

—— 1879. *Victoria Bess: The Ups and Downs of a Doll's Life*. London: John F. Shaw, n.d.

—— 1880. *Little Cousins or Georgie's Visit to Lotty*. London: John F. Shaw, n.d.

—— 1884. *Old England's Story in Little Words for Little People*. London: Hatchards, n.d.

—— 1885. *The Pilot's House or The Five Little Partridges*. London: John F. Shaw, n.d.

Burnett, Frances Hodgson. 1887. *Sarah Crewe, or What Happened at Miss Minchin's*. London: Frederick Warne, 1888.

—— 1911. *The Secret Garden*. London: Penguin, 1994.

Childe-Pemberton, Harriet L. 1882. "All My Doing; or Red Riding Hood Over Again." *The Fairy Tales of Every Day*. London: Society for Promoting Christian Knowledge, n.d. 223–305.

—— 1888. *Birdie: A Tale of Child-Life*. London: Griffith, Farran, Odeden and Welsh, n.d.

Clifford, Lucy Lane. "The New Mother." *Anyhow Stories—Moral and Otherwise*. London: Macmillan and Co., 1882. 8–47.

Edgeworth, Maria. 1796. "The Purple Jar." *Rosamond—A Series of Tales*. Roehampton Digital Library. London: George Routledge, 1918. (wordsworth.roehampton.ac.uk/digital/chlit/edgeros/ind.asp). June 4, 2006.

Giberne, Agnes. 1879. *Sun, Moon, and Stars: A Book for Beginners*. London: Seeley and Co., n.d.

Horowitz, Antony. *Stormbreaker*. London: Walker, 2000.

—— *Skeleton Key*. London: Walker, 2002.

Leslie, Emma. 1889. *Saved by Love: A Story of the London Streets*. Edinburgh: T. Nelson and Sons, 1904.

Molesworth, Mrs 1880. *Hermy: The Story of a Little Girl*. London: W.R. Chambers, n.d.

—— 1882. *Rosy*. London: Macmillan and Co., 1896.

—— 1889. *Great-Uncle Hoot-Toot*. London: Society for the Promotion of Christian Knowledge, n.d.

Montgomery, Florence. 1869. *Misunderstood*. London: Richard Bentley and Son, 1876.

—— 1875. *Wild Mike and His Victim*. London: Richard Bentley and Son, n.d.

Newman, Lesléa. *Heather Has Two Mommies*. Los Angeles: Alyson, 1989.

O'Loughlin, Elizabeth. *Mum and Dad Split Up*. Stroud: Pangolin Books, 2005.

Rowling, J.K. *Harry Potter and the Philosopher's Stone*. London: Bloomsbury, 1997.

—— *Harry Potter and the Order of the Phoenix*. London: Bloomsbury, 2003.

—— *Harry Potter and the Half-Blood Prince*. London: Bloomsbury, 2005.

Sherwood, Mary Martha. 1818. "Story on the Sixth Commandment." *The History of the Fairchild Family*. London: James Nisbet and Co., n.d.

Sinclair, Catherine. 1839. *Holiday House: A Book for the Young*. London: Ward Lock and Co., n.d.
Stretton, Hesba. 1867. *Jessica's First Prayer*. London: The Religious Tract Society, n.d.
—— 1867. *Jessica's Mother*. New Bouverie Series. The Religious Tract Society, n.d.
—— 1869. *Alone in London*. London: The Religious Tract Society, n.d.
—— 1873. *Lost Gip*. London: The Religious Tract Society, n.d.
—— 1883. *The Lord's Purse Bearer*. London: The Religious Tract Society, n.d.
Thorn, Ismay. 1889. *Quite Unexpected*. London: Gardner, Darton and Co., n.d.
—— 1889. *A Flock of Four*. London: Wells, Gardner, Darton and Co., n.d.
Turner, Ethel. *Seven Little Australians*. London: Hodder, 1894.
Wilson, Jacqueline. *The Story of Tracy Beaker*. London: Doubleday, 1991.
—— *Dustbin Baby*. London: Doubleday, 2001.
—— *Clean Break*. London: Doubleday, 2005.
Yonge, Charlotte M. 1856. *The Daisy Chain: Or Aspirations: A Family Chronicle*. London: Macmillan. 1888.
—— 1861. *The Young Step-mother*. London: Macmillan and Co., 1889.
—— 1862. *Countess Kate*. London: Faber and Faber, n.d.
—— 1885. *The Two Sides of the Shield*. London: Macmillan and Co., 1889.

## Secondary Sources

A Stepmother. "The Difficulties and Trials of Stepmothers." *The British Mother's Journal*. Vol. IV. April 1848. 88–9.
Abbott, Mary. *Family Ties: English Families 1540–1920*. London: Routledge, 1993.
Alston, Ann. "There's No Place Like Home: The Ideological and Mythological Construction of House and Home in Children's Literature." *New Voices in Children's Literature*. Ed. Sebastien Chapleau. Lichfield: Pied Piper Publishing, 2004. 55–62.
Anderson, Michael. *Family Structure in Nineteenth Century Lancashire*. Cambridge: Cambridge University Press, 1971.
—— "Household Structure and the Industrial Revolution: mid-century Preston in comparative perspective." *Household and Family in Past Time*. Cambridge: Cambridge University Press, 1972. 215–35.
—— *Approaches to the History of the Western Family, 1500–1914*. Prepared for the Economic History Society. London and Basingstoke: Macmillan, 1980.
—— "Households, families and individuals: some preliminary results from the national sample from the 1851 census of Great Britain." *Continuity and Change*. 1988. 3.3. 421–38.
Anger, Suzy. *Knowing the Past: Victorian Literature and Culture*. Ithaca: Cornell, 2001.
Ariès, Phillipe. *Centuries of Childhood*. Trans. R. Baldick. Peregrine: London, 1973.
Armstrong, Nancy. *Desire and Domestic Fiction: A Political History of the Novel*. Oxford: Oxford University Press, 1987.
Auerbach, Nina and U.C. Knoepflmacher, eds. *Forbidden Journeys: Fairy Tales and Fantasies by Victorian Women Writers*. Chicago and London: University of Chicago Press, 1992.
Author Unknown (1). "The Life-story of 'The Quiver Waifs'." *The Quiver: An Illustrated Magazine for Sunday and General Reading*. (1888) 2. n.p.
Author Unknown (2). "Step-Mothers: Sketches from Life." *The British Mothers' Journal and Domestic Magazine*. No. LXXII. December 1861. n.p.
Author Unknown (3). "To a Step-child." *The British Mother's Magazine*. Vol. VIII. September 1862. 201.
B.B.B. "The Two Step-Mothers." *The British Mother's Journal*. August 1858. 203–7.
Bakewell, Mrs J. 1843. *The Mother's Practical Guide in the Physical, Intellectual, and Moral Training of Her Children*. London: John Snow, n.d.
"Barbie's Pregnant Friend Gets the Push." BBC World News Edition. 2002. (http://news.bbc.co.uk/1/hi/world/americas/2608867.stm18). April 2006.
Bean, Philip and Joy Melville. *Lost Children of the Empire: The Untold Story of Britain's Child Migrants*. London: Unwin Hyman, 1989.
Behlmer, George. *Friends of the Family: The English Home and its Guardians, 1850–1940*. Stanford: Stanford University Press, 1998.
Bettelheim, Bruno. 1976. *The Uses of Enchantment: The Meaning and Importance of Fairy Tales*. London: Penguin, 1991.
Booth, Wayne C. *The Company We Keep: An Ethics of Fiction*. Berkeley and London: University of California Press, 1988.

Bratton, Jacqueline. *The Impact of Victorian Children's Fiction*. London: Croom Helm, 1981.

"British Newspapers." (www.britishnewspapers.co.uk). May 2, 2003.

Buettner, Elizabeth. "Parent-child separations and colonial careers: the Talbot family correspondence in the 1880s and 1890s." *Childhood in Question: Children, parents and the state.* Eds Anthony Fletcher and Stephen Hussey. Manchester: Manchester University Press, 1999. 115–32.

—— *Empire Families: Britons and Late Imperial India*. Oxford: Oxford University Press, 2004.

Carpenter, Humphrey and Mari Prichard. 1984. *The Oxford Companion to Children's Literature*. Oxford: Oxford University Press, 1995.

Chambers, Aidan. "The Reader in the Book." *The Signal Approach to Children's Literature*. Ed. Nancy Chambers. Harmondsworth: Kestrel, 1980. 250–75.

Chase, Karen and Michael Levenson. *The Spectacle of Intimacy: A Public Life for the Victorian Family*. Princeton: Princeton University Press, 2000.

Citizenship Past Consortium. "Hidden Lives Revealed." (www.hiddenlives.org.uk). November 8, 2004.

Coveney, Peter. *The Image of Childhood: The Individual and Society: A Study of the Theme in English Literature*. Harmondsworth: Penguin, 1969.

Cuddon, J. A. *The Penguin Dictionary of Literary Terms and Literary Theory*. Harmondsworth: Penguin, 1982.

Cutt, Nancy. *Ministering Angels: A Study of Nineteenth-Century Evangelical Writing for Children*. Wormley: Five Owls Press, 1979.

Davidoff, Leonore, Megan Doolittle, Janet Fink and Katherine Holden. *The Family Story: Blood, Contract and Intimacy, 1830–1960*. Harlow: Longman, 1999.

Davidoff, Leonore and Catherine Hall. 1987. *Family Fortunes: Men and Women of the English Middle Class 1780–1850*. London: Routledge, 2002.

Davidson, Mary. "Waifs, Wealth and Angels: Victorian Child Conundrums." *The Big Issues: Representations of Socially Marginalised Groups and Individuals in Children's Literature, Past and Present.* Eds Pat Pinsent and Sue Mansfield. Roehampton: National Centre for Research in Children's Literature, 2000. 87–93.

Davin, Anna. *Growing Up Poor: Home, School and Street in London 1870–1914*. London: Rivers Oram Press, 1996.

Demers, Patricia. "Smith, Sarah [pseud. Hesba Stretton] (1832–1911, novelist and short story writer. n.p." *Oxford Dictionary of National Biography*. (www.oxforddnb.com/view/article/36158). March 7, 2007.

Dever, Carolyn. *Death and the Mother from Dickens to Freud: Victorian Fiction and the Anxiety of Origins*. Cambridge: Cambridge University Press, 1998.

Dickens, Charles. 1838. *Oliver Twist*. Harmondsworth: Penguin, 1983.

Doan, Laura. "Introduction." *Old Maids to Radical Spinsters: Unmarried Women in the Twentieth-Century Novel*. Ed. Laura Doan. Chicago: University of Chicago Press, 1991. 1–16.

Doughty, Steve. "The age of the troubled teen." *Daily Mail* September 14, 2004. 10.

Duckworth, Jeannie. *Fagin's Children: Criminal Children in Victorian England*. London: Hambledon and London, 2002.

Dunbar, Janet. *The Early Victorian Woman: Some Aspects of Her Life (1837–57)*. London: George Harrap and Co., 1953.

Dusinberre, Juliet. *Alice to the Lighthouse: Children's Books and Radical Experiments in Art*. Basingstoke: Macmillan, 1987.

Economic and Social Research Council. "Society Today: Welfare and Single Parenthood in the UK." (www.esrc.ac.uk). February 21, 2006.

Eliot, George. 1854. "Woman in France: Madame de Sablé." *George Eliot Selected Critical Writings*. Oxford: Oxford's World's Classics, 2000. 37–68.

Flandrin, Jean-Louis. *Families in Former Times*. Cambridge: Cambridge University Press, 1979.

Foster, Shirley and Judy Simons. *What Katy Read: Feminist Re-Readings of "Classic" Stories for Girls*. Basingstoke: Macmillan, 1995.

Gilbert, Sandra M. and Susan Gubar. 1979. *The Madwoman in the Attic: The Woman Writer and the Nineteenth-Century Literary Imagination*. New Haven: Yale University Press, 1984.

Gillis, John. *A World of Their Own Making: Myth, Ritual and the Quest for Family Values*. Cambridge: Harvard University Press, 1996.

Gilmour, Robin. *The Victorian Period: The Intellectual and Cultural Context of English Literature 1830–1890*. London and New York: Longman, 1993.

Gittins, Diana. *The Family in Question: Changing Households and Familiar Ideologies*, Basingstoke: Macmillan, 1985.

Gorran-Haven.com. "Mevagissey Old Cemetery." (www.gorran- haven.com.mevinscr.htm). April 19, 2003.

Green, D. and A. Owens. "Gentlewomanly capitalism? Spinsters, widows and wealth holding in England and Wales, c. 1800–1860." A paper presented at "Power, Knowledge and Society in the City; Sixth International Conference on Urban History." 2002. Social Science Research Network. (www.esh.ed.ac.uk/urban_history/text/GreenOwens55.doc). June 13, 2005.

Greenwood, James. 1869. *The Seven Curses of London.* Oxford: Blackwood, 1981.

Higgs, E. *A Clearer Sense of the Census.* London: HMSO, 1996.

Hollingshead, John. 1861. *Ragged London in 1861.* London: Dent, 1986.

Horn, Pamela. *The Victorian Town Child.* New York: New York University Press, 1997.

Hughes, Christina. *Stepparents: Wicked or Wonderful? An Indepth Study of Stepparenthood.* Aldershot: Avebury, 1991.

Jalland, Pat. *Death in the Victorian Family.* Oxford: Oxford University Press, 1996.

Jalland, Pat and John Hooper. *Women from Birth to Death: The Female Life Cycle in Britain 1830–1914.* Brighton: Harvester, 1986.

James, John Angell. 1828. *A Help to Domestic Happiness.* Morgan: Soli Deo Gloria Publications, 1997.

Jordan, Jane. *Josephine Butler.* London: John Murray, 2001.

Kawabata, Ariko. "The Border Crossings of Frances Hodgson Burnett—Children's Literature and Romance in Fin de Siècle Britain." Ph.D. Diss. Roehampton University, 2005.

Keith, Lois. *Take Up Thy Bed and Walk: Death, Disability and Cure in Classic Fiction for Girls.* London: The Women's Press, 2001.

Kornfeld, John and Laurie Prothro. "Comedy, Conflict and Community: Home and Family in *Harry Potter.*" *Harry Potter's World: Multidisciplinary Critical Perspectives.* Ed. Elizabeth E. Heilman. New York and London: RoutledgeFalmer, 2003. 187–202.

Loudon, Irvine. *Death in Childbirth: An International Study of Maternal Care and Maternal Mortality 1800–1950.* Oxford: Clarendon Press. 1992.

Lurie, Alison. "A Tail of Terror." *New York Review of Books.* 22.20. (1975). (www.nybooks. co./articles/8993). June 25, 2003.

McClintock, Anne. *Imperial Leather: Race, Gender and Sexuality in the Colonial Contest.* Westport, CN, and London: Routledge, 1995.

McGillis, Roderick. "Lame Old Bachelor, Lonely Old Maid: Harriet Childe-Pemberton's 'All My Doing; or Red Riding Hood Over Again'." *Aspects and Issues in the History of Children's Literature.* Ed. Maria Nikolajeva. London: Greenwood Press, 1995.

McPheron, W. "Frederic Jameson". 1999. (www.prelectur.stanford.edu.jameson). March 12, 2003.

Mary H., Rootsweb.com Discussion List. 2002. (archiver.rootsweb.com/th/read/UK-WORKHOUSE-HOSP). February 15, 2006.

Mayhew, Henry. 1861. "Statement of a young pickpocket". *London Labour and the London Poor.* Vol.1. Electronic Text Center, University of Virginia Library. (http://etext.virginia.edu/etcbin/toccernew2?id=MayLond.sgm&images=images/modeng&data=/texts/english/modeng/parsed&tag=public&part=269&division=div). April 12, 2005.

Merrycoz.org. "Children's Books of the Year." *The North American Review.* 236–49. (www. merrycoz./org/books/BOOK1866.HTM 23). November 2005.

Mohan, J. (n.d.) "The Pharmakon: Grounds for Play." (www.lawrence.edu). February 2, 2006.

Molesworth, Mrs 1893. "On the Art of Writing Fiction for Children." *A Peculiar Gift: Nineteenth Century Writings on Books for Children.* Ed. Lance Salway. Harmondsworth: Kestrel, 1976. 340–6.

Moss, Anita. "Mothers, Monsters and Morals in Victorian Fairy Tales." *The Lion and the Unicorn.* 1988.12.2. 47–60.

Natov, Roni. *The Poetics of Childhood.* New York and London: Routledge, 2003.

Needham, Geo. *Street Arabs and Guttersnipes: The Pathetic and Humorous Side of Young Vagabond Life in the Great Cities, with Records of Work for their Reclamation.* Boston: Guernsey, 1884.

Nelson, Claudia. *Boys Will Be Girls: The Feminine Ethic and British Children's Fiction, 1857–1917.* New Brunswick: Rutgers University Press, 1991.

Newland, P. (n.d.) "'On an Eastern Arc': Reading Iain Sinclair's interest in Christ Church, Spitalfields and its uncanny territory through East End Discourse." (www.literarylondon.org/london-journal/newland). February 2, 2006.

Nikolajeva, Maria. "Children's Literature as a Cultural Code: A Semiotic Approach to History." *Aspects and Issues in the History of Children's Literature.* Ed. Maria Nikolajeva. Westport, CN, and London: Greenwood, 1995. 39–48.

Paul, Lissa. "Enigma Variations: What Feminist Theory Knows About Children's Literature." 1987. *Signal* 53. 186–201.

Pearsall, Judy. Ed. *The Concise Oxford Dictionary*. 10th ed. Oxford: Oxford University Press, 1999.

Penny, Anne Judith. 1858. *The Afternoon of Unmarried Life (from the last London edition)*. New York: Rudd and Carleton, 1859.

Peters, Laura. *Orphan Texts: Victorian Orphans, Culture and Empire*. Manchester: Manchester University Press, 2000.

Phillips, Melanie. "Adults behave like infants. Children are treated like adults. No wonder the young are cracking under the pressure!" *Daily Mail* September 14, 2004. 12.

Poovey, Mary. *Uneven Developments*. Chicago: Chicago University Press, 1989.

Proctor, Adelaide. 1881. "A New Mother." *Legends and Lyrics*. London: George Bell and Sons, 1903. 239–49.

Reber, Arthur S. *The Penguin Dictionary of Psychology*. London: Penguin, 1985.

Robson, Isabel Suart. *Story Weavers: or Writers for the Young*. London: Robert Culley, 1900.

Rose, Lionel. *Rogues and Vagabonds: Vagrant Underworld in Britain 1815–1985*. London and New York: Routledge, 1988.

Ross, Ellen. "Long Live the Family." *The Journal of British Studies*. 2002. 41:4. 537–44.

Ruskin, John. 1865. "Of Queen's Gardens." *Sesame and Lilies, the Two Paths and the King of the Golden River*. London: J.M. Dent, 1907. 48–79.

Salmon, E. 1888. "Literature for the Little Ones." *A Peculiar Gift: Nineteenth Century Writings on Books for Children*. Ed. Lance Salway. Harmondsworth: Kestrel, 1976. 46–61.

Salway, Lance, ed. *A Peculiar Gift: Nineteenth Century Writings on Books for Children*. Harmondsworth: Kestrel, 1976.

Samuel, Raphael. "Mrs Thatcher's Return to Victorian Values." *Victorian Values: A Joint Symposium of the Royal Society of Edinburgh and the British Academy 1990*. Ed. Christopher Smout. Oxford: Oxford University Press, 1992. 9–29.

Schectman, Jacqueline. *The Stepmother in Fairy Tales: Bereavement and the Feminine Shadow*. Boston: Sigo Press, 1993.

Schlueter, Paul and June Schlueter. Eds. *An Encyclopedia of British Women Writers*. London: St. James Press, 1998.

Sebag-Montefiore, Mary. "Nice Girls Don't (But Want To): Work Ethic Conflicts and Conundrums in Mrs Molesworth's Books for Girls." *The Lion and the Unicorn*. 2002. 26.3. 374–94.

Shorter, Edward. *The Making of the Modern Family*. London: Collins, 1975.

Showalter, Elaine. 1977. *A Literature of Their Own: From Charlotte Brontë to Doris Lessing*. London: Virago, 1993.

Silver, Anna Krugovoy. "The Didactic Carnivalesque in Lucy Lane Clifford's 'The New Mother.'" *Studies in English Literature*. 2000. 40.4. 727–43.

Snyder, Katherine V. *Bachelors, Manhood and the Novel, 1850–1925*. Cambridge: Cambridge University Press, 1999.

Spearman, Edmund, R. Woods et al. *The Poor in Great Cities: Their Problems and What is Being Done to Solve Them*. London: Kegan Paul, Trench, Trubner and Co., 1896.

Stanley, Mrs H.M. *London Street Arabs*. London: Cassell, 1890.

Stedman Jones, Gareth. *Outcast London: A Study in the Relationship between Classes in Victorian Society*. London: Penguin, 1971.

Stephens, John. *Language and Ideology in Children's Fiction*. London: Longman, 1992.

Sternlieb, Lisa. *The Female Narrator in the British Novel: Hidden Agendas*. Basingstoke: Palgrave, 2002.

Still Waters Revival Books of Canada. "James, John Angell: A Guide to Domestic Happiness." (www.swrb.com/catalog/j.htm). February 1, 2006.

Stone, Lawrence. *The Family, Sex and Marriage in England, 1500–1800*. London: Weidenfeld and Nicholson, 1977.

*The Girl's Own Paper* [1]. II: 57. January 29, 1881. 288.

*The Girl's Own Paper* [2]. II: 81. July 16, 1881. 672.

*The Girl's Own Paper* [3]. XVIII: 880. November 7, 1896. 96.

*The Girl's Own Paper* [4]. XIV: 701. June 3, 1893. 575.

Thiel, Liz. "The Woman Known as 'Brenda'." Diss. University of Surrey, Roehampton, 2002.

Tosh, John. *A Man's Place: Masculinity and the Middle-Class Home in Victorian England*. New Haven, CN, and London: Yale University Press, 1999.

—— *Manliness and Masculinities in Nineteenth-Century Britain*. Harlow: Longman, 2004.

Townsend, John Rowe. 1965. *Written for Children: An Outline of English-language Children's Literature*. London: Bodley Head, 1990.

Vicinus, Martha. *Independent Women: Work and Community for Single Women: 1850–1920*. London: Virago, 1988.

Wall, Barbara. *The Narrator's Voice: The Dilemma of Children's Fiction*. Basingstoke: Macmillan, 1991.

Walvin, James. *Victorian Values*. London: André Deutsch, 1987.

Warner, Marina. 1994. *From the Beast to the Blonde: On Fairy Tales and Their Tellers*. London: Vintage, 1995.

Waters, Catherine. *Dickens and the Politics of Family*. Cambridge: Cambridge University Press, 1997.

Watkins, Tony. 1999. "Space, History and Culture: The Setting of Children's Literature." *Understanding Children's Literature*. 2nd edn. Ed. Peter Hunt. London: Routledge, 2005. 50–72.

Watson, Justin. "A Semiotic Analysis of the Representation of 'The Family' in Children's Commercials." 2001. (www.aber.ac.uk/media/Students/jjw9902.html). March 25, 2006.

Yonge, Charlotte M. "Stepmothers." *Mothers in Council*. VI.23. (1896) 130–135. The Charlotte M. Yonge Fellowship. (www.dur.ac.uk/c.e.schultze.review/issue/The Young Stepmother). April 26, 2005.

Zipes, Jack. Ed. *Victorian Fairy Tales: The Revolt of the Fairies and Elves*. New York and London: Methuen, 1987.

## Unpublished Papers

Andersson, Maria. "Mother as a Figure of Speech: Prefaces as a strategy for self-authorization in Amanda Kerfstedt's books for children." Paper presented at the 4th Norchilnet Workshop: 2005.

Reynolds, Kimberley. "Families of Choice: Children's Literature's Response to the Changing Nature of Family." Paper presented at the 17th International Research Society for Children's Literature Bienniel Congress: 2005.

# Index

CPSIA information can be obtained at www.ICGtesting.com
Printed in the USA
BVOW021534220911

271880BV00004B/6/P

9 780415 899376